The Complete
BICHON FRISE

A family portrait.   Artist: *Diane Ayres*.

The Complete
BICHON FRISE

by
Barbara B. Stubbs

HOWELL
BOOK HOUSE

NEW YORK

Howell Book House
Macmillan Publishing Company
866 Third Avenue, New York, NY 10022
Collier Macmillan Canada, Inc.

Library of Congress Cataloging-in-Publication Data

Stubbs, Barbara B.
    The complete bichon frise / by Barbara B. Stubbs.
        p.   cm.
    Includes bibliographical references.
    ISBN 0-87605-053-4
    1. Bichon frise.   I. Title.
SF429.B52S78   1990   89-35294   CIP
636.7′2—dc20

Macmillan books are available at special discounts for bulk purchases for sales promotions, premiums, fund-raising, or educational use. For details contact:

                        Special Sales Director
                        Macmillan Publishing Company
                        866 Third Avenue
                        New York, NY 10022

10 9 8 7 6 5 4 3 2 1

Printed in the United States of America

Contents

Acknowledgments

I WISH TO THANK my Bichon friends in the United States and abroad who have generously shared photographs with me for this book. Many are "one of a kind," and I appreciate your trust.

To Gertrude Fournier and Mayree Butler, "thanks for the memories" and for your support.

My thanks to Ford McFarlane for making the computer "friendly" and to Sandy Miller and Deborah Mason for their timely contributions.

My gratitude to Lois Morrow for her tremendous assistance with the chapter on grooming—a talented lady and a special friend.

The Bichon fancy is extremely fortunate to have many accomplished artists in its midst. Their impressions vary, but the results are always delightful and I am so pleased to have them represented here. My thanks go to Gerry Paolillo, Rolande Lloyd, Diane Ayres, Bernice Richardson and Alana Schwartz for sharing their talents.

Richard Beauchamp has written the chapter that interprets the Breed Standard. He is at once articulate and precise, with imagery that brings understanding. Who better to write this chapter than the person who was unswerving in his faith for the breed's potential and whose work was unending on the breed's behalf? Thank you, Richard.

Thank you, all.

La Jolla, California

A Bichon, oil on canvas by Henriette Ronner-Knip (1821–1909), owned by Loís Morrow of California. *Transparency by Richard Green.*

1

History and Origin
of the Breed

A FEW BREEDS ARE ABLE to supply a well-documented history that is difficult to challenge. Unfortunately, the history of today's Bichon Frise is not that definitive, but rather a composite of fact and fiction, legend and conjecture that often lacks specific dates and poetic descriptions by the literary giants of antiquity.

There is one fact, however, upon which all sources agree. In the past there was a small, coated dog, often white, an ancestor of which existed before Christ. From the original "small dog" a number of varieties evolved, brought about by the ongoing exploration and eventual isolation that forced each to reproduce his own kind or gene pool.

To get perspective, we need a brief historical review. Egypt developed as a nation about 3100 B.C. This was not a seafaring nation, however. The Minoans (Crete 3000–1400 B.C.) were sailors like most island people, and explored the whole Mediterranean world. The Phoenicians followed and by 1400 B.C. had taken over a brisk trade in the Mediterranean. They ventured past Gibraltar up the west coast of Europe and even landed in England. Not only were they sailors and traders, but they were among the first to send out explorers and colonize throughout the Mediterranean area. By about 1000 B.C. Malta had become a great trade center, and while Phoenician sailors went to the West, Phoenician caravans plodded the deserts of Arabia and northern India.

The Greeks and Romans followed. By 100 B.C., the time of Julius

Caesar, a Greek trader had found his way to Ceylon, and not long after a Roman trader reached China, both via the Red Sea. Meanwhile, the Chinese found a land route to the West, which was the beginning of the rich commerce from the Far East to Europe, with Italy building a seafaring commercial empire as a result.

Now let us return to the "small, coated, often white" dog. One group of specialists claim the little dog of antiquity is indeed the direct ancestor of the Maltese, while acknowledging a variety of names through the ages. He is said to be a descendant of a "Spitz-type dog bred for surf and marsh" in south-central Europe who arrived with the migrations southward. He was eventually found throughout the Mediterranean area, with the trade center of Malta an obvious source of dispersement, and the wealthy and prominent became the owners. A Maltese-type dog representation (dated 600–300 B.C.) was unearthed in Egypt, and numerous historical references and flowery descriptions have appeared in the writings of the Greeks and Romans with Aristotle (384–322 B.C.) the most notable.

The European Toy Breed specialist, Baron Houtart, states: "The ancient people of the Southern Mediterranean had a dwarf breed . . . originated on the island of Malta or Melitz, near Sicily. I would call them Malita dogs rather than Maltese, so as not to confuse them with the modern Maltese dogs, which are absolutely different from the ancient ones." He feels the origins of the modern Maltese are in the crossing of the miniature Spaniel with the miniature Poodle or with the Cayenne dogs. He also claims that these are the sources from which the "Barbichon"—which was later called the "Bichon"—sprang, and believes the Bichon originated in Italy.

Thus we have a second theory for the origin of the Maltese and a first for the Bichon.

Rome declined and western Europe entered the Middle Ages, but the Byzantine Empire survived and prospered and, along with the Greco-Roman culture, so apparently did the Maltese-type dog. As the trade routes affected the growth of civilization, so did it affect the destiny of our little dog. While he was perpetuated by the Byzantine Empire, and went on to Asia on the trade routes, it is also likely that the invaders that brought the decline of Rome absorbed the small white dog into their society, both retaining his identity in some instances, while in others blending with dogs already in their possession.

No one is positive what brought on the great period of exploration and discovery in the 1400s. European nations began searching for new routes to the East to avoid the long journey of traditional routes. Europe's increased demand for the goods of the East were not being met by existing means, and to top it all, Italy was enjoying a trade monopoly in which other nations wanted to share.

This was also the time of the Renaissance, a period of about three hundred years between the Middle Ages and modern times, that began in Italy. While great achievements came in the arts and scholarship, the Renaissance was also an age of adventure, and men set out to explore the unknown.

During this period, several events influenced the history of the Bichon

From the Canary Islands, the Tenerife Terrier.

Left to right: The Yorkshire Terrier, the Havanese and the Bolognese. Note size relationships and the differences in head (muzzle and skull) and coat type, which may denote that all three breeds may have shared a common ancestor. Bred by Brite and Jan Warming, Denmark.

and its close relatives. In 1488 Bartholomeu Dias rounded the Cape of Good Hope (Africa). In 1498 Vasco da Gama reached India. In 1492 Columbus made his first voyage to the New World, which included the discovery of Cuba. In 1493, 1498 and 1502 he made his second, third and fourth voyages. On the second trip it is known he took 1,200 people, animals, tools, seeds and the other necessities of colonization. In 1521 Magellan discovered the Philippines, via the South American route, and in 1526–30 Sebastian Cabot sailed to and explored the Rio de la Plata (Argentina). The explorations were followed by colonization.

A group of islands figured heavily in the history of the Bichon. These were the Canary Islands, lying sixty miles off the northwest coast of Africa. The Phoenicians, Greeks, Romans and Byzantines had all invaded here. It is said the ancients named these islands Canaria from the Latin *canis* (dog) because they found ''large, fierce dogs'' there.

The Renaissance had reached most of Europe by 1400. France came under the influence during the late 1400s, when under Francis I they began a series of invasions of Italy. Francis I, who reigned from 1515 to 1547, was one of the first to bring Italian artists and craftsmen to the French courts, and the French began to adapt Italian ideas to their own tastes during the 1500s.

With this historical and geographical background we can review the names of some of the small, related breeds as they have passed through history. The lists are so lengthy it is no wonder there is confusion on origins. In 1836 a Dr. Reichenback listed the following ''types of Bolonese Toys, the Silky Poodle, the Bouffet, the Burgos, the Brevibilis, the Flammens, the Pyrome, the Bichon, the Maltese and the Lion Dog.''

In the 1935 French magazine *Revue Cynégétique et Canine,* the following are listed as ''being under the same breed name of Bichon'': the Dog of Tenerife, the Dog of Havana, the Dog of Bologna, the Dog of Baleares, the Dog of Peru, the Dog of Holland and the Little Lion Dog of Buffon.

Le Chien (published in Paris, 1959) states that the Bichon is related to the Barbet or Water Spaniel ''through exterior characteristics and certain morphological particularities which confirm mutual descendants.'' (The Barbet is described in yet another source as ''the dog of water and swamp . . . small dogs soft, wooly and frizzled.'') In *Le Chien* two families are distinguished: the Maltese with the straight hair and a second family formed by grouping the other varieties under the name *Bichon à poil frisé* (Bichon of the curly hair). Both families originated in the Mediterranean area, the Maltese definitely being the older of the two groups (a reference is made to an Egyptian artifact representing a dog with similar characteristics), while the curly-haired Bichon is considered to be essentially of Latin origin.

Votre Ami le Bichon, another Parisian publication, states that the family of Bichons includes four categories: (1) the Maltese, (2) the Bolognese, (3) the Tenerife and (4) the Havanese. The origins are remote, although ''we find allusions to this breed in former writings of more than two centuries before

Havanese puppy, six months old.

Holly, the top Bolognese in Europe in 1985. Owned by Brite and Jan Warming, Denmark.

A historical relative of the Bichon Frise: a Havanese sire, dam and puppies. Note color variations.

Christianity'' (another Egyptian reference). They were common throughout the Mediterranean, especially in Italy.

The reference to "Tenerife" is familiar to anyone with the barest knowledge of the Bichon Frise. The oversimplified history of the Bichon Frise has usually been "The Bichon originated from the Barbet in the Mediterranean, the Italian sailors took it to Tenerife, then it came back to the Continent, went to France during the Renaissance and developed into the Bichon Frise of today."

Upon reviewing all sources, there seems little doubt that small dogs of this era were indeed transported from their eastern Mediterranean realm to the countries rimming the West, to the Balearic Islands and beyond Gibraltar to the Canary Islands and Tenerife. We know this is historically feasible. Exactly when this happened, how long they stayed, and to what degree there was interbreeding with existing dogs is uncertain, but gradually they did return to the Continent, doubtless the same way they arrived, with the sailors and traders. What influence the "Tenerife Bichon" (or "Tenerife Terrier," as some sources call it) had upon its return to the Continent cannot be documented, but one would assume that a sojourn in the Canary Islands would have developed a rather hardy little fellow. At any rate, the name and the association with Tenerife persisted through the years, with a few early chroniclers believing the Bichon Frise originated as a specific, identifiable breed on the island of Tenerife.

The dogs that remained on the Continent continued to breed in their isolated geographical pockets. The most prominent of these was the Bolognese, a woolly, curly-coated relative of the family who became especially popular in the city of Bologna in north-central Italy, the obvious source of its name.

There is particular significance in the Bolognese, for in 1521 the French king, Francis I, began the invasions of northern Italy and was one of the first to bring the Italian Renaissance culture to France. He is specifically mentioned for introducing the little dogs to the court (along with the artisans), however, Henry III, who reigned from 1574 to 1589, was said to have been the true aficionado.

There is documentation of Bolognese being sent to both French and Belgian aristocrats as gifts from their Italian counterparts in the late 1600s, which provided an additional infusion into what gene pool might already have existed thanks to Francis I, Henry III and those who followed.

The Havanese is the fourth member to be mentioned as part of the "Bichon family," following the Maltese, Tenerife Bichon and Bolognese. As would be expected from what has gone before, they too have a history drawn from conjecture and historical possibilities rather than documented fact. There are a number of theories:

1. The Havanese is descended from the Bolognese taken to Argentina by the Italians and crossed with a small South American Poodle, thereby creating a new member of the Bichon family. Both the

6

Spaniards and Italians colonized Argentina in the late 1500s, so the Bolognese certainly had transportation, but the issue of a "South American Poodle" does raise a few questions.

2. The Havanese is descended from the Maltese that were brought by Spaniards to the West Indies, where they were called the "Havana Silk Dog."

3. The Havanese was one of the Western Mediterranean (perhaps Tenerife?) small dogs whose ancestors arrived in Cuba during the days of Spanish exploration and colonization.

4. The Havanese descendants were brought to Cuba by the Italians, who utilized them as gifts to curry favor.

Whatever the source, they became the pampered pets of wealthy Cubans, who bred them and gave them as gifts but never sold them. It is not clear when they found their way back to the Continent, but in doing so they became the fourth member in the so-called "traditional" Bichon family classification.

The cast of characters was in place thanks to the quirks of Man and his history; the dogs of antiquity, and his travels through the centuries, the dogs from Tenerife, from northern Italy and those returned from the New World. We will never be able to prove what combinations blended to produce the breed type that evolved as the Bichon Frise. The impact of one upon the other and the introduction of other possible factors can only be a matter of conjecture.

The other dogs listed earlier were obviously the results of colonization in those specific geographical areas and had little impact on the development of the Continental Bichon family. However, there are two breeds worthy of mention. One is often included as a Bichon family member, perhaps mistakenly. The other is more obscure and is unknown to many, but because of similar historical origins and physical characteristics, it *should* be included in the Bichon group.

The first is the Little Lion Dog, the Petit Chien Lion or the Lowchen, for they are all one and the same dog. Once again we have a dog of Mediterranean origins, known since the fourteenth century with concentration in Spain, France and Italy. Those involved with the Lowchen today feel breed type was established very early and offer a strong case against close affiliation with the Bichon family. The Lowchen is a square breed, unlike the Bichon breeds, which call for a longer body length in proportion to height. The double coat has a semiharsh outer coat with a softer undercoat. Unlike the other Bichon members, the coat is never to be curly. There is a range of colors never found in Bichon Frise or Maltese, and infrequently in Havanese. One of the predominant coat colors is the "tan-point" pattern typical of terriers, while the temperament of the Lowchen also leans toward the terrier. It is felt there is an infusion of terrier blood not found, at least to this degree, in other Bichon family members.

In addition there is evidence that a lion-type trim was frequently used on many dogs other than the Lowchen, which further confuses the issue of breed identification.

Unclipped Lowchen. Breeder: Elizabeth Varga. Is this a Bichon relative?

The Coton de Tulear: Tana, male, owned by J. Lewis Russell, Oakshake Kennel. This delightful breed appears to have close ties to the Tenerife Bichon.

From England, Lowchen Ch. Quinbury Gatanya Fondue at Pepperland. Note proportions and color variations.

The second breed is the Coton de Tulear. Dr. Robert Jay Russell, formerly of the Anthropology Department of the University of California at Los Angeles and a world-renowned biologist, encountered the breed during a two-year field study of the lemurs of Madagascar. Intrigued, he sent home breeding stock in 1974. Subsequent research into the history and development of the Coton validated much of the information already available on the Bichon family.

A small descendant of the Barbet family arrived in the Canary Islands, as we previously learned. In the seventeenth century trades routes around Africa to India and the Orient expanded, and the "Tenerife Bichon" made its way to the Isle of Reunion, east of Madagascar in the Indian Ocean. Here it developed as a distinct breed, acquiring its cottonlike coat, perhaps the result of a single mutation, suggests Dr. Russell. Our dog was now known as the Coton de Reunion, and like his European relatives, became a "favorite of the favored." For reasons not clear, the Coton left the Isle of Reunion, where he subsequently became extinct, but reappeared at Tulear, a bustling trading port of southwest Madagascar. Once again he was a success—first with the ruling tribal monarchy, then the French colonials after 1896 and finally the independent Malagasy Republic after 1960. He was known as the Royal Dog of Madagascar and was recognized in 1970 by the Fédération Cynologique Internationale, the august body that oversees the dog activities of most of Europe and South America. Unfortunately, political unrest threatens the current status of the Coton in Madagascar.

Many of the physical characteristics of the Coton are similar to the Bichon Frise. How fascinating it is to consider the influence wielded by our little dog from Tenerife. His journeys to the south resulted in a breed that has survived to modern times, while his return to the Continent undoubtedly influenced the character of the European Bichon family and ultimately the Bichon of today.

At this juncture we return in our history to one of the most enduring and picturesque of the stories regarding our little white dogs. "The kings and their ladies loved their dogs so very much they carried them with them everywhere in traylike baskets attached around their necks by ribbons." This was probably true, as it is compatible with descriptions of court life at this time. Louis XIV (reigned 1643–1715) eliminated the centuries-old custom of allowing hunting dogs into the palace, which reinstated the small dog as the court "pet of choice," since they were easily carried about. It is here we are told that the dogs were so elaborately cared for by their owners that the verb *bichonner* (to curl) remains as evidence. An accurate derivation of this verb is not known. A majority of references feel that the name Barbichon evolved from the French word *barbiche,* meaning "beard," which was ultimately shortened to Bichon.

Many of the art works of this period include a small dog that could be an ancestor of any member of the Bichon family group described earlier: the *millefleurs* tapestry, *The Lady and the Unicorn,* woven at the end of the

Marie-Anne Carolus-Duran, oil on canvas, 1874, by Emile Carolus-Duran (1838-1917). Courtesy of the Fine Arts Museums of San Francisco, Mildred Anna Williams Collection.

fifteenth century; works by Albrecht Dürer (1471–1528), especially his wood-cuts; *Nelly O'Brien,* by Joshua Reynolds (1723–1792); the portrait of the Duchess of Alba, by Francisco Goya (1746–1828). These are but a few of many works claimed by the various Bichon family members as depicting their particular and individual breeds. The dogs of the kings and courtiers and the dogs in art were certainly forerunners of the Bichon family; however, to identify them as immediate ancestors of a specific breed that exists today, with a few possible exceptions, is probably unrealistic.

The popularity of the small dogs diminished with the onset of the French Revolution in 1789, but is said to have revived during the time of Napoleon III (nephew of Napoleon Bonaparte), who in 1852 established the Second Empire and declared himself emperor.

This was during the productive years of the artist Henriette Ronner-Knip, who was born in Amsterdam in 1821 and died in 1909. She is especially noted for her paintings of cats. However, the pets she depicts tend to be in luxurious surroundings that reflected the wealth of her international following, with patrons coming from New Orleans and from Paris, Rotterdam and other major cities of Europe.

A painting by Henriette Ronner-Knip entitled *A Bichon* was purchased in Belgium by Canadian art connoisseur Nigel Aubrey-Jones. It was later acquired by the Richard Green Gallery in London and in February 1988 by Lois Morrow of California, at whose home it now resides.

This painting shows us a Bichon so close in breed type to the Bichon Frise of today as to be quite astonishing. While the painting was signed, it was not dated. Best professional estimates place it close to one hundred years old. Those Bichon fanciers fortunate enough to have seen the painting, either at the Richard Green Gallery in London or at Mrs. Morrow's home, have been touched by this extraordinary and definitive link with the past.

Following the defeat of France in the Franco-Prussian War, Napoleon III was overthrown and the Third Republic established in 1871. French prosperity grew along with their colonial empire in Africa and Asia. It is not entirely clear why the Bichon lost favor, but by the turn of the century he had become the "dog of the street"—the "little sheep dog." The dog of the aristocrats became the circus dog, the dog of many tricks at the fair and—as legend has it—"the dog of the organ grinder of Barbery," always described as "lively, intelligent and commanding affection with whomever they associate."

Following World War I, it appears that a few isolated dog fanciers in both France and Belgium regained interest in the Bichon à Poil Frisé or Tenerife Bichon (it was called by both names), and early attempts at breeding programs began with what dogs were available following the "circus dog" era and a war that devastated the country. By 1933 enough progress had been made to merit a Breed Standard.

The official Standard of the Breed was adopted on March 15, 1933. It was written by Madame Bouctovagniez, president of the Toy Club of France, in conjunction with the Friends of the Belgian Breeds. However, Mme. Denise Nizet de Leemans as head of the Breed Standards Committee of the

Polka Des Sapins de L'isle, a Bichon owned by Madame Desfarge, France, 1944.

Int. Ch. Gift de Steren Vor, sire of Int. Ch. Jimbo de Steren Vor, appears in the French de Warnabry line.

Bichons on exhibition, France, 1953.

Fédération Canine Internationale was the person who decided on the name Bichon Frise.

J. C. F. (Fred) Peddie, noted breeder and judge from Ontario, Canada, tells the wonderful story of a dinner party in 1972 given in honor of Mme. Nizet de Leemans, who was eighty-two at this time. As a breed of French background that was gaining popularity in the United States, the Bichon Frise was discussed. She told the guests that in 1933, when having a meeting with the founding club representatives of the forming breeds, there was an extremely heated discussion as to what this new breed should be called. Finally, in desperation, she had asked, "What does it look like?" and was told it was a fluffy, little white dog. "Well, then," Mme Nizet de Leemans said, "it shall be called Bichon Frise" (fluffy little dog). And so it was. And so it is.

The Bichon Frise was entered in the *Livre des Origines Françaises* on October 18, 1934. However, despite this official recognition, there continued to be confusion regarding the name, many still using the names Bichon à Poil Frisé or Tenerife Bichon as late as the 1950s and early 1960s.

Early descriptions of the Bichon family members were as numerous and varied as the authors that wrote them. They were not Breed Standards as we know them today, but rather rough characterizations as interpreted by the writers. It is surprising there is not more accuracy, since the Bichon Frise Standard had been available since 1933. But it is interesting, nonetheless, to read these descriptions and contemplate the influence each Bichon family member may have had upon the other.

Dogs of the World (Popular Dogs Publishing Co., Ltd., London) offers the following:

> *Bolognese:* Height under twelve inches, weight under eleven pounds, coat very long and thick and bushy; the whole body covered with a shaggy mass of curls. The hair is short only on the muzzle. Tail tufted. Color, pure white, a few small fawn flecks or stains are permissible.
>
> *Havanese:* Height eleven to twelve and one half inches. Coat furry in silky waves intermingled with large locks. Color—white or beige or solid chestnut brown. Spots on the ears or patches of gray, beige or black permissible.
>
> *Maltese:* Head not too narrow but of terrier shape, not too long, but not apple-headed. Nose black, eyes dark brown with black rims . . . forelegs short and straight. Body short and cobby and low to the ground . . . Hind legs short and nicely angulated. Tail well arched over the back and feathered . . . coat of good length, the longer the better, of silky texture, and not in any way wooly, and straight. Any self color is permissible but pure white is desirable. Slight lemon markings should be penalized. Weight four pounds to nine pounds approved, the smaller the better.
>
> *Tenerife dog:* Height under twelve inches and weight under eleven pounds. Coat in wooly curls neither flat nor twisted and from three to five inches in length. Color white, but slight beige or gray markings, especially on the ears, is permissible . . .

In *The Complete Dog Breeders Manual* (published in England in 1954), the Bichon à Poil Frisé is described as a "Belgian lap-dog related to the

13

Belgian Ch. Youbi of Milton, double grandsire of Lyne of Milton.

Int. Ch. India de la Buthiere, owned by Madame Desfarge.

Bichons from des Closmyons, owned by Madame Laisne, France, 1972.

Bolognese, the Tenerife Dog and the Toy Poodle,'' and the height is given as eleven inches and weight as twelve pounds. The color is white with a long and curly coat, silky in texture, usually clipped. (Note this differentiation between the Bichon à Poil Frisé and the Tenerife Dog.)

According to *Le Chien* (Paris, 1959), "The Bichon à Poil Frisé has a skull a little larger than that of the Maltese, his hair makes him look rounder than he really is. His nose is black, his lips small and well pigmented: his eyes as dark as possible, round and not almond like those of his cousin the poodle. The tail is not cropped and must turn back in an elegant curve not falling to the side, the point and plume falling back toward the middle of the back. The Bichon Frise is wooly in appearance, curly and long, never stringy and always white in color.''

Breeders in the early years did not have a vast selection of foundation stock, so it was inevitable that pedigrees would reveal an incredible amount of inbreeding. The Milton line of M. and Mme. A. Bellotte of Belgium offers a good example of this.

There are a number of Continental breeders whose kennel names have become familiar to Bichon breeders around the world, in addition to the Milton line already mentioned: de Warnabry (Mme. Suzanne Mazaes-Nicholas of France), des Closmyons (Mme. E. Laisne of France), des Frimoussettes (Mme. Jeannine Miligari of France), de la Lande de Belleville (Madame Darlot of France), de la Buthiere (Mme. C. Defarge of France), de la Roche Posay (M. Guiter Stoll of France), de Steren Vor (Madame Abadie of France), des Bourbiel (Mademoiselle Mayieu of France), de Villa-Sainval (Madame Baras-Berben of Belgium, former wife of Albert Baras), de la Persaliere (Mme. Albert Baras of Belgium), de Chaponay (Madame Vaansteenkiste-Deleu of Belgium), du roi des Lutines (Mademoiselle Naudet), de Dierstein (Madame Nemeiller of Germany), Goldfischbrunnen (Schaphusen Forthmann of Germany).

Our "little white dog"—our Bichon Frise—was about to enter an extraordinary phase of his history; he was destined to reach a pinnacle of recognition and fame far beyond the wildest imagination of these early Continental breeders.

Etoile de Steren Vor, one of the original French imports, photographed at sixteen years old.

2

The Bichon Frise
Comes to America

THE BICHON FRISE has achieved a meteoric rise from obscurity to prominence unequaled by few other breeds. Its documented arrival in the United States in October 1956 to full breed recognition by the American Kennel Club was less than seventeen years. This was an amazing feat considering the breed came from a position of minimal popularity abroad.

In Dieppe, France, in 1952 Helene and François Picault acquired their first Bichon Frise. Captivated by the breed, they purchased Etoile de Steren Vor from Madame Abadie of de Steren Vor Kennels, and with thoughts of breeding they purchased a third Bichon, Eddy White de Steren Vor.

The Picault daughters had married Americans and left France, and the parents had given much thought to joining them. Subsequent conversations with Madame Abadie convinced the Picaults that a "fortune" awaited them as Bichon breeders in the United States. So the die was cast, and in October of 1956 the Picaults and the three original Bichons—plus four additional females and the registration name of de Hoop, newly acquired from the French Kennel Club—sailed for America, where they joined their daughter, Rene Dahl, in Milwaukee. Two additional Bichons, Gypsie de Warnabry and Gavote, would follow in six months.

In later years letters were written to the National Bichon Club stating that individuals had purchased Bichons while traveling in Europe during the twenties, thirties and forties, dogs that had become the "beloved family pet." While undoubtedly true, no organized effort had been made on their behalf,

Helene and François Picault, two pioneer Bichon breeders. This photo was taken in 1965.

Mayree Butler (*left*) with Monsieur Mieux du Pic Four and Gertrude Fournier with Lyne of Milton and Judge Thelma Brown (*rear*) 1965.

so the documented history of the breed must begin with the Picaults' arrival in the United States.

Unfortunately, neither the Picaults nor Madame Abadie reckoned with reality. The American Kennel Cub did not recognize the breed, and they were disappointed to learn that such recognition was highly improbable for many years to come. Those who saw the dogs thought them charming, but there was no clamor to own one, and in that first year only a few puppies were placed.

In 1958 the Picaults met Azalea Gascoigne of Pewaukee, Wisconsin. Mrs. Gascoigne had become involved with sporting breeds in 1947, then in 1954 began a successful decade as a Dachshund breeder. She purchased her first Bichon at this time, for she felt the breed had potential. Her faith was sufficient to occasion a trip to the Bichon kennels in France; she returned home with Lady des Frimoussettes, whose son, Dapper Dan de Gascoigne, was destined to have an enormous impact on the future of the breed.

In 1960 the Picaults' daughter moved to California, and the parents followed. In a letter sent to the author dated in 1969:

> Having left Milwaukee with ten females and three males we were due for a new disappointment for, lacking the necessary space conditions, we had to board our thirteen dogs at a veterinarian's hospital for $200 a month, and this for three months, until we were able to secure a place in Coronado for $75 a month. I used to take them out by groups of three or four mornings or evenings and, although everyone stopped to admire them, not one was bought.
>
> We then decided to place them with some people who were willing to give us three puppies from the first litter, which represented for us an indemnification; in exchange they would become actual owners of the dogs and will receive the French pedigree.
>
> That is when one of these persons, Mrs. Huer, enjoying these privileges and having recently fulfilled her obligations, introduced us to Mrs. Fournier . . . in 1961.

Mrs. Fournier, who had bred and exhibited Collies under the Cali-Col prefix, was delighted with this new little dog and felt there was indeed a future for them. Arrangements were made, and Mrs. Fournier took possession of Eddy White de Steren Vor, Etoile de Steren Vor, Gypsie de Warnabry and Gigi de Hoop, and the name Pic Four was taken to represent the partnership.

In spite of considerable effort on the part of Mrs. Fournier, widespread popularity for the Bichon was not forthcoming. The "fortune" envisioned by the Picaults never materialized, and their interest in actively pursuing the project waned. Thus, after two years, Mrs. Fournier became the sole owner of Eddy White, Etoile, Gypsie and Gigi, and once again assumed her original Cali-Col prefix.

Fortunately for the future of the Bichon, Mrs. Fournier continued her efforts to promote the breed and foster interest. When Mrs. Mayree Butler lost a favorite pet, her son encouraged her to investigate a "new breed" he had seen on a local television program. Mrs. Fournier was at work! Thus the two

19

San Diego ladies met, and Mrs. Butler acquired her first Bichon Frise, Kupkake du Pic Four.

Mrs. Fournier continued her promotional efforts through advertisements in a national dog magazine; she wisely saw the need for gaining exposure on this level and was pleased when responses were received from Goldie Olsen of Washington and Jean Rank of Pennsylvania. However, through the ongoing interest and endeavors of both Mrs. Fournier and Mrs. Butler, southern California remained the focal point of Bichon activities for a number of years.

At this juncture some sort of formal organization was deemed necessary. From the list of Wisconsin Bichon owners obtained earlier from the Picaults, Mrs. Fournier discovered that Mrs. Gascoigne with her "Azavic" Dachshunds was the only person with any involvement in purebred dogs.

A phone call revealed an existing club in the Milwaukee area, which to Mrs. Gascoigne's regret was more social than dog oriented. In May 1964 a meeting was held in San Diego to establish a national "parent" club and to discuss plans for the future of the Bichon Frise. The club was called the Bichon Frise Club of America, with Mrs. Gascoigne designated as the first president and Mrs. Fournier as secretary and registrar.

The Bichon Frise Club of America and subsequent local clubs played an enormous role in the eventual recognition of the breed by the American Kennel Club and are discussed in detail in a later chapter.

Local groups around the country came together because of their mutual interest in the Bichon and began holding match shows, the first being held in San Diego. Unfortunately, in the show rings of Continental Europe emphasis on meticulous care was lacking. It was, and still is, the custom to exhibit with little or no grooming. Dogs were unwashed, unbrushed and unscissored and in general lacked the basics of show presentation that are taken for granted in the American show ring. Therefore, it is not surprising that the early Bichon supporters were openly ridiculed by U.S. judges and exhibitors of recognized breeds that had seen the Bichon in show rings abroad. The Bichon Frise's road to "stardom" in the United States was not without pitfalls.

Talk of getting the breed recognized began to flourish. A few initial sorties were made to the American Kennel Club. Their response? More dogs, more people, more clubs, more match shows and more geographical distribution was needed. Actually, these things would come almost automatically, provided that enough genuine and dedicated interest could be built, and that became the issue—how to attract the people that would provide this.

The real problem became clear—*image*. At this time the Bichon was not being taken seriously. The dog fancy was patronizing at best and disinterested generally. In Rare Breed matches held around the country, the Bichons appeared in the rings clean (usually), brushed out (occasionally) and scissored (rarely)—scarcely a picture to incite a riot of interest. A concerted effort began to change this image of the breed. Even the most doubting enthusiast realized that the Bichon had to compete on a level of presentation equal to the recognized breeds, or it would never take its place beside them.

In January 1969 Frank Sabella (then a top professional handler, today

Azalea Gascoigne with Lady des Frimoussettes, dam of famous Mex. Ch. Dapper Dan de Gascoigne.

Jean Rank with Lochinvar du Pic Four (*foreground*) (King of Rayita ex Etoile de Steren Vor).

21

Goldy L. Olsen with French import puppies, 1966.

Ombre de la Roche Posay and Oree de la Roche Posay, imported by Goldy Olsen, 1966.

an internationally known judge) came to the Bichon Frise Club of America Annual Meeting and Seminar and gave his ideas and suggestions on Bichon presentation. His program included a start-to-finish demonstration of washing, blowdrying and scissoring a dog plus a handling exhibition showing table procedure, movement patterns and techniques that offer a dog to his best advantage.

Miracles were not achieved overnight, but this seminar set the stage for the appealing rounded, contained look that has evolved today, both here and around the world, and was directly responsible for a brochure published by the national club that gave the first detailed information on grooming. This proved to be a milestone.

So progress was made, but that progress would be worthless unless the general public could be made aware of it. What was needed was the support and assistance of an extremely knowledgeable and highly respected individual with a background in dogs of long standing. Someone was needed with connections in the dog "media" in order to spread the word and foster interest in the breed on a level denoting both quality and dedication. The ideal person was, of course, Richard Beauchamp, editor of the premier dog magazine in the United States. A visit to his offices by the author and a trio of Bichons aroused his interest and created a challenge, and he agreed to join the fight for breed recognition. With his participation, the long road to success grew shorter.

In 1971 the Bichon Frise was accepted into the Miscellaneous Class, and in 1973 was given full breed recognition. In 1976 the Bichon Frise Club of America, Inc., held its first licensed Specialty show. In 1985 the final organizational goal was reached when the BFCA was accepted for membership into the American Kennel Club, with a voting delegate to represent the parent club and the breed.

In the formative years of the 1960s and the early 1970s, there were many problems shared by all breeders. It is to the everlasting credit of the early breeders that, through dedicated and often heartbreaking selective breeding, the quality increased from year to year and a dog emerged with amazing rapidity to take its place as a serious contender for Best in Show and Group awards. Indeed, Bichon owners and breeders of today owe a debt of gratitude to the breeders of early years who waged the dual battle of gaining breed acceptance and respectability while engaged in the arduous task of evolving a breed of merit.

It should be stated here that in the early 1970s the Bichon breeders, via the parent club, fought valiantly (and successfully) for placement in the Non-Sporting Group versus the Toy Group. It was the firm belief that the size required for success in the American Toy Group would bring about a reduction of quality in a breed that was striving to go forward. Furthermore, the American breeders did not consider the Bichon to be "toy" in either attitude, type or substance.

The first Standard of the breed was adopted by the original twenty-eight charter members of the Bichon Frise Club of America in 1964; a second version was modified and adopted by the membership in 1968. But while the

Four generations *(left to right):* Cali-Col's Ne'er Do Well (four months), Mon Ami du Pic Four (three years), Kord du Pic Four (six years), and Eddy White de Steren Vor (ten years).

Bottom, left to right: Perky, Kord du Pic Four, Monsieur Mieux du Pic Four, Lassy of Milton. *Top:* Mon Ami du Pic Four *(left)* and Cali-Col's Ne'er Do Well. Seventh Bichon is not identified; can you find him?

Standard was approved by the Kennel Club in November of 1974, the years that followed showed that judges needed additional clarification, so a more detailed Standard was offered and approved in 1979.

In 1987 the American Kennel Club began a project to standardize the format of all breed standards. The Bichon Frise Club of America completed its work, and the current Standard, reflecting the format changes and some additional word modifications, was adopted in 1988.

The Bichon had arrived in the United States in 1956 from a position of relative unimportance in Europe; but after American Kennel Club recognition in 1973, the breed was on its way. As the dogs became top contenders in the American show ring and people experienced the enormous delight of having them as loving companions, interest in the Bichon Frise ignited on an international level.

Dr. Harry Spira, noted international dog show judge and veterinarian from Australia, has said, "The Bichon Frise is an American breed." While acknowledging that the origins of the breed were indeed on the Continent, he maintains that it is the American breeder who has achieved the degree of quality and presentation that has brought the Bichon Frise to the level of distinction and respect that it enjoys today.

Ch. Cali-Col's Robspierre, one of two foundation dogs for Chaminade. Sire of Ch. Chaminade Mr. Beau Monde. *Photo by Missy, 1970.*

3

Breeders—
Then and Now

THE PRINCIPAL BREEDERS during the early 1960s dominated early pedigrees and continue to appear behind top winners and producers of today. It is a rare pedigree that does not ultimately trace back to one or more of these early breeders.

De Gascoigne (Wisconsin)

Azalea Gascoigne was the first American breeder of Bichons. She introduced the French des Frimoussettes Bichons to complement the de Steren Vor and de Warnabry lines of the Picaults' original dogs. Andre de Gascoigne bred to the import, Lady des Frimoussettes, produced Dapper Dan de Gascoigne, a dog of enormous influence, as will be seen shortly. Ch. Gabby de Gascoigne (Darnit de Gascoigne ex Leslie des Frimoussettes) was the sire of six champions, including a top producing bitch, Ch. Gabby's Angel of Willow Wink. Diable de Gascoigne and Napoleon de Gascoigne appear in many pedigrees. De Gascoigne is behind de Noel and Vintage Years pedigrees, but it is the dominance of Dapper Dan that Bichon history will record. Mrs. Gascoigne retired from active breeding in the mid-1970s.

Cali-Col (California)

Gertrude Fournier has been a major breeder for many years. Not only has she bred forty-three champions, but—equally importantly—produced

Mex. Ch. Dapper Dan de Gascoigne.

BIS and Specialty BOB winner, Ch. Cali-Col's Scalawag, CD; handler, Michael Dougherty. Bred by G. Fournier.

Dapper Dan de Gascoigne with Mayree Butler; Dan's son, Cali-Col's Scalawag, shown by Bernice Richardson; and Scalawag's daughter, Reenroy's Ami du Kilkanny, shown by Barbara Stubbs, May 1972.

28

Ch. Cali-Col's Shadrack, influential producer; handler, Michael Dougherty.

Ch. Cali-Col's Octavius Caesar, owned by Martin and Roberta Rothman, 1970.

Seascape the Captain's Choice, owned and bred by Pamela Sharp and Keith Nelson, 1970.

many dogs and bitches that became the foundation Bichons for other notable breeders. Shortly after assuming the Picaults' Bichons, she imported the sisters Lyne of Milton and Lassy of Milton (products of a brother-sister breeding) and later Marquis of Milton. Gipsie de Warnabry (Int. Ch. Bandit de Steren Vor ex Cybelle de Steren Vor) was an additional import that added much to the Cali-Col line. These plus the American-bred Mon Ami du Pic Four, Monsieur Mieux du Pic Four and Lochinvar du Pic Four would have an impact through the Cali-Col line. When Mrs. Gascoigne came to California for the 1964 meeting, she brought Dapper Dan de Gascoigne with her, and fortunately for the future of the Bichon he remained there with Mrs. Fournier and later Mrs. Butler. Dan produced a number of offspring destined to influence the Cali-Col line. Bred to Lyne of Milton he produced Ch. Cali-Col's Robspierre, Ch. Stardom's Odin Rex, Jr., Ch. Cali-Col's Octavius Caesar and Ch. Cali-Col's Candida, all of whom would prove not only to be dominant producers in the United States, but the influence of their offspring would be felt in Canada, England and ultimately Australia and New Zealand. Bred to Cali-Col's Our Daphne (daughter of Gipsie) Dan produced the brothers Ch. Cali-Col's Scalawag, C.D., and Ch. Cali-Col's Shadrack. The former was an outstanding winner in the days following AKC recognition with three Bests in Show, eighteen Group Firsts and two Specialty wins. Shadrack was the sire of fourteen champions, several of which became foundation dogs for other breeders. Ch. Cali-Col's Rhapsody of Reenroy and Ch. Shabob's Nice Girl Missy are among the top ten producing dams with nine and ten champions respectively. While no longer an active breeder and exhibitor, it is obvious the Cali-Col name *and* Mrs. Fournier occupy dominant positions in the development of the breed in the United States.

Reenroy (California)

Mayree Butler's acquisition of KupKake du Pic Four signaled the beginning of a long career as a breeder of forty-one champions, with four that are especially notable: Reenroy's Riot Act, sire of twenty-one champions; his daughter, Ch. Reenroy's Image of Ami, the foundation bitch for Norvic Bichons; Ch. Reenroy's Royal Flush de Noel (a foundation dog for Del Noel and the sire of one of the breed's top producing sires); and Ch. Reenroy's Ami du Kilkanny, foundation bitch for Chaminade, destined to become famous through her top producing son, Ch. Chaminade Mr. Beau Monde. A litter sister to Ami, Reenroy's C'est Bon de Pigalle, was the dam of the first Bichon bitch to win a group, Ch. Chaminade Phoenicia. In the late 1960s Mrs. Butler had acquired Dapper Dan de Gascoigne. Bred to Little Nell of Cali-Col, he produced Ami and Royal Flush (from different litters). Ch. Reenroy's Double Trouble (co-owned with Sandy Miller of Cromwell Bichons) is the sire of seven champions, while Ch. Reenroy's Robespierre produced six champions. Ch. Reenroy's Ragtime Reuben, Ch. Reenroy's Ready Freddy Welbey, owned by Mary Ann Pichel of Balverne Bichons, and Ch. Reenroy's Riot Squad each produced four champions. Ch. Reenroy's Ritzy Doll (Reenroy's

Roxene Du G.W., bred by Goldy Olsen; owned and shown here by Marie Winslow, Win-Mar, 1971.

Ch. Stardom's Odin Rex, Jr., owned and shown by Stella Raabe, Rava. Bred by Cali-Col Kennels, reg. 1972.

Reenroy's Riot Act, a top producer, owned and bred by Mayree Butler, 1971.

Romeo ex Reenroy's Rebecca), owned by Dorothy Goodwin of Heydot Bichons, was a success in the show ring in the early 1970s and won many friends for the breed during that pivotal period. As will be seen, the Reenroy Bichons appear in the pedigrees of many of the top breeders of today.

Goldysdale (Washington)

Goldy Olsen used the Goldysdale prefix in the early days and changed to the G.W. suffix in later years, which often produces confusion when reviewing pedigrees. Natchen of Cali-Col was a foundation bitch. Ombre de la Roche Posay and Oree de la Roche Posay were imported in the mid 1960s; however, their major influence would not be felt until the early 1970s, most notably in the C and D Bichons of Dolores and Charles Wolske. In 1967 Mrs. Olsen went to Europe for a prolonged visit and returned with five puppies: Qukette de la Roche Posay, Orlanda de la Roche Posay, Quetty de Warnabry, Quintal de Warnabry and Quillet des Frimoussettes. Quillet was acquired by Iradell Kennels (Mrs. Clarkson Earl, Jr., New York), where he became a factor in the East Coast pedigrees. Mrs. Olsen did not exhibit, but dogs bred by her became the foundation for a number of eastern and midwestern Bichon lines, i.e., Teeny Teepee, L'Havre Joyeux, Dove-Cote, Mel-Mar and the Win-Mar Bichons of Marie Winslow, who later became heir to some of these historic imports.

Rank (Pennsylvania)

Jean Rank obtained her first Bichons from Cali-Col. While producing thirty-four champions, Rank Bichons would become important as foundation stock. Lochinvar du Pic Four, Rank's Gay and Rank's Treasurer are familiar names in early pedigrees. Ch. Rank's Eddie (Martin's Frostie Muffin ex Rank's Treasure), owned by Robert Koeppel, was the first Bichon to win Best of Breed at the prestigious Westminster Kennel Club show in 1974. Ch. Rank's Raggedy Andy, sire of ten champions (owned by Belle Creek Kennels, Lorrie Conrad, Michigan), was the 1981 National Specialty winner. The co-breeder was Judy Thayer. Ch. Rank's Tar Baby of Lejerdell was the top producing bitch of Mrs. Rank's breeding, with seven champions to her credit, owned by C and D. Rank's Leading Lady had five champions. Once again we have a breeder whose Bichons became influential in the breeding programs for subsequent breeders, one of the most successful being the Brereton Bichons of Margaret Britton and Mary Spruiell.

INTERIM BREEDERS

There were a number of individuals who had an active interest in the Bichon Frise in the late 1960s who either acquired or bred specific Bichons that occupied a prominent place in the pedigrees of succeeding years. These

Ch. Cali-Col's Candida, foundation bitch for Bobbye McKelvey and Works D'Arte.

Ch. Tarzan de la Persaliere, imported by Lejerdell Kennels of Jerome Podell, pictured here with his four-month-old son, Rank's Tar-son de Lejerdell, 1972.

individuals, along with the original breeders, contributed to an increased public awareness of the breed by exhibiting their Bichons in early matches, Rare Breed exhibitions and finally the Miscellaneous Classes at the American Kennel Club shows prior to full recognition. Some are breeding and exhibiting today; others are no longer active.

Staramour (Pennsylvania)

Celeste Fleishman was one of the earliest of the East Coast Bichon supporters. Her French import, Ch. Titan de Warnabry (Jimbo de Steren Vor ex Janitzia des Frimoussettes), and his son, Ch. Stardom's Nicki de Staramour, sire of eight champions and Q La Jolie Bibi de Reenroy, were successful entrants on the early show scene. Mrs. Fleishman imported Ch. Azara Zardin from Australia, and now, with his offspring in the ring, her exhibiting continues.

Lejerdell (New Jersey)

Jerome Podell imported Ch. Tarzan de la Persaliere (Quintan of Milton ex Maya of Milton), a sire of four champions, which brought more of the Belgian line to the country. Ch. Lejerdell's Leo D Lion of Rank, a son of Tarzan, and Lejerdell's Polar Bear were also champion producers. Tarzan ultimately went to England and the Cluneen Kennels of Elish Banks.

Braymar (New York)

Martin and Roberta Rothman's acquisition of Ch. Cali-Col's Octavius Caesar brought the famous Dapper Dan ex Lyne of Milton breeding across the continent to blend with their Reenroy bitches and a French import. His son, Ch. Braymar's Jackpot, was a noteworthy competitor of the era, and his daughter, Ch. Braymar's Nicole, was the dam of a top producing bitch, Braymar's Bali Hai. The Rothmans were active breeders and exhibitors in the early 1970s.

Teeny Tepee (Ohio)

Elizabeth (Betty) Shehab acquired Teeny Tepee's Mauri Julene as her foundation bitch. With Ombre de la Roche Posay as her double grandfather and Orlanda de La Roche Posay as a grandmother, Mauri Julene became one of the earliest influential results of the Goldysdale imports. Mauri Julene was the dam of five champions, two of which were top producing sons, Ch. Teeny Tepee's Cherokee Prince (with fourteen champion offspring) and Ch. Teeny Tepee's Chief of Diandee (with thirty-six champions). They were sired by Reenroy's Regal Beau and Ch. Reenroy's Royal Flush de Noel respectively, both of which were sons of Dapper Dan de Gascoigne. Mrs. Shehab acquired her first Bichon in 1968 and continues to be a staunch supporter of the breed.

Teeny Tepee's Mauri Julene, foundation
bitch for Elizabeth Shehab, 1971.

Ch. BoDan's Geronimo, owned and bred
by Bonnie Caison.

Mel-Mar (Michigan)

Melvin and Marvel Brown in 1967 acquired their foundation bitch, Ch. Mel-Mar's Randee of Goldysdale, another of the Ombre and Oree (de la Roche Posay) import daughters to arrive in the Midwest. Randee's son, Ch. Mel-Mar's Imperial du Chaminade (sired by Petit Galant de St. George) was one of the breed's earliest champions, and a daughter, Ch. Mel-Mar's Chou Chou de Noel (ex Diable de Gascoigne) would anchor the de Noel line. Mr. and Mrs. Brown have continued their interest in the breed and today are breeding in conjunction with Linda Lewis and Ladywood Bichons.

De Noel (Illinois)

Virginia Haley was the breeder of sixteen champions, seven by Ch. Mel-Mar's Chou Chou de Noel. Mrs. Haley introduced into the Midwest both Ch. Reenroy's Royal Flush de Noel, who would sire a top producing son, and Ch. Cali-Col's Winston de Noel, the sire of eight champions. Mrs. Haley was not active after the mid-1970s.

Ee's R Bichons (California)

Eva and Erwin Schroeder's foundation bitch, Ee's R Cali-Col's Ritzy Ruffles (Dapper Dan de Gascoigne ex Cali-Col's Our Daphne) was the dam of three especially notable offspring: bred to Petit Galant de St. George she produced Ee's R Royal Trinquette, dam of eight champions, including the 1978 National Specialty winner, Ch. Beau Monde the Iceman, and Canadian Ch. Ee's R Regal Prince of Henruf, sire of seventeen Canadian champions. Bred to Ch. Ee's R King George of KrisKanu she produced Ch. Beau Monde Ee's R Express, who became the foundation dog for Tres Beau Bichons and the sire of twelve champions. The Schroeders have been active since 1967.

Works D'Arte (Arizona)

Bobbye McKelvey was a breeder-exhibitor for a relatively short period of time, but she produced several Bichons of considerable influence. Her foundation bitch was Ch. Cali-Col's Candida, of the now-famous Dapper Dan and Lyne of Milton combination. Candida bred to Petit Galant de St. George produced Works d'Arte Miro a Chaminade, who was the dam of the first Australian Bichon champion, and Ch. Kahil's Color Me White, a foundation bitch for Cameo Bichons. A littermate was Works d'Arte Renoir, granddam of Ch. Works D'Arte Witty, the foundation bitch for Windstar Bichons.

Sarkis (Nevada)

Marie Sarkissian and Teena Sarkissian Runyon's foundation bitch at Sarkis, Ch. Chaminade Phoenicia, was a refreshing sight with owner-handler

Foundation bitch Ch. Mel-Mar's Randee of Goldysdale, owned by Marvel and Melvin Brown, 1969.

Ch. Rank's Eddie, first Bichon to win the breed at Westminster Kennel Club, in a 1973 photograph. Owner: Robert A. Koeppel; breeder: Jean Rank.

Teena during those early days of matches, exhibitions and Miscellaneous Classes. At thirteen years old, this talented young handler with her showy little Bichon won many fans for the breed at a time when this was important. Upon recognition, Phoenicia became the first Bichon bitch to win a Group First. Her granddaughter, Ch. Sarkis T. C. White Magic, was Winners Bitch at the 1982 National Specialty.

Seascape (California)

Pamela Sharp acquired Vintage Year's Rubion, who produced three sons of note: Seascape the Captain's Choice, sire of seven champions, and Ch. Seascape the Seafarer, both sons of Cali-Col's Shadrack; Rubion was later bred to Reenroy's Riot Act and produced Ch. Seascape the Tidal Wave.

Charda (Illinois)

Charlotte Trebonsky acquired both Ch. Seascape the Seafarer and Ch. Seascape the Tidal Wave. Their presence in the Midwest was a stroke of good fortune. Seafarer, aside from being a fine showman, was the sire of twelve champions, seven of these for the Legacy Bichons of Dorothy Siebert (Illinois). Tidal Wave was the sire of Ch. Nerak's Sweet Stuff of Charda, who was the dam of one of the top producing bitches of all time, Ch. Jalwin's Panache of Win-Mar, a foundation bitch for Jalwin Bichons and Ann D. Hearn.

Rava (Florida)

Stella Raabe, formerly of Virginia, has been a long-time Bichon enthusiast. Ch. Stardom's Odin Rex, Jr. (Dapper Dan ex Lyne of Milton), and Reenroy's Riot Act went to the East Coast and Mrs. Raabe and became available to the breeders in that area. Her foundation bitches were Ch. Rava's Royal Velvet of Reenroy, a Riot Act daughter out of Cali-Col's Rhapsody of Reenroy, one of the all-time top producing bitches; a second bitch was Reenroy's Rava BeBe (Cali-Col's Joset ex Reenroy's Quesar). Rava's Royal Valour went to Hilda Murphy and Vale Park Bichons in Canada, while Rava's Real Valor of Reenroy, an Odin Rex daughter, went to Mrs. J. Sorstein of Carlise Bichons in England.

TODAY'S BREEDERS

The following are Bichon breeders who are breeding and exhibiting at this writing. A mere handful can claim over twenty years as fanciers, while others became active during the seventies. The eighties brought additional enthusiasts to the ranks. These breeders have made significant contributions to the advancement of the Bichon Frise, and they are presented on the following pages with an effort made to trace the progress of the various lines.

Chaminade (California)

Barbara Stubbs acquired Petit Galant de St. George (ten champions), Ch. Reenroy's Ami du Kilkanny (five champions) and Ch. Cali-Col's Robspierre (fourteen champions) as foundation dogs in 1966. The breeding of Ami and Robspierre produced Ch. Chaminade Mr. Beau Monde, who became the top producing sire in breed history. Mr. Beau Monde's litter sister, Ch. Chaminade Sonata, was bred to Petit Galant. That combination produced Ch. Chaminade Syncopation (co-breeder, Richard Beauchamp), the first Best in Show Bichon, owned by Mrs. William B. Tabler of New York. Syncopation was an outstanding showman with an ingratiating temperament that won many fans for the breed in those early days when the breed began to show in point competition and support was needed. He ultimately won seven Bests in Show and sixty Group Firsts and became a top producer with fourteen champion offspring. Braymar's Bali Hai (Ch. Chaminade Mr. Beau Monde ex Ch. Braymar's Nicole), in co-ownership with Roberta Kuester Rothman, produced eleven champions. Bred to Ch. Chaminade Tempo (Petit Galant ex Ami), a championship litter was produced that included Ch. Braymar Chaminade Pavanne (owned by Dale and Norma Morgan), who was owner handled to Best of Opposite Sex wins at three National Specialty shows (1978, 1979 and 1983, from the Veteran Bitch class).

This litter also included Ch. Braymar Caprice du Chaminade, whose son, Ch. D'Shar's Rendezvous du Chamour (fourteen champions), produced a multiple Best in Show winner. Another Bali Hai top-producing daughter was Ch. Chaminade Cantata (five champions), whose own two daughters, Ch. Chaminade Sugar Baby and Ch. Chaminade Blue Velvet, have each produced Specialty and all-breed Best in Show–winning sons. Chaminade has produced forty-two champions at this writing.

Beau Monde (California)

Richard Beauchamp obtained his first Bichon, Ch. Chaminade Mr. Beau Monde, in 1971. This proved to be a stroke of good fortune for the Bichon world both here and abroad—a dog who would prove to be a dominant sire in the hands of a man with thirty years of experience in breeding and showing a number of different breeds. Through his owners' watchful efforts, Mr. Beau Monde became the top producing sire in the history of the breed, with sixty-five champions. Many of these champion offspring became top producing foundation dogs and top winners in England, Scandinavia, South America, South Africa, Australia (Beau Monde produced the first Bichon to come to this country) and New Zealand, as well as here in the United States. He produced four Best in Show winners and a three-time National Specialty

Ch. Reenroy's Ami du Kilkanny, foundation bitch for Barbara Stubbs. Dam of Ch. Chaminade Mr. Beau Monde.
Photo by Missy, 1970.

Petit Galant de St. George, second foundation dog at Chaminade, in 1969.

Ch. Chaminade Mr. Beau Monde, the all-time top producing sire, in 1974. Owned by Richard G. Beauchamp and Pauline Waterman.

40

show winner and number-two top producing sire of all time, Ch. Vogelflight's Music Man.

From 1973 to 1986 Pauline Waterman joined Mr. Beauchamp in a partnership under the Beau Monde prefix. To date Beau Monde has produced fifty champions, including the top producing bitch of all time, Ch. Beau Monde the Firecracker (seventeen champions); the number-four all-time top producing sire, Ch. Beau Monde the Huckster (Ch. Teeny Tepees Chief of Diandee ex Ch. Beau Monde the Stripper), with thirty-six champions; and the 1979 National Specialty winner, Ch. Beau Monde the Iceman. Ee's R Royal Trinquette, with Patricia Craige as co-owner (Petit Galant de St. George ex Cali-Col's Ritzy Ruffles), was a successful producer for Beau Monde with eight champions, several of which became foundation dogs for other lines.

C and D (Illinois)

Charles and Dolores Wolske have bred an amazing 103 champions at this writing! This is an extraordinary accomplishment for any breeder and must be a source of pride to this husband-and-wife team who through the years have consistently presented their own dogs. Their first Bichons were Ch. C and D's Countess Becky and Ch. C and D's Count Kristopher. The grandsires of these littermates were two of the Goldysdale imports, Quintal de Warnabry and Ombre de la Roche Posay. A grandam was Oree de la Roche Posay. Becky is the number-two top producing bitch of all time with sixteen champions, thirteen of these by Ch. Chaminade Mr. Beau Monde. This includes the first Best in Show Bichon bitch, from the famous "Sun" litter, Ch. C and D's Beau Monde Sunbeam (owned by Mrs. Jonathan Slocum) with four Bests in Show. Two of these Mr. Beau Monde–Becky daughters became foundation bitches and top producers for Crockerly and Tres Beau Bichons, while a third was a successful producer for the Wolskes themselves.

Ch. C and D's Count Kristopher was yet another outstanding sire for C and D, with thirty-one champions. Offspring of note were Ch. C and D's Beau Monde Blizzard, Best in Show winner and sire of ten champions (his dam, Ch. C and D's Sunbonnet, was dam of eight champions), and Ch. Bunnyrun the Heartbreaker, sire of ten champions, including a Best in Show winner (his dam, Ch. C and D's Katie Did, was another Sunbonnet offspring and a foundation bitch for Bunnyrun Bichons). More producing and winning Count Kristopher sons: Ch. C and D's King of the Road (seven champions) and Ch. C and D's Xmas Knight, who was not only a sire of fourteen champions but also an owner-handled Best in Show dog for the successful C and D Bichons. The Wolskes have been active since the early 1970s.

Vogelflight (Virginia)

Mary and John Vogel's and Kathy Vogel Hayes's Vogelflight foundation bitch was Ch. Vogelflight's Be Be Zwingalee. Her sire was from the Goldysdale lines at Iradell (Mrs. Clarkson Earl, Connecticut), and her dam was from the Cali-Col and Reenroy crosses at Thur-Em (Vicki Stowell, Virginia). She was bred back to her father and produced Vogelflight's Diandee Pouf, who in turn was bred to Ch. Teeny Tepee's Cherokee Prince, a Reenroy-Goldysdale cross. A daughter of this breeding, Ch. Vogelflight's Diandee Amy Pouf, was bred to Ch. Chaminade Mr. Beau Monde, and in February of 1975 a litter was born that proved to be one of the most famous of all Bichon litters by virtue both of its success in the show ring and its impact on future pedigrees.

Four males were the result, including Ch. Vogelflight's Music Man, the top winning Bichon in 1977 and 1978 with eight Bests in Show and eighty Group Firsts. He was also the winner of the Bichon Frise Club of America National Specialty Show three consecutive years, 1976, 1977, and 1978, a feat that has never been repeated. A most impressive statistic is his producing record; as the sire of forty-seven champions he is second only to his sire, Mr. Beau Monde. Especially successful were the breedings to Ch. Beau Monde the Firecracker, as they produced eleven champions. Ch. Vogelflight's Choir Master followed his brother as the top winning Bichon in 1979 and was also a successful sire with eleven champion offspring, which included the number-four top producing bitch, Ch. Vogelflight's Fantasia, dam of twelve champions. Ch. Vogelflight's Choir Boy completed his U.S. championship and then went to England to the noted Leander Kennels of John and Wendy Streatfield, where he was integrated into their Bichon breeding program. He also won two Bichon Frise Club of Great Britain Specialty Shows, in the tradition of his brother, Music Man. Ch. Vogelflight's Linus Diandee was the final champion in this litter, and was himself the sire of two champions.

In addition to the twenty-two champions bred at Vogelflight, another interesting aspect has been the mother-daughter team of Mary Vogel and Kathy Vogel as handlers, Kathy eventually pursuing a career as a professional handler. In the early years this duo made an especially attractive and talented addition to the Bichon ring.

Crockerly (California)

Rosmarie Blood's foundation bitch for Crockerly Bichons was a daughter of the second or "Moon" litter of Ch. Chaminade Mr. Beau Monde ex Ch. C and D's Countess Becky cross, Ch. C and D's Beau Monde Moonshine. She was the dam of nine champions, five from Ch. Beau Monde the Huckster and four from Ch. Vogelflight's Music Man. She herself was the Best of Winners at the first Bichon Frise Club of America National Specialty in 1976, where her sire won the Stud Dog Class and her half brother, Music Man, won Best of Breed. Her most celebrated offspring was Ch. Crockerly's Beau Monde Eclipse (sired by Ch. Beau Monde the Huckster), owned by Nancy Shapland of Devon Bichons, the 1980 National Specialty winner and top Bichon for that year. A recent addition to Crockerly has been Ch. Azara Crockerly Rose, C.D. (Ch. Nagazumi Mr. Frosty of Zudiki ex Ch. Leijazulip

Eng. and Am. Ch. Vogelflight's Choir Boy with owner Wendy Streatfield, of Leander Kennels, England.

Ch. Vogelflight's Linus Diandee with breeder and owner Mary Vogel.

Left to right: Ch. Vogelflight's Diandee Amy Pouf, dam of the brothers, and her sons Ch. Vogelflight's Music Man and Ch. Vogelflight's Choir Master, 1977.

Angelique), imported from Australia from the Azara Kennels of Rudi Van Voorst. Mrs. Blood is an AKC licensed judge.

Kobold (Texas)

Sherry and Lee Fry's early Bichons at Kobold were Ch. Puck de Bossange (Cali-Col's Prince Charming ex Samba des Closmyons) and Rava's Royal Valkyrie of R'nr (Ch. Stardom's Odin Rex, Jr., ex Reenroy's Samee) with five and four champions respectively. Their son, Ch. Kobold's Kilimanjaro, was an early group winner and sire of six champions. The coming of Ch. Beau Monde the Firecracker (Ch. C and D's Count Kristopher ex Ch. C and D's Beau Monde Sunbeam), co-owned with Richard Beauchamp for her first litter, initiated a producing bitch record that is unequalled to date. She is the number one top producing bitch of record with seventeen champions, eleven of these from Ch. Vogelflight's Music Man. A second bitch, Ch. Vogelflight's Fantasia (co-owned with Jim Taylor), is the number four all-time top producing bitch, with thirteen champions. Kilimanjaro bred to Fantasia produced Ch. Kobold's Windjammer, sire of five champions. In turn, Windjammer bred to Firecracker produced Ch. Kobold's Skyrocket, who is the sire of thirteen champions. Kobold has produced forty-eight champions at this writing.

Devon (Illinois)

Nancy Shapland tells us that the first Bichon at Devon was Ch. C and D's Star Gazer (Ch. C and D's Sunburst ex C and D's Windsong), a multiple Group winner and sire of nine champions, including the 1978 National Sweepstakes winner, Ch. C and D's Katie-Did. Ch. Beau Monde the Huckster (Ch. Teeny Tepee's Chief of Diandee ex Ch. Beau Monde the Stripper) was the next multiple Group winner for Mrs. Shapland. He became the number four all-time top producing sire with thirty-six champions, many of whom became top producers themselves. Next came the Huckster daughter, Ch. Crockerly Beau Monde Eclipse (dam, Ch. C and D's Beau Monde Moonshine), who was the top winning Bichon in 1980, the year in which she won the Fifth Bichon Frise Club of America National Specialty. She is the dam of three champions, which includes the 1985 National Sweepstakes winner, Ch. Beau Monde the Magic Crystal.

Mrs. Shapland was yet another breeder to acquire a bitch of the Ch. Chaminade Mr. Beau Monde ex Ch. C and D's Countess Becky cross; from their third litter came Ch. C and D's Devon Hell's Lil Angel. She is the dam of five champions, but it is her breeding to Ch. Tomaura's Moonlite Sonata (Ch. Loftiss Reenie ex Ch. Tomaura's Touch of Elegance) that would rewrite the books and break all existing records. Ch. Devon Puff and Stuff became the top winning Bichon in the history of the breed, with 60 all-breed Bests in Show and 165 Group Firsts. Puff won the Bichon Frise Club of America National Specialty in 1985, again in 1986 and was, of course, the top Bichon in those years as well as the top Non-Sporting dog. In 1986 she was the number two dog of all breeds. Puff won many friends for the breed with her exuberant showmanship, and hers is an extraordinary feat. It is doubtful if this record will be equaled for many years to come. A littermate of Puff's, Ch. Devon Vive Poncho, owned by Mary Ellen and Gene Mills and Richard Beauchamp, has gained a reputation as a top producing sire with fifteen champions.

Tres Beau (Florida)

Laura Keator acquired the foundation dog for Tres Beau Bichons in Ch. Beau Monde Ee's R Express (Ch. Ee's R King George ex Ee's R Cali-Col's Ritzy Ruffles), the sire of twelve champions. The foundation bitch was Ch. C and D's Beau Monde Moondust, another of the Mr. Beau Monde and Countess Becky offspring, the dam of six champions, all by Express. Ch. Tres Beau Baccaro was the Sweepstakes winner at the First Bichon Frise Club of America National Specialty in 1976 and was subsequently the sire of four champions. Ch. Tres Beau Arch de Triumph was the sire of four, and Ch. C and D B Ann Tres Beau was the dam of three champions. Ch. Tres Beau Impeccable Imp, dam of three champions, was a foundation bitch for Paw Mark Bichons and produced a multiple Best in Show winner for that line. Ch. Tres Beau Decor was a winning and producing foundation dog for Hillwood. Express and Moondust proved to be a successful and influential cross that would ultimately influence several lines.

Hillwood (Maryland)

Ellen MacNeille's first Bichon at Hillwood was Ch. Larica's Ondine of Hillwood (Ch. Paw Paw Punjab ex Ch. Mainbrace Alice Beau Monde), dam of three champions. Ch. Tres Beau Decor (Ch. Beau Monde Ee's R Express ex Ch. C and D's Beau Monde Moondust) was the foundation dog and sire of sixteen champions. He was the winner of two all-breed Bests in Show and eighteen Group Firsts. Bred to Ondine he produced Ch. Hillwood Brass Band, winner of two all-breed Bests in Show, seventeen Group Firsts and the 1983 Bichon Frise Club of America National Specialty. Brass Band sired six champions, the most notable being Ch. Camelot's Brassy Nickel, who became a top competitor in 1984 and 1985. Ellen MacNeille is an AKC licensed judge.

Camelot (New Jersey)

Pam Goldman is the breeder and owner of Ch. Camelot's Brassy Nickel (Ch. Hillwood Brass Band ex Renada's Lady Pooky V. Camelot). He was the winner of eight all-breed Bests in Show and forty-one Group Firsts, one of which occurred in 1984 at the prestigious American Kennel Club centennial show in Philadelphia. He was also the winner of the 1984 Bichon Frise Club of America National Specialty. He produced four champion offspring, including Ch. Unicorn Nickolas Nickelbee.

Unicorn (New Jersey)

Joann Failla is the breeder-owner of Ch. Unicorn's Nickolas Nickelbee (Ch. Camelot's Brassy Nickel ex Sandy Bert's Amanda Puff). He was the top winning Bichon in 1987 with seven all-breed Bests in Show and thirty-seven Group Firsts.

Win-Mar (Illinois)

Marie Winslow is the breeder of twenty-three champions, including her top producing and influential sire, Ch. Win-Mar's Magnificent Scamp (Reenroy's Riot Act ex Scille de Warnabry). Scamp produced nineteen champion offspring, including a top producing daughter, Ch. Jalwin's Panache of Win-Mar, who, with fourteen champions, was a mainstay of Jalwin Bichons. Ch. Win-Mar's Lucy Lucille (seven champions) and Am. and Can. Ch. Win-Mar's Little Elf (five champions) are highlights of the Elfins Bichons of John Hoglund. In addition, Win-Mar has provided foundation Bichons for Druid and Sumarco.

Mrs. Winslow had been in touch with Goldy Olsen over the years. As the latter became less active in Bichons following her initial involvement, Win-Mar became the recipient of some Bichons of historical interest and importance, including (1) the French imports Scille de Warnabry (Int. Ch. Jimbo de Steren Vor ex Int. Ch. Janitizia des Frimoussettes), Qukette de la Roche Posay (Igor Prince des Frimoussettes ex Fourmi de Dierstein), Sariette de Warnabry (Int. Ch. Jimbo de Steren Vor ex Int. Ch. Janitizia des Frimoussettes; (2) bred by Goldy Olsen, Roxene du G.W. (Quintal de Warnabry ex Orlanda de la Roche Posay), Ch. G.W.'s Fantastic Rose-el (Quilet des Frimoussettes ex Quetty de Warnabry), Win-Mar's Triumph du G.W. (Sweet du Roi des Lutins ex Sariette de Warnabry); and (3) bred by Gertrude Fournier, Natchen of Cali-Col (Eddy White de Steren Vor ex Lassy of Milton). Mrs. Winslow acquired her first Bichons in the late 1960s and has been a dedicated enthusiast through the years.

Druid (Illinois)

Betty Keatley and Betsy Schley produced the forty champions of Druid that are the results of blending Legacy (Dorothy Siebert, Illinois) and Win-Mar bloodlines. Am. and Can. Ch. Lily Gatlock of Druid (Ch. Druid's Diplomacy ex Winmar's Three Coins of Druid), dam of three champions, was a Best in Show winner (Canada), a multiple Group winner in the United States and Best of Opposite Sex at the 1982 Bichon Frise Club of America National Specialty. Win-Mar's Three Coins of Druid produced nine champions including Ch. Barbra Gatlock of Druid, who has ten champions to her credit, and

Multiple BIS winner and a top producer, Ch. Leander Snow Star, with Laura Purnell, of Tomaura Bichons.

Winner of BFCA first Breeders Competition, 1986, Paw Mark Bichons of Pauline Schultz (*left to right*): Ch. Paw Mark's Talk of the Town, Ch. Paw Mark's Tripple Threat and Ch. Paw Mark's September Song. The Breeders Competition is held annually with the National Specialty.

Ch. Win-Mar's Lillian of Druid, who has five. A Lillian son, Ch. Scamper Gatlock of Druid, is a Specialty Best in Show and Group winner and the sire of seven champions. Scamper is co-owned by Laura Fox of Foxlaur Bichons.

Jalwin (Georgia)

Ann D. Hearn says that two bitches were the foundation of the Jalwin line. Ch. Jalwin Illumine de Noel (Ch. Cali-Col's Ulysses ex Ch. Cherokee Candy de Noel) is the dam of five champions. The second, Ch. Jalwin Panache of Win-Mar (Ch. Win-Mar's Magnificent Scamp ex Ch. Neraka Sweet Stuff of Charda) is the dam of fourteen champions, making her the number-three top producing bitch of all time. Six of these were sired by Ch. Diandee Masterpiece and five by Ch. Leander Snow Star. The most famous of her offspring is Ch. Jalwin Just a Jiffy, a top winner and producer owned by Pauline Schultz of Paw Mark. A Jiffy sister from a repeat breeding of Ch. Diandee Masterpiece and Panache was Ch. Jalwin Justice, who also proved valuable to the Paw Mark line. Mrs. Hearn is the breeder of twenty-five champions and is an AKC licensed judge.

Paw Mark (Georgia)

Pauline Schultz began Paw Mark Bichons with Ch. Jalwin Just a Jiffy (Ch. Diandee Masterpiece ex Ch. Jalwin Panache of Win-Mar). Jiffy was the winner of the 1981 Bichon Frise Club of America National Specialty plus seven all-breed Bests in Show and thirty-six Group Firsts. He is the sire of seventeen champions. Bred to Brereton's Cassandra Magic he produced Ch. Paw Mark's Pebbles of Brereton, winner of the Sweepstakes at the 1983 BFCA National Specialty (co-owned with Margaret Britton). Bred to the Paw Mark foundation bitch Ch. Tres Beau Impeccable Imp (Ch. Beau Monde Ee's R Express ex Ch. C and D's Beau Monde Moondust), Jiffy produced Ch. Paw Mark's Talk of the Town. He became the top winning Bichon for 1984 with nine all-breed Bests in Show and forty-eight Group Firsts, ably handled by his owner, Pauline Schultz, once again that rarity, the breeder-owner-handler. A Jiffy granddaughter, Ch. Sandcastle Bikini, has been a Specialty and multiple Group winner for the Sandcastle Bichons of Linda Dickens. The Jiffy sister, Ch. Jalwin Justice, produced eight champions for Paw Mark, notably Ch. Paw Mark's September Song, owned by Pam Lee, Colorado (ABI), a multiple Group winner; and Ch. Paw Mark's Lollipop Labow, a Specialty Best in Show winner and Best of Opposite Sex winner at the 1987 Bichon Frise Club of America National Specialty, owned by Lenora and Robert Wilson, Oregon (Norwil). Both bitches were by Ch. Brereton B.B. Cody. Paw Mark has produced twenty-nine champions to date. Mrs. Schultz and her daughter Deedy Pierce have had great success handling their own Paw Mark Bichons and equal success as professional handlers for other lines and other breeds.

Brereton (Alabama)

Albert and Margaret Britton relate that the early Bichons of Brereton go back to the bloodlines of Jean Rank. Ch. Brereton's Gamblin Dandy (Ch. Rank's Bella Sunshine ex Rank's Diamond Lil) bred to Ch. King's Heidi Ho (Ch. Rank's Rank and Ready ex Brereton Carnisa of Rank) produced Ch. Brereton's Deuces Wild. She in turn produced six champions, five from the Paw Mark's Jiffy and Talk of the Town. Ch. Brereton Happy Hour, a daughter of the Jiffy ex Deuces Wild combination, was bred to Ch. Scamper Gatlock of Druid. A resulting son, Ch. Brereton Stonewall Jackson, returned to Druid, where he was bred to Ch. Win-Mar's Lillian of Druid, producing a litter of five champions. The Jiffy ex Deuces Wild combination also produced Ch. Brereton B. B. Cody, who, bred to Ch. Jalwin Justice, produced well. Albert and Margaret Britton are breeders of twenty-four champions.

Jadeles (Michigan)

Judith Thayer's foundation dog was Ch. Lierre des Champ Jumeaux, who sired nine champions. This included a Best in Show son, Ch. Jadeles the Kid H H Pride (owned and shown by Lorrie Conrad, Belle Creek Bichons) and a daughter, Ch. Jadeles December Blizzard, who produced six champions. Two other males, Ch. Jadeles October Goblin and Ch. Jadeles March Freddy, sired eight and nine champions respectively. The Jadeles foundation bitch, Ch. Jadeles December Snow (Kalon of Goldysdale ex Quillici of Goldysdale—Ombre de la Roche Posay being the double grandsire), produced six champions. Ch. Jadeles May Marigold, a product of the foundation dog and bitch, also produced six champions. Jean Rank and Judy Thayer were co-breeders of the 1981 Bichon Frise Club of America National Specialty winner, Ch. Rank's Raggedy Andy (Ch. Rank's White Blaze ex Rank's Bobbin Along). Andy was owned by Naomi Makeowiec and shown by Lorrie Conrad, Belle Creek Bichons, and was the sire of ten champions. Mrs. Thayer is the breeder of thirty-six champions.

San Don (Ohio)

Sandra and Donald Orr's foundation bitch at San Don is San Don's Rockin Bobbin of Rank (Ch. Lejerdell's Leo D Lion of Rank ex Mary's Bobbin), with three champions to her credit. Most notable of her offspring was Ch. San Don's Friend, sired by Ch. Rank's White Flame. Friend was the sire of thirteen champions and was the first breeder-owner-handled Specialty winner. However, it was his son, Ch. San Don's Friendly Legacy (by Ch. Win-Mar's Lucy Lucille and bred by Mr. and Mrs. John Hoglund) who took Specialty winning to new heights, as he has won six Specialty Bests in Show, three of these in 1988. He is the sire of seven champions. Ch. Chamour Demitasse du San Don (D'Shar Rendezvous du Chamour ex Brayamar's Bouquet) dam of two champions, has been part of the San Don breeding program.

BISS winner Ch. San Don's Friendly Legacy, son of Friend, from San Don Bichons.

BISS winner Ch. San Don's Friend, from the San Don Bichons of Sandy and Donald Orr.

Multiple BIS winner Ch. Norvic's Razzle Dazzle, from the Norvic Kennels of Alice and Norman Vicka.

51

Sandy Orr has competently handled her own Bichon Frises and is also a successful handler of other breeds.

Diandee (Michigan)

Clover and John Allen's first Bichon at Diandee was Vogelflight's Diandee Pouf (Tinker II of Rich-Lo ex Vogelflight's Bebe Zwingalee). She produced three champions, but it was her daughter, Ch. Vogelflight's Diandee Ami Pouf (sired by Ch. Tepee's Cherokee Prince), who made history through her four famous Vogelflight sons. The acquisition of Ch. Teeny Tepee's Chief of Diandee (Ch. Reenroy's Royal Flush de Noel ex Teeny Tepee's Mauri Julene) proved to be the focal point of the Diandee line, as he became the number three all-time top producing sire, with thirty-six champions. An outstanding offspring is Ch. Beau Monde the Huckster, just behind his father as the number four all-time top producing sire, with 36 champions. Ch. Diandee Masterpiece (Ch. Norvic's Nebuchadnezzar ex Diandee Sweet Pollyanna) is the sire of nine champions, notably the top winner and producer, Ch. Jalwin Just a Jiffy, and his sister Ch. Jalwin Justice. Am. and Can. Ch. Diandee Renegade (Ch. Diandee Alba the Aristocrat ex Ch. Diandee Sunshine of Maberhof), a linebred sire, is currently making his mark. The Allens are breeders of thirty-two champions and both are AKC licensed judges.

Norvic (Ohio)

Alice and Norman Vicka purchased Ch. Reenroy's Image of Ami as the foundation bitch at Norvic. She has nine champions to her credit. A daughter, Norvic's Nice N Easy, produced Ch. Norvic's Razzle Dazzle, the sire of six champions and winner of four all-breed Bests in Show and multiple Group Firsts (owned by Robert A. Koeppel) and a second son, Ch. Norvic's Easy Does It, the sire of eight champions. Ch. Norvic's Sweet Stuff produced five champions, including a daughter, Ch. Norvic's Alpine Sparkler (by Ch. Norvic's Dazzle Me), who produced ten champions (owned by Ann Freeman of Alpine Bichons). Early blending of the Diandee and Norvic lines helped develop the type sought by these two breeders. Mrs. Vicka is the breeder of forty-five champions at this writing.

Regal (Ohio)

Evelyn Koziel acquired the foundation bitch for Regal in Ch. My Bit of Honey Lola (Joey Shain du G.W. ex Teeny Tepee's Mauri Julene), who subsequently produced five champions. Several successful producing bitches followed. Ch. Lex Mieux Regal Victoria (Ch. Som-bee's Beau Pirot Le Mieux ex Ch. Bo-Dan Belle Piroette Le Mieux) produced seven champions, while Ch. Beau Monde the Fawn (Ch. C and D's Count Kristopher ex Ee's R Royal Trinquette) was the dam of five champions. Ch. Cali-Col's Robspierre was co-owned by Mrs. Koziel. Bred to the Fawn he produced Ch. Beau

Monde Regal Rose, a multiple Group winner owned by Ellen MacNeille of Hillwood Bichons. Regal Bichons have produced twenty-seven champions.

Tomaura (Kansas)

Laura Purnell has been a successful breeder, with fifty-two champions to her credit. She acquired two males who became top producers: Ch. Loftiss Reenie (Reenroy's Toro ex Reenroy Tanya), sire of twenty-seven champions, and Ch. Leander Snow Star out of Leander Snow Venture and Ch. C and D's Beau Monde Sunflower. (Sunflower and the dam of Snow Venture were litter sisters: Ch. Chaminade Mr. Beau Monde ex Ch. C and D's Countess Becky.) Snow Star, one of the great world travelers, arrived in Kansas by way of England, where he was born, and Australia, where he was shown. His American record was three Bests in Show and a Specialty win. He is the sire of 33 champions. Bred to Ch. Chaminade Sugar Baby he produced his first Best in Show son, Ch. Westoak Wizard of Pawz. Tomaura has produced a number of successful bitches. Ch. Tomaura's Sweet Charity (linebred from Ombre de la Roche Posay) with five champions, Tomaura's Amber de Susa with seven champions and Ch. Tomaura's Touch of Elegance topping the list with ten champions. This is a daughter of Ch. Tomaura's Frosty Snowman out of Ch. Mainbrace Betsy of Tomaura (a Petit Galant de St. George granddaughter). Ch. Tomaura's Moonlight Sonata gained lasting fame as the sire of the top winning Bichon of all time, Ch. Devon Puff and Stuff, owned by Nancy Shapland, Devon Bichons.

Keleb (Kansas)

Judy Fausset says the foundation bitch for Keleb is Ch. Keleb Kriquette of Tomaura (Ch. Loftiss Reenie ex Tomaura's Bundle of Joy), who produced five champions. Bred to Am. and Can. Ch. Keleb's Bang-a-way Bear she produced Ch. Keleb's Majestic Reason, sire of eight champions, most notable being a top producing son, Ch. Keleb's A Touch of Deja Vu, sire of seven champions and a foundation dog for the Deja Vu Bichons of Karla Matlock. Bred back to her sire Kriquette produced Ch. Keleb's Snowbear O'Tomaura, a Group winner and sire of five champions. Two Keleb Bichons were imported by the Australian Azara Kennels of Rudy Van Voorst and Frank Valley, Keleb Majestic Image and Keleb Snuggle Dumpling. Keleb has produced twenty-one champions to date.

Sumarco (New Jersey)

Roy Copelin credits two Bichons with making an impact on the Sumarco line, Ch. Tomaura's Symphony of Sumarco (Ch. Loftiss Reenie ex Ch. Tomaura's Touch of Elegance) and her half brother, Ch. Tomaura's Mor Bounce to the Oz, sired by Ch. Leander Snow Star. The former has four champions to her credit, and the latter has seven. Ch. Win-Mar's Windsong

Best in Show winner Ch. Lambo of Loch Vale, bred, owned and handled by Diane Ayres, Loch Vale Bichons.

Ch. Bunnyrun Still the One, eleven months, youngest Best in Show Bichon. Bred, owned, and handled by Kurt James.

de Sumarco (Ch. Win-Mar's Magnificent Scamp ex Ch. Nerak's Sweet Stuff of Charda) is the dam of four champions and a sister to the top producing bitch, Ch. Jalwin Panache of Win-Mar. Cathy Jones (Alafee) and Jacqueline Kartanos (Kraig Kourt) combined with Sumarco to import Ch. Montravia Jazz M Tazz (Leijazulip Jazz of Zudiki ex Montravia's Snow Dream) from the English breeder Pauline Gibbs. Alafee and Sumarco imported the bitch Paper Lacy of Zudiki from a second English breeder, Jo Brown-Emerson. These two English imports produced Ch. Sumarco Alafee Top Gun, the first American-bred champion of an English-bred sire and dam. Top Gun (owned by Mrs. William B. Tabler) is a multiple Best in Show and Group winner.

Bunnyrun (Kansas)

Beth and Kurt James have had the good fortune of being breeder-owner-handler of both a Specialty Best in Show winner (1981) and an all-breed Best in Show winner (1988). First is Ch. Bunnyrun the Heartbreaker (Ch. C and D's Count Kristopher ex Ch. C and D's Katie-Did), the sire of fourteen champions. This includes an all-breed Best in Show winner, Ch. Bunnyrun the Quarterback, who himself is the sire of nine champions. The second is Ch. Bunnyrun Still the One (Ch. Diamant's Le Magnifique ex Ch. Bunnyrun Over the Rainbow), who broke all records by winning his Best in Show at the tender age of eleven months! Mr. James comes from a family with a long-term involvement in purebred dogs, and he himself was a professional handler for many years. Beth James is the breeder of twenty-two champions.

Loch Vale (Kansas)

Diane Ayres piloted one of only five American Bichons that have been breeder-owner handled to an all-breed Best in Show. Two of these five live in Kansas! Mrs. Ayres took Ch. Lambo of Loch Vale (Ch. Chaminade Mr. Beau Monde ex Ch. Cali-Col's Alouette) to this win in 1980, the first Bichon breeder to do so. Ch. Muguet of Loch Vale, litter sister to Lambo, is the dam of five champion daughters, three of whom are champion producers. One, Ch. Avalanche Lily of Loch Vale, produced Ch. Tres Jolie Mr. Vagabond (sired by Ch. Craigdale's Ole Rhondi), who won three all-breed Bests in Show and forty-five Group Firsts.

Darkel (New York)

Dorothy Wilson, an early 1970s breeder, says her foundation Bichon was Parkway LaFemme (Quilet des Frimoussettes ex SaMajestic de la Persaliere). Bred to Ch. Beau Monde the Actor she produced Am. and Can. Ch. Darkel's Artic Star, Am., Can. and Bda. C.D. Artic Star produced two American champions but is recognized even more for his ten Canadian champions. His daughter, Can. Ch. Darkel's Cameo Souvenir, was bred to Ch.

Windstar's Aristotle. An offspring of this breeding, Am., Can. and Bda. Ch. Darkel's Imperial Gamble, was the sire of ten American champions. Once again the Darkel line proved highly successful in Canada, for Imperial Gamble is the sire of twelve champions in that country.

Paw Paw (New York)

Amy Costello acquired the foundation bitch, Ch. Tanya (Int. Ch. Gift de Steren Vor ex Gueule D'Amour des Frimoussettes) when she was imported in the early 1970s. Tanya produced eight champions, several of whom proved influential. Three of these were by Mex. Ch. Dapper Dan de Gascoigne: Ch. Paw Paw Kimberly Kate, Ch. Paw Paw Ramona and Ch. Paw Paw Sir Lancelot. An additional three champions were by Dan's grandson, Ch. Chaminade Mr. Beau Monde, most notable being Ch. Paw Paw Punjab, sire of five champions. Paw Paw produced sixteen champions, and the prefix can be seen in the pedigrees of Ardezz (Stephanie Ezzard), Glen Elfred, (Eleanor Grassick), Keleb (Judy Fausset), Petit Four (Judith Hilmer) and others.

Windstar (New York)

Estelle and Wendy Kellerman are breeders of twenty and twenty-three champions respectively. This mother and daughter duo have been active since the early 1970s, when they acquired Ch. Jaronda Bon Vivant (Jaronda Raincheck of Reenroy ex Genifred of Iradell), the sire of eight champions. Their foundation bitch was Ch. Beau Monde Works D'Arte Witty (Reenroy's Sir Bernard ex Works D'Arte Renoir), who also produced eight champions. Four of Witty's champions were by Ch. Chaminade Mr. Beau Monde. One of these, Ch. Windstar's Aristotle, produced four American champions before going to Argentina, where he became a Group Winner and successful producer. His son, Am. Ch. Darkel's Imperial Gamble, was an impressive producer both in the United States and in Canada. Witty bred to Bon Vivant produced Ch. Belinda of Windstar, who was the dam of seven champions. This included Ch. Windstar's the Minstrel Singer, sire of nine champions. Another Belinda son, Ch. Windstar's Fig Newton, sired a current winner, Ch. Windstar's Charisma. Wendy Kellerman was a fine junior handler as a youngster and today is a successful professional handler.

Glen Elfred (New York)

Eleanor Grassick explains that unique circumstances provided the foundation dog for Glen Elfred. Ch. Glen Elfred Mr. Chips (Napoleon de Gascoigne ex Golden Rules Lottie) was a rescue dog who was not acquired until he was three and a half years old. Despite his inauspicious early years, he completed his championship, sired twelve offspring and proved to be a dominant factor in the Glen Elfred line. A notable son was Ch. Ardezz Mr. Showman, sire of seven champions. The litter sisters Ch. Ballade de Lizette

Ch. L'Havre Joyeux Desi, an influential producer for the L'Havre Joyeux Bichons of Dr. Donald and Rolande Lloyd.

Ch. Petit Four Super Trouper, Group winner, BOS 1985 National Specialty, bred and owned by Judith L. Hilmer.

Ch. Beau Monde Works D'Arte Witty, foundation bitch for Windstar Kennels of Estelle and Wendy Kellerman.

and Ch. Ballade de Babette (Paw Paw Ulysses ex Libit Chez Rivage d'Ami) were champion-producing foundation bitches. The latter was Best of Opposite Sex winner at Westminster Kennel Club in 1978 and dam of four champions, including Ch. Glen Elfred's Ego Trip, grandsire of Ch. Glen Elfred's Billy Boy, a multiple Group winner. Glen Elfred has produced thirty-four champions to date and has been influential in the pedigrees of Stephanie Ezzard (Ardezz) and Le Beau Chien Bichons of Lisa DeGregorio, second winner of the Breeder of the Year award for the Bichon Frise Club of America.

Diamant (California)

Kay Hughes's foundation Bichons of Diamant were in co-ownership with Stephanie Ezzard (Ardezz), formerly of New York and currently a California resident. Ch. Ardezz Jacques Diamant (Ch. Ardezz Mr. Showman ex Ardezz Spoonful of Sugar) and Ch. Ardezz Juliette Diamant (Ch. Ardezz Mr. Showman ex Ardezz Satin Pillow) became successful producers for the Diamant Bichons of the 1980s. Jacques is the sire of seven champions to date. The most celebrated is Ch. Diamant's Le Magnifique, winner of two all-breed Bests in Show, a Specialty Best in Show and forty-two Group Firsts. He in turn is the sire of six champions, including an all-breed Best in Show–winning son of his own, Ch. Bunnyrun Your the One. He was owned during his show career by Jill Cohen of Seastar Bichons. Juliette is the dam of six champions. Bred to Ch. Beau Monde the Huckster she produced Ch. Diamant Dominique, dam of Le Magnifique.

Miri-Cal (Pennsylvania)

Miriam Barnhardt's Miri-Cal foundation bitch, obtained from the Fran-Dor line of Doris Homsher, was Ch. Fran-Dor's Chantilly (Ch. Kettle Lane Dandelion ex Braymar's Oleana), dam of five champions. Four of the five were by Ch. Vogelflight's Choir Master: Ch. Miri-Cal's Sound of Music, with four champions; Ch. Miri-Cal's Motet (owned by Ed and Anne Jones of Enjoue Bichons), with three champions; and Ch. Miri-Cal's Berceuse, with three champions. Sound of Music bred to a Berceuse granddaughter produced Ch. Miri-Cal's All That Jazz, a 1984 all-breed Best in Show winner who also won fifteen Group Firsts and is making a name for himself as a producer, with thirteen champion offspring at this writing.

Petit Four (New York)

Judith Hilmer relates that an early producer for Petit Four was Ch. Petit Four Beau Peep (Ch. Chaminade Mr. Beau Monde ex Ch. Paw Paw Kimberly Kate). Her son, Ch. Petit Four Quite White (sired by Ch. C and D Petit Four White Xmas) became a sire of seven champions. Ch. C and D Petit Four White Xmas, bred by Dolores Wolske, was the sire of ten champions. Ch. Petit Four Super Trouper (Petit Four American Express ex Ch. Petit Four

Ch. Miri-Cal's All That Jazz, BIS and Group winner for Miri-Cal Bichons of Miriam Barnhardt. *Photo by Missy.*

BIS and BISS winner Ch. Diamant's Le Magnifique from Diamant Bichons of Kay Hughes.

Sparkle Plenty) was Winners Dog at the American Kennel Club Centennial Show in Philadelphia in 1984, following that up with a Best of Opposite Sex win at the Bichon Frise Club of America National Specialty Show in 1985. Mrs. Hilmer is the breeder of thirty-six champions to date.

L'Havre Joyeux (Massachusetts)

Rolande and Donald Lloyd, D.V.M. were among the breeders in the late 1960s who acquired their foundation dogs from Goldysdale. Ch. Rickel du G.W. (Ombre de la Roche Posay ex Natchen of Cali-Col) and Richel du G.W. were the first. (Doris Hyde and Dove-Cote Bichons acquired a full sister to these two as a foundation bitch.) They produced Ch. Mon Monsieur de L'Havre Joyeux and L'Havre Joyeux Tina Tart. The latter was the dam of two notable offspring. The first was Ch. L'Havre Joyeux Lucy, dam of the 1982 Bichon Frise Club of America National Sweepstakes winner, Ch. L'Havre Joyeux Mighty Might, sired by Ch. Vogelflight's Choir Master. The second was Ch. L'Havre Joyeux Desi, who sired Ch. Parfait Coming Home, a top producing sire for the Bichons of Druid, Parfait Bichons and the Pere Jacque line.

Chanson (Florida)

Carol Sommers's Chanson foundation bitch, Starlette de la Persaliere, was bred to Petit Galant de St. George, producing Ch. Chanson's Clouds of Mainbrace. This dog, bred in turn to Chaminade Fantasie, owned by Mainbrace (Tom Howell, Virginia), produced Ch. Mainbrace Betsy O Tomaura, an important producer for the Tomaura line. A second bitch of the Chanson Bichons, Joanne's Elke of Chanson (Ch. Chaminade Mr. Beau Monde ex Chanson's Gift of Sunnyknoll), became important to the Parfait line of Joanne Spilman.

Parfait (Massachusetts)

Joanne Spilman says the foundation bitch, Joanne's Elke of Chanson, proved to be an important element in the Parfait breeding program. Bred to Ch. Cameo Temptation Chaminade she produced Ch. Parfait Apple Crisp and Ch. Parfait Apple Crunch. Ch. L'Havre Joyeux Desi and Apple Crunch produced Ch. Parfait Coming Home, a notably influential sire of twenty-one champions to date, who themselves have become successful producers, i.e., Ch. Parfait Ebony and Ivory, Ch. Pere Jacque Samson D'Parfait, Ch. Win-Mar's Lillian of Druid. As the last bitch ever bred to Ch. Chaminade Mr. Beau Monde, Apple Crunch produced the two final champions of his career. Apple Crisp, bred to Cotton R. Nell, produced Ch. Parfait Hellsapopin of Druid (co-owned with Betty Keatley, L. Kilduff and T. Lao), winner of the 1988 Bichon Frise Club of America National Specialty Show, only the third

60

bitch to achieve that honor in the thirteen years of Specialty shows. Joanne Spilman is the breeder of twenty-one champions.

Pere Jacque (North Carolina)

Jane Lageman acquired Ch. Pennywise Triple Trouble (Ch. Parfait Coming Home ex A Bit O Cotton) as a foundation bitch for Pere Jacque. Bred back to Ch. Parfait Coming Home she produced Ch. Pere Jacque Samson D'Parfait. With four champions in one year he appears on his way to being a top producer for his breeder-owner. Ch. Pennywise the Challenger, a half brother to Triple Trouble (by Ch. Win-Mar's Magnificent Scamp), is also the sire of four champions. Ch. Parfait Ebony and Ivory (Ch. Parfait Coming Home ex Parfait Candy Apple) is the second producing dam, with nine champions to her credit.

Chamour (California)

Lois Morrow's interest in Bichons at Chamour took a different turn from most, in that the males became the dominant factor as opposed to the bitches. Ch. Chaminade Tempo (Petit Galant de St. George ex Ch. Reenroy's Ami du Kilkanny) was acquired in 1973. A multiple Group winner, Tempo was the sire of eight champions, including Best in Show and Specialty winner Ch. Cameo Temptation Chaminade (ex Ch. Kahil's Color Me White), who was himself the sire of seven champions. (Mrs. Morrow was the co-breeder with Ginger LeCave and co-owner with Jim and Carla Denney.)

Tempo also sired a champion litter from Braymar's Bali Hai that proved influential. A bitch, Ch. Braymar Pavanne du Chaminade (owned by Norma and Dale Morgan), was the Best of Opposite Sex winner at the 1978, 1979 and 1983 National Specialties. A son was the 1979 National Sweepstakes winner, and a daughter, Ch. Larkshire Paper Doll, is the dam of six champions. A second daughter, Ch. Braymar's Caprice du Chaminade (owned by Dorothy Spear), bred to her half brother, Cameo Chaminade Chant, produced the second major dog at Chamour, Ch. D'Shar Rendezvous du Chamour. This Specialty Best in Show and multiple Group winner is the sire of fifteen champions, the most notable being Ch. Craigdale's Olé Rhondi (ex Ch. Wicked Music of Craigdale and bred by Dale Hunter). Olé was the number one Bichon in 1983 with eight all-breed Bests in Show, sixty Group Firsts and four Specialty wins. He is the sire of eighteen champions to date, including two Best in Show sons, Ch. Tres Jolie Mr. Vagabond and Am., Mex. and Int. Ch. Chaminade Le Blanc Chamour. Ole has two daughters who have produced Best in Show sons, Ch. Chaminade Sugar Baby (Ch. Westoak Wizard of Pawz) and Ch. Chaminade Blue Velvet (Ch. Alpenglow Ashley du Chamour). Ashley was the 1987 BFCA National Specialty winner, with ten Bests in Show and seventy Group Firsts. He was the number one Non-Sporting dog for 1987–88. Mrs. Morrow proficiently owner-handled many of

Ch. Chaminade Tempo, the first of several influential sires for Lois Morrow, Chamour Bichons.
Handled by Ric Chaschoudian. *Photo by Missy.*

Ch. D'Shar's Rendezvous du Chamour, a Tempo grandson, another important sire for Chamour owned by Lois Morrow. Sire of cover dog, Ch. Craigdale's Olé Rhondi.

Photo by Missy.

Ch. Alpenglow's Ashley du Chamour, also a Tempo grandson, is number three all-time top winning Bichon, a 1988 Non-Sporting Group winner and 1987 BFCA National Specialty winner. Owned by L. Morrow and J. McClaren; bred by B. Stubbs and L. Daye; handled by Michael Kemp.

the Tempo, Rhondi and Olé offspring to their championships and is the breeder of twenty champions.

Cameo (California)

Ginger LeCave notes that the Cameo foundation Bichons were a blending of the early bloodlines. Ch. Kahil's Color Me White (Reenroy's Riot Act ex Works D'Arte Miro du Chaminade) was the dam of Ch. Cameo Temptation Chaminade, winner of the 1977 National Sweepstakes with the largest entry to date, in addition to being a Specialty and all-breed Best in Show winner. Ch. Jacelene Chanedelle (Cali-Col's Shadrack ex Reenroy's Jacelene Lily) produced three champions, and a son, Cameo Chaminade Chant, was the sire of Ch. D'Shar's Rendezvous du Chamour, a top producer, and Ch. Cameo Catastrophe, whose son, Ch. Drewlaine the Cameo Kid, is another top producer.

In recent years Mrs. LeCave has worked closely with Dibbet (Betty Shuck, Oregon). Mrs. LeCave and Mrs. Schuck have imported a male and a female from England to complement their breeding programs. Rouska's Cameo Dance (Shamaney Stepping Out at Kynismar ex Rouska's Dance of Love) is co-owned with breeder Den Thomas of England. This youngster won Best Puppy at the Bichon Club of Great Britain Open Show in the winter of 1988, then came to the United States and won the Sweepstakes at the BFCA National Specialty and was also the Sweepstakes winner at the Bichon Frise Club of Northern California Specialty. The female is Jaylea Dibbet Royal Duchess (Eng. Ch. Tiopepi Mad Louie of Pamploma ex Jaylea Son et Lumiere).

Drewlaine (California)

Mary Ellen and Gene Mills's first lady at Drewlaine was Ch. Cali-Col's Villanelle (Cali-Col's Shadrack ex L'Amour du G.W.). A dam of three champions, she was also Best of Opposite Sex winner at the first BFCA National Specialty in 1976. Her daughter, Ch. Drewlaine Eau du Love (sire, Ch. Chaminade Mr. Beau Monde) was Best of Opposite Sex winner at the 1977 National Sweepstakes with the largest entry to date. Eau du Love was the dam of four champions sired by Ch. Beau Monde the Huckster, including Ch. Drewlaine Beau Monde Deja Vu, the third generation from Villanelle. Ch. Drewlaine the Cameo Kid (Cali-Col's Chaminade Drum Song ex Ch. Cameo Catastrophe) has been a successful producer for Drewlaine with six champion offspring, including Ch. Beau Monde the Magic Crystal, Sweepstakes Winner at the 1985 BFCA National Specialty (ex Ch. Crockerly Beau Monde Eclipse) and Ch. Chamour Melody of Drewlaine (ex Ch. Larkshire Paper Doll), dam of four champions from her first litter. She is the foundation bitch for Hollyhock Bichons of Ford and Diana McFarlane and Linda Rowe. Ch. Devon's Vive Poncho, in co-ownership with Richard Beauchamp, was the top sire for 1987 and 1988, with fifteen champions to his credit.

64

Deja Vu (Arizona)

Karla and Les Matlock owned Ch. DeDeb's Deja Vu Prelude Major, C.D. (Ch. Rank's Raggedy Andy ex Rank's Southern Belle), the first Bichon with twelve champion offspring. The foundation bitches were two linebred Music Man daughters (ex Ch. Bella Lucianna), Ch. Bella Graziella of Deja Vu, with six champions to date, and Ch. Bella Angelina of Deja Vu with five champions. Ch. Keleb a Touch of Deja Vu (Ch. Keleb Majestic Reason ex Ch. Keleb's Wait N See Desusa) has produced eight champions and was obviously another successful addition to the line. In four years of breeding, the Deja Vu line has produced eighteen champions, five Group-winning Bichons and six with Obedience titles. All have been owner handled, of which the Matlocks are justifiably proud.

All of these breeders have made their special contributions and all should be justifiably proud of their achievements. It bears repeating that few breeds have accomplished so much in so short a time. The dedicated breeders and love of the Bichon Frise made it happen.

Bichons of Leander (*clockwise*): Am. Ch. Vogelflight's Choir Boy of Leander, Leander Beau Monde the Fanfare and Leander Snow Dragon. Owned by Wendy Streatfield.

4

The Bichon Frise
Around the World

THE BICHON FRISE continues to grow in popularity around the world. Breeders in many countries have accepted the challenge of establishing quality lines for perpetuating and protecting the breed. This chapter highlights the efforts of just some of the breeders who have met that challenge.

CANADA

In July 1975 the Canadian Kennel Club granted full recognition to the Bichon Frise, due largely to the efforts of Kay Calderbank. In contrast to the United States, Canada did not have a national club and the means of promoting interest in the breed, which makes Mrs. Calderbank's individual accomplishment even more remarkable.

An application for Canadian Kennel Club recognition required a list of twenty-five Bichons that had or could get American Kennel Club papers as well as Bichon imports from Europe whose sire and dam were registered there; in 1971 there were only nineteen known Bichons in Canada. In May of 1973 Mrs. Calderbank began her efforts toward recognition, and in March 1974 the application was filed with the Canadian Kennel Club. A year later, in March 1975, the Bichon was accepted and placed in the Non-Sporting Group.

The Breed Standard was adopted in 1975, once again through the efforts of Mrs. Calderbank, and is still the Standard in use as of this writing.

The Canadian Bichon Frise shares ancestry with the American, as most of the foundation stock was imported from the United States. The breed developed in specific geographical areas, due to the great distances in Canada. There was little exchange of the gene pool among the different regions, as it was usually easier for breeders to go south to the American bloodlines than to ship across the expanses of their own country.

The first Bichons appear to have arrived in Canada in 1966 and 1967 but did not contribute to breed development. Mrs. Calderbank also acquired her first Bichon in 1967, which in essence marked the beginning of the progress of the breed in Canada.

Myworth Reg. (British Columbia)

Owned by Kay Calderbank, the first three Bichons were Quentelly of Goldysdale (de la Roche Posay line), Vintage Year's Sauterne (de Gascoigne line), Sariette de Wanabry (de Steren Vor and des Frimoussettes) and Ch. Myworth's Tinker Terrific (Diable de Gascoigne ex Odelis of Goldysdale). Sariette and Tinker Terrific produced Myworth's Miss Muffet, a top producing bitch for the Myworth line. In 1972 Mrs. Calderbank imported Can. and Am. Ch. Ee's R Regal Prince of Henruf (Petit Galant de St. George ex Cali-Col's Ritzy Ruffles), who would have a profound effect upon Canadian Bichon Frise. A fine showman, Henruf received sixty Bests of Breed and thirty-nine Group placements in a limited show career. He was the sire of seventeen champions, and his offspring provided many of Canada's most influential breeders with their foundation stock.

Kay Calderbank was the breeder of Canada's all-time top winning Bichon and top producing sire, Can. and Am. Ch. Myworth's Enchantment (Ch. My Windy K ex Ch. Lejerdell Tar-Esa), a Henruf grandson, owned by Helen Kasper. "Chante" was to Canada what Ch. Chaminade Syncopation was to the United States—the first great showman and ambassador for a breed newly recognized. From 1976–78, in a total of 141 shows, there were 128 Bests of Breed, 12 Bests in Show, 39 Group Firsts and 76 other Group placements. It was a fitting tribute to the lady who had given so much to the breed.

Drurylane Reg. (Alberta)

Andrea Crowe was among the first to own Bichons in Canada. Her foundation dog was Can. and Am. Ch. My Windy K (Can. and Am. Ch. Ee's R Regal Prince of Henruf ex Myworth's Tiffany), who made his mark as sire of Can. and Am. Ch. Myworth's Enchantment. She is also the owner of Myworth's Winter Folley (Lejerdell's Target of Myworth ex Myworth's Miss Muffett), dam of six champions.

Am. and Can. Ch. Ee's R Regal Prince of Henruf, the first Bichon to appear in Canada's Miscellaneous Class, February 1973. Owned by Kay Calderbank.

Ch. My Windy K., son of Henruf. Owned by Andrea Crowe.

Ch. Myworth's Enchantment (*extreme left*), grandson of Henruf and all-time top winning Canadian Bichon, with his offspring (*left to right*): Ch.Vassalys Bugler (top winner, 1982–83), Ch. Vassaly's Ruffian (a top winning bitch) and Ch. Chante's Image of Kibbatt (top Bichon, 1979, 1980 and 1981).

Ch. Vale Park Special Edition, Best in Show winner, top winning Bichon of 1986–87.

Ch. Vale Park Perce Neige, also a Best in Show winner and sister to Special Edition.
Photo by Missy.

Am. and Can. Ch. Cherrie My Fair Lady, foundation bitch for Deborah Mason, Kibbatt Bichons. Dam of the top Bichon for 1979, 1980 and 1981.

Vale Park (Saskatchewan)

Hilda Murphy is another of the premier breeders of Canada. Her blending of the Myworth line of Canada and Rava and Crockerly produced an identifiable line of her own. She is the breeder of Ch. Vale Park Kylie (Ch. Ee's R Regal Prince of Henruf ex Rava Royal Valour), dam of seven champions, whose daughter, Ch. Kenningway Vale Park Vivace (sired by Ch. Rava's Regal Victory), was also the dam of seven champions.

Vivace bred to Can. and Am. Ch. Crockerly's Beau Monde Moonglo produced Can. and Am. Ch. Vale Park Classic Masterpiece, another top producer with nine champion offspring. Masterpiece bred to Vale Park Crystal Snowflake produced two Best in Show winners: Ch. Vale Park Perce Neige (owned by Gerald Phillips) and Ch. Vale Park Special Edition (owned by Carman and Rick Fehler). The latter was Canada's top winning Bichon for 1986 and 1987, with a total of nine Bests in Show and seventy-five Group Firsts. When Vivace was bred to Ch. Kenningway's Friendly Persuasion (Ch. San Don Friend ex Ch. Vale Park Kyle), another Best in Show winner was produced, Ch. Vale Park the Challenger (owned by Gerald Phillips).

Kenningway (Saskatchewan)

Kendra James's foundation bitch, Ch. Vale Park Kylie, bred to Ch. Rava Regal Victory produced the influential Ch. Kenningway Vale Park Vivace. A second bitch, Ch. Vale Park Craigdale Classic (Can. and Am. Ch. Crockerly Beau Monde Moonglo ex Ch. Kenningway Vale Park Vivace), bred to Ch. Vale Park the Challenger produced Ch. Kenningway's Mercedes Benz, winner of the 1987 Bichon Frise Club of Canada National Specialty.

Kibbatt (British Columbia)

Deborah Tanner Mason's foundation bitch, Can. and Am. Ch. Cherrie My Fair Lady (Burlington Burt ex Myworth's Rene, a Henruf daughter), bred to Can. and Am. Ch. Myworth's Enchantment produced four champion offspring, including Can. and Am. Ch. Chante's Image of Kibbatt's, Canada's top winning Bichon for 1979, 1980 and 1981.

Vassaly's Reg. (Alberta)

Helen Kasper was the owner of Can., Am. and Bda. Ch. Myworth's Enchantment. He was bred to her foundation bitch, Ch. Sonatina of Kibbatt's, a litter sister to Ch. Chante's Image of Kibbatt's, and produced Ch. Vassaly's Ruffian, one of Canada's top winning bitches. A son from this breeding, Can. and Am. Ch. Vassaly's Bugler, was the top winning Canadian Bichon for 1982 and 1983 and winner of the first Canadian National Specialty in 1983. Bugler is the sire of nine champions, including a multiple Best in Show son,

Ch. Dyon Las Vegas Bandit, bred by Diane Wiley and owned by Helen Kasper.

Craigdale (British Columbia)

Dale Hunter's foundation bitch was Beau Monde Works d'Arte Wicked (Reenroy Sir Bernard ex Works d'Arte Renoir). Bred to Ch. Vogelflight's Music Man she produced Can. and Am. Ch. Wicked Music by Craigdale, dam of five champions. One of these five was Can. and Am. Ch. Craigdale's Olé Rhondi (sired by Ch. D'Shars Rendezvous du Chamour), who was a multiple Best in Show winner and top Bichon in the United States in 1983. Ch. Craigdale's Great Classic (Ch. Cali-Col's Beau Monde Brummel ex Beau Monde Works d'Arte Wicked) bred to Can. and Am. Ch. Tarawn's Cheyenne Sundance (Vande le Buthiere ex Myworth Miss Muffett) produced Can. and Am. Ch. Craigdale and the Sundance Kid, multiple Group winner owned by Garda Johnstone.

Saddlebrook (Quebec)

Pat Hardisty is the breeder of one of Canada's top producing dams, Ch. Saddlebrook's Lady Tara (Ch. Knightwood White Tornado, a Ch. C and D's Beau Monde Blizzard son, ex Paw Paw Crystal, Ch. Chaminade Mr. Beau Monde daughter). Lady Tara is the dam of seven champions. Saddlebrook Bichons have become the foundation dogs for some of eastern Canada's most prominent breeders.

Trevor (Ontario)

Joan Trevor is the breeder and owner of Canada's top winning Bichon for 1985, Can. and Am. Ch. Tevor's Damien 1st (Ch. Trevor's Only Sir Fredrick ex Ch. Trevor Miss Mandy). Damien is a multiple Best in Show Bichon and also winner of the 1985 and 1986 Canadian National Specialties. His dam, Miss Mandy, has produced five champions.

Snopuff (New Brunswick)

Carole Mineault's foundation bitch for Snopuff is Susaru's Charm of Carealot (Ch. Susaru's Monsieur Maurice ex Phaedo Letita Violette), who produced two of Canada's recent Best in Show winners, Ch. Snopuff's Goodluck Bear, owned by Carole Mineault, and Can. and Am. Ch. Snopuff's Ami de Neigenveau, owned by Florence Erwin. Both were sired by the French import, Ch. Pablo de la Buthiere (U'Sam de Villa Sainval ex Natacha de la Buthiere).

In eastern Canada two American breeders—Diandee (Clover Allen, Michigan) and Darkel (Dorothy Wilson, New York)—have figured prominently.

Am. and Can. Ch. Wicked Music by Craigdale, owned and bred by Dale Hunter. Dam of cover dog, Am. and Can. Ch. Craigdale's Olé Rhondi. *Photo by Missy.*

Diandee

Clover Allen's Can. and Am. Ch. Teeny Tepee's Chief of Diandee was Canada's top winning Bichon in 1975 and also one of the country's top producers, with eleven Canadian champions. By Reenroy's Royal Flush de Noel ex Teeny Tepee's Mauri Julene, he was bred by Elizabeth (Betty) Shehab. Diandee Bichons figure prominently in the pedigrees of many of eastern Canada's winning and producing Bichons.

Darkel

Dorothy Wilson produced two of Canada's most influential sires: Can., Am., Bda., P.R. and Int. Ch. Darkel's Imperial Gamble (Ch. Windstar's Aristotle ex Ch. Darkel's Cameo Souvenir) and Can. and Am. Ch. Darkel's Artic Star (Beau Monde the Actor ex Parkway La Femme). Imperial Gamble was the number two Bichon in Canada in 1980, owner handled, and is the sire of twelve Canadian champions. His daughter, Ch. Darkel's Ruffles and Lace (ex. Ch. Darkel's Beaux Yeux Artic Hope), was the number three Bichon in 1983. Artic Star was the sire of ten Canadian champions.

The Bichon Frise has grown in popularity in Canada. While acknowledging the influence of the American-bred Bichon, the Canadian breeders are firmly establishing their lines and are making their mark.

Canada Top Winning Bichon Frise

1975	Can. and Am. Ch. Teeny Tepee Chief of Diandee (Reenroy's Royal Flush de Noel ex Teeny Tepee's Mauri Julene) Breeder, Betty Shehab; owner, Clover Allen
1976	Can., Am. and Bda. Ch. Myworth's Enchantment (Ch. My Windy K ex Ch. Lejerdell's Tar-Esa) Breeder, Kay Calderbank; owner, Helen Kasper
1977	Can., Am. and Bda. Ch. Myworth's Enchantment
1978	Can., Am. and Bda. Ch. Myworth's Enchantment
1979	Can. and Am. Ch. Chante's Image of Kibbatt's (Can., Am. and Bda. Ch. Myworth's Enchantment ex Can. and Am. Ch. Cherrie My Fair Lady) Breeder, Deborah Tanner Mason; owner, Lynne Carson
1980	Can. and Am. Ch. Chante's Image of Kibbatt's
1981	Can. and Am. Ch. Chante's Image of Kibbatt's
1982	Can. and Am. Ch. Vassaly's Bugler (Can., Am. and Bda. Ch. Myworth's Enchantment ex Ch. Sonatina of Kibbatt's) Breeder-owner, Helen Kasper
1983	Can. and Am. Ch. Vassaly's Bugler

1984	Can. and Am. Ch. Culford's B Major
	(Cali-Col's Drum Major ex Culford's The Naughty Nun)
	Breeder, L. Ford; owner, Angela Baldwin
1985	Can. and Am. Ch. Trevor's Damien 1st
	(Ch. Trevor's Only Sir Fredrick ex Ch. Trevor's Miss Mandy)
	Breeder-owner, Joan Trevor
1986	Ch. Vale Park Special Edition
	(Can. and Am. Ch. Vale Park Classic Masterpiece ex Vale Park Crystal Snowflake)
	Breeder, Hilda Murphy; owners, Rick and Carman Fehler
1987	Ch. Vale Park's Special Edition

ENGLAND

In order to fully appreciate the efforts of English breeders in establishing the Bichon Frise in England, the reader should first be aware that all dogs imported into England must spend six months in quarantine. As there were no known Bichons in the United Kingdom in the early 1970s, when interest in the breed was first aroused, all the foundation stock had to go through this expensive and time-consuming procedure.

Another point of interest for the reader is the English championship system. Three Challenge Certificates (CC) are needed to complete a championship. In the United States dogs and bitches do not compete against existing champions for the "points," or in this case, the Challenge Certificate. This is not so in the United Kingdom. Here there is no Best of Breed class where the champions compete against each other. The dogs and bitches usually must defeat an existing champion in order to earn the CC. A further detriment is the limited number of championship shows that are held each year. Thus it should be obvious that the percentage of dogs completing their championships is low and such titles are indeed an exceptional feat.

There is one final point of interest. When a dog is imported into England from the United States, or anywhere else, for that matter, the new owner is allowed to add *his* kennel name to the name already given to the dog by his breeder. This is true in several countries. You will notice that, as a result, there are some overly long and occasionally awkward registered names.

The first Bichon Frise arrived in England in 1973, the year that saw the American Bichon gain full recognition by the American Kennel Club. Mr. and Mrs. J. Sorstein of the Carlise prefix imported a dog and a bitch from the United States, Rava's Real Valor of Reenroy (Am. Ch. Stardom's Odin Rex, Jr., ex Reenroy's Tina Tilton) and Jenny Vive de Carlise (Beauchaun High Cotton ex Snowbee de Beauchaun) (High Cotton was an Odin Rex son).

The first English Bichon litter was born in 1974. From this litter Aus. Ch. Carlise Cicero of Tresilva and Carlise Circe of Tresilva would be of

Carlise Cicero of Tresilva, a foundation dog for Tresilva that would later go to Australia. Owned by Jackie Ransom.

Leander Beau Monde Snow Carol, top Bichon in England, 1978, and first Bichon in the Toy Group at the famous 1978 Crufts show.

importance. Cicero, who eventually went to Australia, was the sire of Int. Ch. Tresilva Don Azur, who became influential in Sweden.

A second litter from the two original imports produced foundation bitches for three kennels. Chris Cooley (Glenfolly), Betty Mirylees (Beaupres), who sent the first Bichons to New Zealand, and finally Derek Chiverton and Vera Goold (Leijazulip), who acquired Carlise Calypso Orion, who was destined to become the granddam of the top winning English Bichon of all time, Ch. Tiopepi Mad Louie at Pamploma.

Leijazulip

In 1975 Mrs. Goold imported two Bichons from the noted de la Buthiere Kennels of Madame Desfarges, located outside of Paris. Jazz de la Buthiere of Leijazulip and Leilah de la Buthiere had an enormous impact on the development of the breed in England and eventually Australia. We are told the Leijazulip prefix was formed from the names of Mrs. Goold's Bichons Leilah, Jazz and Tulip. Their son, Leijazulip Guillaume, was a top stud dog in England, then gained his International titles (and a great show reputation) when sent to Sweden. Another bitch, Ninon de la Buthiere of Leijazulip, was the dam of Leijazulip Kipling and Leijazulip Jazz of Zudiki (this is a second Jazz) who were important both in England and Australia and eventually New Zealand. The Leijazulip prefix is known worldwide.

Tresilva

Jackie Ramsom was another of the early English breeders. In addition to the acquisitions from Carlise, there were two Belgian imports (the first to arrive in England), Zethus de Chaponay of Tresilva and Zena de Chaponay of Tresilva. The famous Int. Ch. Tresilva Don Azur and his sister, Tresilva Donnà Azur, were the offspring of Carlise Cicero and the Belgian import Zena. Cicero was sent to Australia, as were other foundation dogs from Tresilva. In addition to its success in England, the Tresilva line is also found throughout Scandinavia.

Cluneen

Elish Banks imported a number of Bichons from the American Lejerdell Bichons as well as from the French Warnabry Kennels. Cluneen Lejerdell's Tarzanna was the first Bichon to be exhibited in England. Am., Fr., Dtch., Germ., Bel., Mex. and Int. Ch. Tarzan de la Persaliere (Quintan of Milton ex Maya of Milton) was certainly one of the most titled Bichons in history. He was imported by Mrs. Banks from the United States and the Lejerdell Kennels of Jerome Podell, who had originally imported him from France in late 1970. Tarzan sired four American champions before returning to the Continent.

Eng. and Ir. Ch. Tiopepi Mad Louie at Pamploma, all-time top winning Bichon in England and Toy Group winner at Crufts, 1989. Owned by Michael Coad.

Ch. Melsel Cracklin Rosie, all-time top winning bitch, owned by Chris Belcher.

Ch. Snarsnoz Show Quest at Melsel, a top winner and sire of Cracklin Rosie. Owned by Chris Belcher.

Ch. Kynismar Blackeyed Susie, a top producing bitch for Kynismar Bichons of Myra Aikens.
Photograph by Roger Chambers.

Ch. Kynismar's Heaven Sent, top bitch, and
Ch. Kynismars Boogie Boy, top dog for 1988.
Owner: Myra Aikens.

Eng. and Ir. Ch. Sulyka Snoopy, Best of Breed
at Crufts, 1984 and 1985; Top Stud Dog, 1987.
Owned by Sue and Roger Dunger.

Twinley

Pauline Block, noted breeder of the Pharaoh Hound, Long coated Chihuahuas and Tibetan Terriers, visited the United States in 1973 and acquired Cottonmops Jolie Ivette of Twinley from the Rothmans' Braymar Bichons. While in quarantine, Jolie produced a litter by Ch. Cali-Col's Octavius Caesar, the first of the Twinley Bichons. In 1977 Mrs. Block imported Astir de Chaponay of Twinley from Belgium. He made his mark in England and later went on to Australia, where he gained his championship. The Twinley Bichons continue to be outstanding, and many have become foundation dogs and winners for kennels in Scandinavia and Australia, while Ch. Twinley Pantomime Prince of Melsel is a recent multiple Best in Show winner at home.

Leander

John and Wendy Streatfield were Poodle breeders of considerable reputation when they became interested in the Bichon. Their first import from the United States, in 1974, was a bitch who became internationally prominent, Am. and Aust. Ch. C and D Beau Monde Sunflower of Leander. She had been bred to Am. Ch. C and D Beau Monde Blizzard and whelped a litter while in quarantine; Leander Beau Monde Snow Carol, Leander Snow Venture and N.Z. Ch. Leander Snow Puff (one of the earliest Bichons in New Zealand). Leander Bichons figure prominently in English, Australian and New Zealand Bichon pedigrees.

The Streatfields and their associate, Sally Wheeler, added a number of other Bichons from the Beau Monde and C and D lines. In 1977 they imported Am. Ch. Vogelflight's Choir Boy, one of the four famous brothers who had been so successful in the United States. Choir Boy fulfilled his legacy and became equally successful as a winner and producer.

In addition to producing outstanding Bichons in England and foundation dogs for "down under," Wendy Streatfield is noted for another special contribution to English Bichons. As a Poodle breeder and exhibitor, her dogs had always been presented in impeccable fashion. Bichons in England had previously been shown in the Continental fashion, which in essence means no grooming. Mrs. Streatfield went to work and produced a Bichon style like that found in the United States. Needless to say there was resistance, but the beautiful results couldn't be denied, and she won her point. Today the American style of grooming is almost universal except in France and Belgium.

Other Bichons from the French de la Buthiere and Closmyons lines were added by both established and new breeders. From this combination of Continental and American breeding comes the English Bichon of today.

In addition to the early breeders mentioned, a number of individuals have established themselves as breeders of note in the current English Bichon world:

Sue and Roger Dunger (Sulyka) with Eng. and Ir. Ch. Sulyka Snoopy (Eng. and Aust. Ch. Leijazulip Jazz of Zudiki ex Shammaney My

Ch. Bobander Toot the Flute, a top winning bitch shown by owner-breeder Chris Wyatt.

All-breed championship BIS winner Twinley Pantomine Prince, owned by Pauline Block.

The fabulous "Breeding Group" of Babro Jonsson, Xanbos Kennel, three-time BIS winners (*left to right*): Ch. Xanbos Carlie Team, Ch. Xanbos Special Teamwork, Ch. Xanbos Rainbow Warrior, Ch. Xanbos Rainbow Illusion and Ch. Xanbos Hunkidori Team.

Choice of Sulyka), winner at Crufts 1984–85 and the breed's top stud dog in 1987.

Peter and Pauline Gibbs (Montravia) with another top champion and sire, Ch. Montravia Persan Make Mine Mink, sire of the top record holder, Ch. Tiopepi Mad Louie at Pamploma.

Chris Belcher (Melsel) with Ch. Snarsnoz Show Quest at Melsel and his daughter, Ch. Melsel Cracklin Rosie, top winning bitch in the United Kingdom for 1987.

Jo Brown-Emerson (Zudiki) with Aust. and Eng. Ch. Leijazulip Jazz of Zudiki and his son Nagazumi Mr. Frosty of Zudiki, who have had such a great impact on the Australian Bichons.

Chris and Bob Wyatt (Bobander) with Bobander the Muffin Man and his daughter Ch. Bobander Toot the Flute.

Den Thomas (Rouska) with Ch. Rouska's Song and Dance, Rouska's Dancemaster and Rouska's Cameo Dance, who won the Puppy Dog Stakes in England in February 1989. This youngster was imported to the United States and won the Bichon Frise Club of America National Sweepstakes in May 1989 and the Bichon Frise Club of Northern California Sweepstakes in October 1989, and completed his American championship three weeks later.

Myra and Robert Aikens (Kynismar) with their Ch. Kynismar Blackeyed Susie, her son, Kynismar's Blackeyed Bugaloo, and grandson Kynismar's Boogie Boy have had great success. Kynismar Bichons have taken Best of Breed at Crufts in 1988 and 1989; and N.Z. Ch. Kynismar's Hidden Destiny won Best in Show at the 1986 Special Open show with 223 entries, the largest Bichon entry in the world to date. He was sent to New Zealand, where he became the number one Bichon.

The Bichon has become extremely popular in England, and the fancy is very active. The Bichon Frise Club of Great Britain was organized early in 1976 and in 1982 was approved to hold its first championship show. The Northern and Midland Bichon Frise Club was approved in March 1982. The Southern Bichon Frise Breeders Association is a third Bichon group offering seminars and educational activities.

It is interesting to note that a number of English-bred Bichons have been imported into the United States in recent years. The English blend of the early American Bichons with the more contemporary Continental lines has had appeal for several of the American breeders, and this introduction into their bloodlines has been highly successful.

SWEDEN

Azur

Jane Martinsson-Vesa imported the first Bichons into Sweden in 1976. From the United States came Nord. Ch. Paw Paw Rhinestone Cowboy (Am.

Jane Martininsson-Vesa and Int. Nor. Ch. Leijazulip Guillaume winning Best in Show Veteran, 1984—a dog of great impact, first in England, then in Scandinavia and Europe.

1988 Bichon Specialty of Sweden. Judge: Sally Wheeler, Leander Bichons of England. BIS Bichonette's Charming Cross (Rigmor Offoson, owner and breeder), and Reserve BIS, S.SF. Ch. Inghedens Breeze's Unexpected Lass (Inger Adeheimer, owner-breeder).

Int. Ch. Allan Aventurer of Twinley, winning Group 1 in Norway. Owner: Ester Stray.

Danish Ch. Azzjazz Danish Blue, breed winner at the largest show on the Continent, the World Show held in Copenhagen, June 1989. Bred by Maureen Adams of England and owned by Katina Christopherson of Denmark. Also a Specialty winner and top Toy dog for 1988.

Ch. Paw Paw Punjab ex Bellissima Biji), bred by A. Costello and L. Goldwater. From England Mrs. Martinsson-Vesa brought Int. and Nordic Ch. Tresilva Don Azur (Carlise Cicero of Tresilva ex Zena de Chaponey of Tresilva) and his little sister Tresilva Donna Azur from Jackie Ransom. Don Azur was the first English Bichon to become a Nordic champion, while Rhinestone Cowboy bred to Donna Azur produced the first Swedish champion, Azura Andre.

Not long after, there were more English imports by Mrs. Martinsson-Vesa: Nord. Ch. Beaupres Candida of Tresilva (Zethus de Chaponey of Tresilva ex Carlise Canny Caprise of Beaupres), Nord. Ch. Leijazulip Dominique (Aust. Ch. Jazz de la Buthiere ex Carlise Calypso Orion) and Leijazulip the Tinker (Aust. Ch. Beau Monde the Snowdrift of Leander ex Carlise Calypso Orion).

In 1980 Int. and Nord. Ch. Leander Snow Maiden (Leander Snow Venture ex Am. and Aust. Ch. C and D's Beau Monde Sunflower of Leander) arrived in Sweden. She was three years old when she arrived, but she made a lasting impression on the Azur line with only two litters, for her children were both champions and producers.

In 1981 Int. and Nord. Ch. Leijazulip Guillaume (Aust. Ch. Jazz de la Buthiere ex Leilah de la Buthiere of Leijazulip) arrived from Vera Goold and Derek Chiverton, who had bred and shown the dog in England, but it was in Sweden that he made his mark. Mrs. Martinsson-Vesa states: "Willi has meant a lot to the breed in Scandinavia. He is a multiple Best in Show winner, including a Best in Show Veteran at the age of ten years. . . . He has many offspring in Europe, forty of them were champions at the end of 1987." Two of his most famous sons are Eng. Ch. Leijazulip Kipling and Eng. Ch. Leijazulip Jazz of Zudiki. Mrs. Martinsson-Vesa has been a successful breeder of twenty-eight champions at this writing.

Xanbos

In 1979 Mrs. Babro Jonsson won the first Breeding Class ever held in Sweden, at the Stockholm International Show. Mrs. Jonsson has had continued success exhibiting "breeding groups," which means the breeder shows *five* dogs of his or her own breeding in a given competition! In 1988 Mrs. Jonsson placed eighth on the "best breeder" list for All Breeds.

Other noted breeders include:

Lars and Inger Adeheimer, who began their breeding program with four imports from the Beau Monde Kennels in the United States: Nord. Ch. Beau Monde the Lone Ranger (Ch. C and D's Beau Monde Blizzard ex Ch. Keystone Christine), Am. and Nord. Ch. Beau Monde the Kobold Kaddie (Ch. Vogelflight's Music Man ex Ch. Beau Monde the Firecracker), Beau Monde the Sky Song (Ch. C and D's Beau Monde Blizzard ex Ch. Beau Monde the Vamp) and Nord. Ch. Beau Monde the Fantasy (Ch. Chaminade Mr. Beau Monde ex

Aust. Ch. Beau Monde the Snowdrift of Leander, the first Bichon Frise to arrive in Australia, making his show debut in October 1976. Imported from the United States by Harry McKenzie-Beggs.

Aust. Ch. Jazz de la Buthiere of Leijazullp, all-time winner and top sire, owned by Azara Bichons.

Aust. Ch. Azara Le President, top Australian-bred Bichon, owned by Betty Brown, bred by Azara Bichons.

Beau Monde the Echo). From Australia and breeder F. H. Wilson the Adeheimers obtained Aust. Nord. Ch. Planhaven Fire and Ice (Aust. Ch. Cannondale Cleva Clyde ex Leander Snow Girl). Mr. Adeheimer is a noted Terrier breeder and judges a great deal internationally.

Ann Margaret Ericson, who imported Nord. Ch. Tsingfu's Dixie Doodle (Nord. Ch. Hunkidori Bobbi Dazzler ex Hunkidori Tittletattle) from Norway; he subsequently became one of the top producing sires. She also is the owner of Int. and Nord. Ch. Skydds Beatrice (Int. and Nord. Ch. Tresilva Don Azur ex Nord. Ch. Leijazulip Dominique), who has been a successful producer; she was bred in Sweden by K. Davidson.

The Twinley line of England's Pauline Block had early representation through Nord. Ch. Twinley King Kassius (Twinley Tiberius ex Katrinka of Carlise of Twinley), imported by Eva Soderqvist.

The Bichon Frise has had significant popularity in Sweden. The following statistics show the registration figures of the Bichon in recent years.

1981	1982	1983	1984	1985	1986	1987	1988
91	117	164	256	277	314	415	496

An interesting note: All puppies born in Sweden have to be registered.

Sweden has a very active Bichon Frise club, which was founded in November of 1982. Everyone who acquires a Bichon is asked to join, and at this writing membership is at five hundred. The club is totally computerized. Frequent seminars are offered on general care, grooming and scissoring, and there is a good deal of helpful interchange among the members. Several Bichon shows are arranged each year, the largest being held in Stockholm. The first was held in 1983 and was judged by Judy Fender of Hunkidori Kennels, England. The most recent show, with an entry of 124 dogs, was judged by Sally Wheeler (Leander), also of England. Best in Show was S. Ch. Bichonettes Charming Cross (Nord. Ch. Tsingfu's Dixie Doodle ex S. Ch. Rhapsody's Afrodite). The breeder-owner was Rigmor Offosson. Top Bitch and Reserve Best in Show was S.SF. Ch. Inghedens Breeze's Unexpected Lass, breeder-owner Inger Adeheimer.

Sweden has imported Bichons from Australia, England, Norway and the United States with great success. The breed is popular and obviously well organized, quality is there and the future looks bright.

AUSTRALIA

Like England, Australia has a quarantine system that adds considerable dimension to the problems of introducing a new breed or importing new bloodlines for a breeding program. Bichons imported from the United States or the Continent went to England for the standard six-month quarantine, then

Aust. Ch. Leijazulip Angelique, Australia's top producing dam, owned by Azara Bichons.

Eng. and Aust. Ch. Leijazulip Jazz of Zudiki, top winner in England and Australia, owned by John and Wendy Hutchinson, Monjoie Bichons.

Aust. Ch. Monjoie Babelle Sophia, one of Australia's top bitches, bred by John and Wendy Hutchinson, owned by Peter and Jill Eerden, Dobrana Kennels.

on to Australia for an additional three-month quarantine. It is obvious then why so many Australian pedigrees often closely parallel the English pedigrees.

Margaret and Harry McKenzie-Beggs were well-known breeders and exhibitors of Afghans and Salukis in New South Wales. As time went on they looked for a smaller breed, and after visiting the Leander Kennels of Wendy and John Streatfield in England, became captivated by the Bichon Frise. Arrangements were made, and in 1976 the first Bichon was imported into Australia, Am. Ch. Beau Monde the Snowdrift of Leander (Ch. Chaminade Mr. Beau Monde ex Works D'Arte Miro Chaminade). They subsequently imported a dozen Bichons, including Aust. Ch. Carlise Cicero of Tresilva (Rava's Real Valor of Reenroy ex Jenny Vive de Carlise), a son of the first two Bichons imported into England; Aust. Ch. Beau Monde the Dove of Leander (Am. Ch. C and D's Count Kristopher ex Am. Ch. Beau Monde the Vamp); and Am. and Aust. Ch. C and D's Beau Monde Sunflower of Leander (Am. Ch. Chaminade Mr. Beau Monde ex Am. Ch. C and D's Countess Becky). Without question Mr. and Mrs. McKenzie-Beggs initiated what became a deep-seated interest in the Bichon Frise throughout Australia.

Twenty-four Bichons were imported into Australia of Leander bloodlines. These offered foundation dogs for Dianne Crosby-Brown (Ancrowns) and France Wilson (Planhaven). These two women initially imported four Bichons: Leander Snow Scout and Leander Snow Bubbles (both: Am. and Aust. Ch. Beau Monde the Snowdrift of Leander ex Am. and Aust. Ch. C and D's Beau Monde Sunflower of Leander). Sunflower herself was eventually imported to Australia. The second pair were Leander Snow Cap and Leander Snow Girl (both: Am. Ch. C and D's Beau Monde Blizzard ex Val Va Don's Chantee of Leander.) Snow Cap and Bubble produced the first litter born in Australia in April 1977.

Azara

The most consistently successful breeders over the years, who have gained international recognition, have been Frank Vallely and Rudi Van Voorst of the Azara Kennels in Victoria. In 1974 they saw a picture of a Bichon—Am. Ch. Stardom's Nicki de Staramour, owned and bred by Celeste Fleishman (Pennsylvania)—in an American dog magazine and decided this was the breed for them. In 1977 Azara imported Aust. Ch. Leander Snow Mittens (Leander Snow Venture ex Am. and Aust. Ch. C and D's Beau Monde Sunflower of Leander, a sister to Am. and Aust. Ch. Leander Snow Star), who became one of Australia's top producing bitches. However, without a doubt the most influential import was Aust. Ch. Jazz de la Buthiere of Leijazulip (Int. Ch. If de la Buthiere ex Fr. Ch. Vanda de la Buthiere), acquired from Vera Goold in England. With twenty Bests in Show and thirty-one champion offspring, his show and producing records have yet to be equaled. A second male, Aust., Fr., Germ., Sw. and Int. Ch. Looping de la Buthiere (Int. Ch. If de la Buthiere ex Int. Ch. Vania de Villa Sainval) was

Ch. Dunnrhoen Chartres, bred and owned by Loretta Smart, Dunnrhoen Bichons, Best in Show at the Adelaide Royal, 1985, top win for a Bichon in Australia.

Aust. Ch. Dolorado Demis, a winner and producer of several BIS winners, from the Tejada Kennels of Geraldine Griegg.

Amer. and Austr. Ch. Beau Monde Drewlaine Demon, a current top winner on the Australian scene, was imported from the United States via the United Kingdom. CC winner at Expo '89, Melbourne, owned by noted breeder Geraldine Griegg.
Photography by Twigg.

Aust. Ch. Azara Petit Fleur, a multiple BIS winner at all-breed championship show, winner of Victoria's Toy Dog of the Year, 1982, for Azara Bichons.

Aust. Ch. Daldorado Charisma, two Reserve Bests in Show all Breeds, Specialty Best in Show winner (BFC of Victoria), Toy Group winner, Breed winner at Royal Easter show of New South Wales. Another outstanding winner for owner Geraldine Griegg, breeder of twenty-one champions and seven Best in Show winners. *Pet Portraits.*

imported from Madame Desfarges, directly from France. A third male, Aust. Ch. Nagazumi Mr. Frosty of Zudiki (Aust. and Eng. Ch. Leijazulip Jazz of Zudiki ex Shining Star of Zudiki) came from Jo Brown-Emerson of England. Aust. Ch. Leijazulip Angelique (Aust. Ch. Jazz de la Buthiere of Leijazulip ex Leilah de la Buthiere of Leijazulip) was the second major bitch imported, and she has become a top producing dam, with fourteen champions. A male and a female from Judy Fausset's Keleb Kennels in the United States added to the foundation dogs at Azara.

Aust. Ch. Azara Le President is the top Australian-bred Bichon, while the three bitches—Aust. Ch. Azara Petit Fleur, Aust. Ch. Azara MaBelle Ami and Aust. Ch. Azara Desiree—have been extraordinarily successful as winners (among them they have won twenty-one Bests in Show) and as producers. The Azara line has produced thirty champions and has provided foundation Bichons for numerous Australian and New Zealand kennels, while several have returned to England. In 1985 Azara Zarden was imported by Celeste Fleishman, and in 1986 he was Best of Winners at Westminster Kennel Club show, an interesting twist of circumstance that brings the Azara story full circle.

Monjoie

Wendy and John Hutchinson of Victoria imported the first English champion to Australia, Ch. Leijazulip Jazz of Zudiki (Int. Ch. Leijazulip Guillaume ex Ninon de la Buthiere), where he became a consistent winner at all-breed and Specialty shows. The bitch, Aust. Ch. Azara MaBelle Ami (Aust. Ch. Jazz de la Buthiere of Leijazulip ex Aust. ch. Leijazulip Angelique) was yet another successful acquisition for Monjoie, both as an all-breed Best in Show and Best in Show Specialty winner and as a top producer; bred to Jazz of Zudiki, she has produced thirteen champions at this writing. Monjoie Bichons have been successful in Australia and have provided foundation Bichons for breeders of New Zealand.

Tejada

Geraldine Griegg, also a noted Yorkshire Terrier breeder, is the breeder of Best in Show winner Aust. Ch. Tejada French Conxion (Aust. Ch. Tejada Le Fanfaron ex C and D's Little Snowwhite of Leander), owned by Peter and Jill Eerden of Dobrana Bichons. Mrs. Griegg is also the owner of Aust. Ch. Dolorado Demis, bred by Rob and Judy Lawson, Dolorado (Aust. Ch. Jazz de la Buthiere of Leijazulip ex Aust. Ch. Leander Snow Baby). He is the sire of fourteen champions, six of which are all-breed Best in Show winners. Included in this number is Ch. Dunnrhoen Chartres, bred by Loretta Smart of Dunnrhoen, who was Best in Show at the Adelaide Royal in 1985, probably the top win for a Bichon in Australia. He continued his show career by becoming South Australia's top Bichon for 1985, 1986 and 1987.

Wyndalon

Mrs. N. G. Thomson imported Aust. Ch. Astir de Chaponay of Twinley (Xorba de Chaponay ex Xcarlet de Villa Sainval) from Belgium and, from England, Aust. Ch. Leander Snow Whirl (Huntglen Leander Arden ex Am. Ch. Val Va Don Demi Chantee of Leander). Along with the English import, Leander Snow Shower, they added to the early dogs who would produce Australian champions and foundation dogs for other lines.

One of the world's best traveled Bichons is Am. and Aust. Ch. Leander Snow Star (Leander Snow Venture ex Ch. C and D's Beau Monde Sunflower). He was born in England and as a puppy sent to Australia, where he was owned by Mr. and Mrs. McKenzie-Beggs and later Lee Benyon. He won six Bests in Show and was the first Bichon in New South Wales to take Best in Show honors. He was then sent to the United States and arrived to a new owner, Laura Purnell (Tomaura). In the United States he won three all-breed Bests in Show and has become one of the top producing sires of the breed. Happily, his days as a great world traveler are over.

As in all countries, the popularity of the Bichon Frise continues to grow: in 1980 there were 160 Bichons registered; in 1987 there were 535.

NEW ZEALAND

New Zealand is another country where interest in the Bichon Frise was precipitated by seeing a photo of a Bichon in an American book. Margaret and Allan Crooks, Silverlea Kennels, Christchurch, saw a picture of Mrs. William Tabler's Bichon, Am. Ch. Chaminade Syncopation, which triggered their interest in the breed. In 1976 correspondence to England began. Betty Mirylees of Beaupres Kennels sent them their first Bichon, a puppy dog, Beaupres Casanova, out of the bitch Carlise Canny Caprice of Beaupres. He arrived in New Zealand in August of 1977 and would eventually become the first New Zealand Bichon champion.

Mr. and Mrs. Crooks subsequently imported Beaupres Astrid, and on November 7, 1978, the first Bichon litter was born in New Zealand. From that litter Mystic Miss of Silverlea and Andre of Silverlea became the first New Zealand–born Champions.

Shandau

From 1977 to 1980 interest surged, both in the North Island and the South Island. Elsie Rennie imported Leander Snow Jingle (the first English import in the North Island) plus Leander Snow Petal and a dog, Leander Snow Print. Later she imported Beau Monde White Wine, a Ch. Chaminade Mr. Beau Monde daughter. White Wine arrived in England bred to Am. Ch. Beau Monde the Huckster. Sometime later White Wine and a daughter were sent to

Ch. Leander Beau Monde Snow Puff, BIS and Group winner in England and New Zealand for owner Jean Fyfe and Mutiara Bichons.

Ch,. Kynismar Hidden Destiny, imported from England by Jean Fyfe of Mutiara Bichons. All-time top winning Bichon in New Zealand.

Ch. Puffin Billy of Sulyka, imported from England by Elsie Rennie of Shandau Bichons.

Ch. Blancheur Chou-Choute, owned and bred by Shery Schou, won Best Puppy in Show.

Ch. Monjoie D'Amour, multiple BIS Australian import for Blancheur Bichons and Shery Schou.

94

New Zealand, both in whelp, the dam to Am. Ch. Leander Beau Monde Snow Puff, the daughter to Eng. Ch. Cluneen Jolly Jason of Hunkidori. Ch. Shandau Iceberg (Eng. Ch. Leander Snow Puff ex Beau Monde White Wine) was a successful winner in 1985. In 1987 Shandau imported Puffin Billy of Sulyka, son of Sue and Roger Dunger's famous Eng. Ir. Ch. Sulyka Snoopy. He quickly obtained his championship and went on to be a multiple Best in Show winner.

Mutiara

Jean Fyfe, of Auckland, imported Eng. Ch. Leander Beau Monde Snow Puff, another of the great travelers, having been conceived in the United States, born in England, then sent to New Zealand at the age of five, having sired three English champions.

In 1982 Mrs. Fyfe began a series of imports from the Azara Kennels of Australia, most from the foundation Bichons imported by them. Two especially outstanding additions were the sisters N.Z. Ch. Azara Zarina and N.Z. Ch. Azara Zabo (Aust. Ch. Nagazumi Mr. Frosty of Zudiki ex Aust. Ch. Azara Petit Fleur). The imported Ch. Azara Ramon (Ch. Jazz de la Buthiere of Leijazulip ex Ch. Leander Snow Mittens, two of the earliest Australian imports from England) was the first Bichon in New Zealand to win a Best in Show at an all-breed championship show.

In August of 1986 Jean Fyfe imported Ch. Kynismar Hidden Destiny (Shamaney Stepping Out at Kynismar ex Kynismar Campanula). In March of 1986 Destiny had won Best in Show at the Bichon Frise Club of Great Britain show with an entry of 223 under judges Dale Hunter (Canada) and Barbara Stubbs (U.S.A.). In New Zealand he compiled the top show record of any Bichon to date with eleven Bests in Show, twenty-four Toy Group firsts and thirty-eight Challenge Certificates in championship shows.

Blancheur

Shery Schou imported N.Z. Ch. Monjoie D'Amour, one of the first sons of Eng. and Aust. Ch. Leijazulip Jazz of Zudiki to come to New Zealand. He was a multiple Best in Show winner and has proven to be a top producer.

Parfait

Raewyn Rainsford has done well in the show ring with Ch. Blancheur de L'Aube, a Ch. Monjoie D'Amour son. Imports have been Petit Bijou Charm (Ch. Dobrana Le Corsair ex Ch. Monjoie Kylie) from Australia and, from England, Rushmar Magic Night, who was the top winning puppy for 1988. This youngster is the grandson of Myra Aikens's well-known English champion, Kynismar Blackeyed Bugaloo.

*   *   *

In the South Island, Nigaire Ross of Christchurch has imported, from the Australian Dobrana Kennels of Peter and Jill Eerden (who have combined the best from the early Azara and Monjoie imports) Aust. Ch. Dobrana Debonaire (Jazz of Zudiki ex Ch. Dobrana Belle Moyrann). She has imported additional Dobrana stock, which she plans to blend with the outstanding dogs now available in New Zealand.

Registered with the New Zealand Kennel Club through 1988 are 70 champions, 316 litters, 888 individual registrations and 53 imported Bichons. The Bichon has become very popular in New Zealand, not just as a show dog but as a family pet, and the breeders are making a great effort to educate the pet owners in the details of care and grooming. Jean Fyfe compiled a detailed book with articles, pictures and diagrams on all aspects of Bichon care, and to date six hundred have been distributed—quite astonishing, considering the size of the country and the number of Bichons involved. As in Sweden, an all-out effort is being made to educate at all levels of ownership, a concept that should be considered and acted upon everywhere, with all breeds, but is too often ignored in the interests of profit.

JAPAN

The best records indicate that the first Bichons (seven of them) were imported into Japan from France in April of 1970. About the same time two Bichon puppies were imported from the United States. In 1972 the Bichon Frise was recognized by the Japanese Kennel Club, and thirty-nine Bichons were registered, which number included the imported Bichons and their puppies.

In 1974 the first advertisement of the Bichon Frise appeared in the *Aiken no Tomo* (Friends of Pets), and the general public began to show some interest in acquiring them. Around 1975 pet importers came to the United States and attended the American dog shows, where they saw the ''American'' version of the Bichon, a fluffy white groomed dog, reminiscent of an appealing stuffed animal, and they began seriously to import Bichons to Japan. Most of the imports during this era were puppies.

The first imported American champion was a male, Am. Ch. Bo-Dan's Regal Puff (Master Toby of Bo-Dan ex Cupid's Moonglow); however, it appears that he was not used very much for breeding at this time.

One of the early champion males imported from the United States was Am. Ch. Vogelflight's Banjo Eyes (Am. Ch. Vogelflight's Music Man ex Am. Ch. Vogelflight's Kandi Tres Bon), bred by Mary Vogel. Of special interest is the fact that Banjo Eyes was the first champion offspring of the noted winner and producer, Music Man. Am. Ch. Vogelflight's Banjo Eyes was owned by Koki Iijima, then the president of the Japanese Kennel Club and the Maltese Club; the Maltese has also been a popular breed in Japan.

Am. Ch. Tenerife's Artful Dodger (Am. Ch. Beau Monde the Huckster ex Am. Ch. C and D's Queen Victoria) joined other American champions in

Ch. C and D's Bit O'Honey, a foundation bitch from C and D Bichons for Mr. and Mrs. Satoki Hayashi.

Port Washington of Narita Hayashi-so, BOB and Group 3 in the FCI Asian International Dog Show, Japan, spring 1989. Bred by S. Hayashi and owned by M. Enokida.

Am. Ch. C and D's Flying Tiger of Devon and son, their first Bichon import, photographed in Japan for owners Mr. and Mrs. Satoki Hayashi.

The first Specialty Best of Breed winner, a Japanese-born Bichon, 1985.

Am. and Jap. Ch. Dibbet Maximillian shown taking "Reserve King" (Reserve BIS) in Japan, handled by owner Eriko Sasada.

Japan, where he became noted as a producer. Dodger was bred by Ethel Herman.

In 1978 Mr. and Mrs. Satoki Hayashi imported a male from Charles and Dolores Wolske, Am. Ch. C and D's Flying Tiger of Devon (Am. Ch. C and D's Billy the Kid ex Am. Ch. C and D's Sunbonnet), who became the foundation for Bichon breeding in Japan. Mr. and Mrs. Hayashi also imported two bitches from Sherry and Lee Fry, Am. Ch. Kobold's Daytona (Am. Ch. Vogelflight's Music Man ex Am. Ch. Beau Monde the Firecracker) and Am. Ch. Taylored for Show (Am. Ch. Kobold's Kilimanjaro ex Am. Ch. Vogelflight's Fantasia).

From this period until the early 1980s, the Wolskes sent a number of Bichons to Mr. and Mrs. Hayashi, who ultimately became significant breeders in Japan: Am. Ch. C and D's B'Ann Tres Beau (Am. Ch. Beau Monde Ee's R Express ex Am. Ch. C and D's Beau Monde Moondust), Am. Ch. C and D's Victor of the Road (Am. Ch. C and D's King of the Road ex Am. Ch. C and D's Princess Victoria), Am. Ch. C and D's Petit Four Quite a Guy (Am. Ch. Petit Four Quite White ex Am. Ch. C and D's Bewitching Lady), Am. Ch. C and D's Bit O'Honey (Am. Ch. Adelridge Romeo de Beau Monde ex Am. Ch. C and D's Milkmaid) and Am. Ch. C and D's Dragon Lady (Am. Ch. C and D's Petit Four White Xmas ex Am. Ch. C and D's Moonglory).

Dragon Lady was sent to Japan in whelp, having been bred to Am. Ch. Win-Mar's Magnificent Scamp. One of the resulting puppies, born in Japan, was returned to the Wolskes, Am. Ch. C and D's Taro the Great.

Another of the American champions now living in Japan is Am. Ch. Dibett Maximillian. This Bichon has the distinction of being one of the few personally selected by his Japanese owner. In most cases the selections are made by a pet importer, an individual knowledgeable in specific breeds who travels to the countries necessary to obtain top dogs for designated clients.

The case of Maximillian was unique. Eriko Sasada spent nearly two years in the United States studying the American dog show, handling and grooming of various breeds, both on the East Coast and the West Coast. In Washington State she spent several months as guest of Dean and Beverly Passe, professional handlers, and at this juncture fell in love with the Bichon. Betty Shuck of Dibbet Bichons was approached; Eriko met Maximillian and decided he was the one for her. Max was purchased by Eriko's father, Keizo Sasada, who is an international judge and has been a top breeder of Dobermans in Japan. Max was shown in this country, where he obtained his American championship, then went to Japan, where he became the top winning Bichon in 1984, taking "Reserve King" (Reserve Best in Show) several times handled by Eriko Sasada.

At a later date, Eriko obtained a female puppy, Dibbet's Coming Up Roses, who also finished her Japanese championship and took "Reserve Queen" on several occasions.

Originally, the Bichon Frise was classified by the Japanese Kennel Club in the Toy Group, but in 1977 they were changed to the Non-Sporting Group. There they remained until April of 1988, when the Japanese adopted the FCI

(Fédération Cynologique Internationale) system, and the Bichon was once again returned to the Toy Group.

In 1976 the first Bichon earned his Japanese championship. Then followed five champions in 1977, two in 1978, seven in 1979 and two in 1980. As grooming techniques improved, the Bichon began to compete successfully on the all-breed level.

The first Bichon Frise club was organized in 1978 but dissolved after a year and a half of operation. In 1980 a group of Bichon fanciers organized the International Bichon Frise Club, which is still in operation today, with Satoki Hayashi as president. During the early years, Richard Beauchamp was a guest speaker with his noted presentation on the Bichon Frise.

The first Japanese Specialty show was held in 1985, with sixty entries. The second Specialty was in 1988, with an entry of fifty. In April 1989 the FCI Asian International Dog Show was held in Japan with Port Washington of Narita Hayashi-so taking a very respectable third place in the group. This Bichon was bred by M. Hayashi and owned by M. Enokida.

At the present time there are about 4,000 Bichons registered with the Japanese Kennel Club; however, it would appear that major interest in the breed is on the decline, as registration of the Bichon has dropped from approximately 300 per year to 200, and membership in the Bichon club has gone from 150 to 100. It will be interesting to see what the future holds for the Bichon Frise in Japan.

OTHER COUNTRIES

The Bichon Frise is found in other countries but not in significant numbers, with the possible exception of Mexico. That county now has a Specialty club that is putting on shows, and interest is certainly growing. Geraldine Church has been an active fancier for a number of years.

There have been a few individual dogs, imported from the United States, that have done well at the international shows in Argentina, Brazil and Venezuela, but interest in the Bichon has not developed in South America as it did in the United Kingdom and Scandinavia.

South Africa has imported from both England and the United States, and the Bichon has been in that part of the world for over a decade.

5

The International
Bichon Frise Congress

ON MAY 6, 1986, Richard Beauchamp was in Scotland judging a large entry of Bichons at the Edinburgh Kennel Club show. That evening he made a phone call to Barbara Stubbs in California. "I have an idea. I think we should hold an International Bichon Congress. It should be held in London, perhaps in conjunction with Crufts. Yes, that's it—Crufts—February 1988."

Thus the idea was born—perhaps a bit jokingly at first, as the complexities of organizing such a venture became apparent. But by the fall of 1986 mailing lists had been assembled from Bichon organizations, exhibitor lists and catalogs from around the world, and in November 1986 the introductory announcement of the event went out from the congress mailing address in San Diego. A London hotel was booked, a program and tentative scheduling arranged and the Bichon Frise Club of Great Britain contacted. Through the efforts of Secretary Pauline Block and other working members, the British club offered to hold a Special Open Show and host a day of hospitality prior to the official opening of the congress.

There were a few skeptics who felt such a congress was premature. The breed was too young, they said. But supporters felt this was exactly *why* such a gathering was expedient at this time; the breed was indeed young, and this opportunity of sharing ideas and concepts on an international level could promote a harmony of purpose, objectives and direction. The stated goal of the congress was to bring about international agreement on the "essence" of

FIRST INTERNATIONAL BICHON FRISE CONGRESS - 1988

Logo for the First International Bichon Frise Congress, London, February 1988.

Judges at the Special Open Show and participants in the International Bichon Congress. *Left to right*: Lars Adeheimer (Sweden), Lois Morrow (United States), Rudi Van Voorst (Australia), Gertrude Fournier (United States) and Wendy Hutchinson (Australia), all Bichon breeders.

A rare group picture of English Bichon champions assembled in honor of the international visitors at the Special Open Show, London, February 1988.

the Bichon Frise, and everyone's efforts were focused on achieving that goal.

The response to the concept of a Bichon congress was as enthusiastic as had been anticipated, and reservations arrived from around the world. The summer of 1988 saw a second mailing detailing the plans and projected activities. The idea conceived in that first transatlantic call was fast becoming a reality.

On Sunday, February 6, 1988, the buses arrived at the Mount Royal Hotel, Mayfair, London, for the hour trip to Langley Community Center, Langley, Slough, for the Special Open Show hosted by the Bichon Frise Club of Great Britain. (We remind the reader that due to the six-month quarantine policy of the United Kingdom, there were no foreign Bichons present.) There was an outstanding entry of nearly two hundred Bichons. The catalog was an incredible effort on the part of the British show committee that offered a three-generation pedigree for each entry—an invaluable record for every foreign visitor. Trophies for the event had been donated by Bichon fanciers from around the world, and the judging panel was a gathering of Bichon breeders that emphasized the international flavor of the day: The dog classes—Lars Adeheimer of Sweden; Bitch classes—Rudi Van Voorst of Australia; Best Puppy in Show and Best Opposite Puppy, Best in Show, Reserve Best in Show and Best of Opposite Sex—Gertrude Fournier of the United States; Puppy Dog Stakes—Lois Morrow of the United States; Puppy Bitch Stakes— Yanna Leinonen of Finland; Special Beginners Stakes, Dogs and Bitches— Wendy Hutchinson of Australia.

The midday buffet luncheon hosted by the British club offered enviable opportunities to make new friends, talk with the exhibitors and have a "hands on" experience with the English Bichons that represented both Continental and American bloodlines and the resulting blends. The day was long but satisfying and provided a perfect prologue for the seminar days of the congress that would follow.

On the afternoon of February 8, Pauline Block, president of the Bichon Frise Club of Great Britain, called the congress to order and introduced Ferelith Hamilton, club patron and internationally known figure in the world of dogs, who officially opened the congress and welcomed the 160 individuals attending from England, Ireland, Scotland, Finland, Norway, Sweden, Denmark, Belgium, Holland, New Zealand, Australia, Japan, Mexico, Canada and the United States. Miss Hamilton then introduced Richard Beauchamp, who must have felt great personal satisfaction in seeing his concept of the congress become an accomplished fact. In addition to the Bichon breeders and owners, there were judges and fanciers from other breeds in attendance for this "learning experience" and also the press, which showed great interest in this unique event staged by this "young" breed. It was, in short, a stellar attraction.

Mr. Beauchamp opened the congress with a slide and lecture presentation on the "essence of the Bichon," which set the stage. This was followed by Dr. Harry Spira, noted Australian veterinarian and international all-breed judge, who spoke on artificial insemination, and Dr. Jane Corrigan, with

Lars Adeheimer judged Dog Classes, Gertrude Fournier judged Best Puppy and Best in Show, and Rudi Van Voorst judged the Bitch entry. Susan Dunger owner-handler of Best in Show, Snuggle Up to Sulyka, and the owner of Reserve Best in Show, Sulyka Samantha, handled by Stephen Thomson.

Best Puppy Bitch, Azzjazz Sweet Angel (*left*), bred, owned and handled by Maureen Adams, and Reserve Puppy Bitch, Twinley Crystal Gazer, bred by Pauline Bloc and handled by Den Thomas.

105

fourteen years of specialized interest in the breed with "A Veterinary Overview of the Bichon." Monday evening featured a cocktail party and banquet that offered additional opportunities to pursue new friendships.

Tuesday's activities began at 9:00 A.M. with Dr. Biodne Eskeland from Norway and a lecture on the nutrition of the Bichon Frise. A Bichon breeder himself and an internationally known specialist in the field of nutrition, Dr. Eskeland was not only highly informative but quite literally left the crowd asking for more.

The remainder of the morning was a breeder's panel moderated by Richard Beauchamp and focusing on the similarities and differences of breeding concepts from an international point of view. Members of the panel were Rosmarie Blood (United States), Lars Adeheimer (Sweden), Geraldine Griegg (Australia), Pauline Block (England) and Andrew Brace (England).

The afternoon program offered one of the most popular events of the congress. Three different judges independently judged five different Bichons. To add interest, three of the Bichons were not presented in show trim, as they were to be part of the grooming demonstration on the following day. This offered a challenge for both judges and audience alike. The judges were Ferelith Hamilton (England), Dr. Harry Spira (Australia) and Dr. Samuel Draper (United States). Each evaluated the entry, made his placements, then left. The audience made its selections by written ballot. The open forum that followed, with the judges and the audience participating, was enlightening for everyone.

Wednesday morning brought the grooming demonstration by Lois Morrow (United States), Den Thomas (England) and Lee Walmsley (Australia). The spectators moved freely around the grooming areas while video cameras rolled and shutters clicked.

Upon completion of the grooming, the five Bichons were shown once again to the audience and the placements tallied by ballot. The results differed from the previous day, showing the importance and effect of the scissor work.

The morning emphasis on grooming led to the closing discussions of the congress. The breed Standard as defined by the FCI does not allow for the refined grooming that originated in the United States and subsequently spread to other countries as interest in the breed developed. Judges in countries operating under the FCI Standard or in countries with similar limitations have quietly overlooked these grooming restrictions and exhibitors have presented their dogs as if in the American show ring. However, France, as home of the FCI, remains adamant that the brushed and scissored Bichon is not acceptable.

A show of hands indicated the international breed representatives present at the congress applauded the grooming presentation as demonstrated that day. Thus a resolution was passed asking that Bichon organizations around the world write to the Fédération Cynologique Internationale (FCI) requesting the FCI Bichon Frise Standard be changed to state that grooming and presentation should henceforth be a matter of choice.

The success of the congress was undeniable. It was agreed that a Second

106

Geoff Corish (*left*) handling Michael Coad's Ir. Ch. Pamplona Gay Crusader and Den Thomas handling his Reserve Dog and Best Puppy in Show Roushka's Cameo Dance.

Grooming Seminar at the International Bichon Congress, London, February 1988, with a demonstration by Lois Morrow of the United States.

Grooming Seminar at the International Bichon Congress, London, February 1988, with a demonstration by Lee Walmsley of Australia.

Congress would be held in five years (1993). Officially, the congress ended the afternoon of February 10. Unofficially, it marked the beginning of new friendships, understanding and an easy exchange of ideas that continues to this day.

In February 1989, one year later, Barbara Stubbs and Inger and Lars Adeheimer of Sweden met in New York City on the occasion of the Westminster Kennel Club show. Mr. Adeheimer, a Terrier and Bichon breeder and an international judge, commented that the Bichon Frise offered a higher degree of uniformity on the international level than any other breed he knew. He credited this with an unprecedented degree of communication that existed among Bichon breeders worldwide. The 1988 International Congress became the focal point of that "communication." Without question, the Bichon can anticipate reaching new heights in the future.

6

The Bichon Frise Standard in the United States

THE CURRENT STANDARD of the Bichon Frise stands among the best written and most accurately descriptive of the American Kennel Club breeds. It provides proportions and relationships that accurately portray the breed's structure. Even more important, when these relationships are accomplished, they create an exceptionally sound animal that is capable of the most effortless and efficient movement in the canine world.

STANDARD FOR THE BICHON FRISE

General Appearance

The Bichon Frise is a small, sturdy, white powder puff of a dog whose merry temperament is evidenced by his plumed tail carried jauntily over the back and his dark-eyed inquisitive expression.

This is a breed that has no gross or incapacitating exaggerations and therefore there is no inherent reason for lack of balance or unsound movement.

Any deviation from the ideal described in the standard should be penalized to the extent of the deviation. Structural faults common to all breeds are as undesirable in the Bichon Frise as in any other breed, even though such faults may not be specifically mentioned in the standard.

The look is bright, alert and sassy. It makes you expect something naughty at any moment.

Size, Proportion, Substance

Size—Dogs and bitches 9½ to 11½ inches are to be given primary preference. Only where the comparative superiority of a specimen outside this range clearly justifies it should greater latitude be taken. In no case, however, should this latitude ever extend over 12 inches or under 9 inches. The minimum limits do not apply to puppies.

Proportion—The body from the forwardmost point of the chest to the point of rump is ¼ longer than the height at the withers. The body from the withers to lowest point of chest represents ½ the distance from withers to ground.

Substance—Compact and of medium bone throughout: neither coarse nor fine.

Head

Expression—Soft, dark-eyed, inquisitive, alert. *Eyes* are round, black or dark brown and are set in the skull to look directly forward. An overly large or bulging eye is a fault as is an almond shaped, obliquely set eye. Halos, the black or very dark brown skin surrounding the eyes, are necessary as they accentuate the eye and enhance expression. The eye rims themselves must be black. Broken pigment, or total absence of pigment on the eye rims produce a blank and staring expression, which is a definite fault. Eyes of any color other than black or dark brown are a very serious fault and must be severely penalized. *Ears* are drop and are covered with long flowing hair. When extended toward the nose, the leathers reach approximately halfway the length of the muzzle. They are set on slightly higher than eye level and rather forward on the skull, so that when the dog is alert they serve to frame the face. The *skull* is slightly rounded, allowing for a round and forward looking eye. The *stop* is slightly accentuated.

Muzzle—A properly balanced head is three parts muzzle to five parts skull measured from the nose to the stop and from the stop to the occiput. A line drawn between the outside corners of the eyes and to the nose will create a near equilateral triangle. There is a slight degree of chiseling under the eyes, but not so much as to result in a weak or snipey foreface. The lower jaw is strong. The *nose* is prominent and always black. *Lips* are black, fine, never drooping. *Bite* is scissors. A bite which is undershot or overshot should be severely penalized. A crooked or out of line tooth is permissible, however, missing teeth are to be severely faulted.

Neck, Topline and Body

The arched *neck* is long and carried proudly behind an erect head. It blends smoothly into the shoulders. The length of neck from occiput to withers is approximately ⅓ the distance from forechest to buttocks. The *topline* is level except for a slight, muscular arch over the loin.

Body—The chest is well developed and wide enough to allow free and unrestricted movement of the front legs. The lowest point of the chest extends at least to the elbow. The rib cage is moderately sprung, and extends back to a short and muscular loin. The forechest is well pronounced and protrudes slightly forward of the point of shoulder. The underline has a moderate tuck-up. *Tail* is

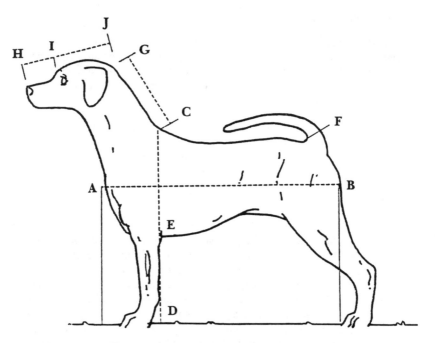

PROPORTIONS OF THE IDEAL BICHON FRISE
A–B: BODY LENGTH (sternum to buttocks) ¼ longer than C–D: HEIGHT (withers to ground). C–E: BODY DEPTH (withers to lowest point of chest) ½ of C–D (withers to ground). E–D: LENGTH OF LEG (elbow to ground) ½ of C–D (withers to ground). C–F: (WITHERS TO TAIL) ¼ less than C–D (withers to ground). C–G: NECK (back of skull to withers) ⅓ length of body A–B. H–J: HEAD ⅜ muzzle, H–I (nose to stop) and ⅝ skull, I–J (stop to occiput).

An exceptionally sound animal that is capable of the most effortless and efficient movement in the canine world.

well plumed, set on level with the topline and curved gracefully over the back so that the hair of the tail rests on the back. When the tail is extended toward the head it reaches at least halfway to the withers. A low tail set, a tail carried perpendicularly to the back, or a tail which droops behind is to be severely penalized. A corkscrew tail is a very serious fault.

Forequarters

Shoulders—The shoulder blade, upper arm and forearm are approximately equal in length. The shoulders are laid back to somewhat near a forty-five degree angle. The upper arm extends well back so the elbow is placed directly below the withers when viewed from the side. *Legs* are of medium bone; straight, with no bow or curve in the forearm or wrist. The elbows are held close to the body. The *pasterns* slope slightly from the vertical. The dewclaws may be removed. The *feet* are tight and round, resembling those of a cat, and point directly forward, turning neither in nor out. *Pads* are black. *Nails* are kept short.

Hindquarters

The hindquarters are of medium bone, well angulated with muscular thighs and spaced moderately wide. The upper and lower thigh are nearly equal in length meeting at a well bent stifle joint. The leg from hock joint to foot pad is perpendicular to the ground. Dewclaws may be removed. Paws are tight and round with black pads.

Coat

The texture of the coat is of utmost importance. The undercoat is soft and dense, the outercoat of a coarser and curlier texture. The combination of the two gives a soft but substantial feel to the touch which is similar to plush or velvet and when patted springs back. When bathed and brushed, it stands off the body, creating an overall powder puff appearance. A wiry coat is not desirable. A limp, silky coat, a coat that lies down, or a lack of undercoat are very serious faults.

Trimming—The coat is trimmed to reveal the natural outline of the body. It is rounded off from any direction and never cut so short as to create an overly trimmed or squared off appearance. The furnishings of the head, beard, moustache, ears and tail are left longer. The longer head hair is trimmed to create an overall rounded impression. The topline is trimmed to appear level. The coat is long enough to maintain the powder puff look which is characteristic of the breed.

Color

Color is white, may have shadings of buff, cream, or apricot around the ears or on the body. Any color in excess of 10% of the entire coat of a mature specimen is a fault and should be penalized, but color of the accepted shadings should not be faulted in puppies.

Gait

Movement at a trot is free, precise and effortless. In profile the forelegs and hind legs extend equally with an easy reach and drive that maintain a steady topline. When moving, the head and neck remain somewhat erect and as speed increases there is a very slight convergence of legs toward the center line. Moving away, the hindquarters travel with moderate width between them and the foot pads can be seen. Coming and going, his movement is precise and true.

Temperament

Gentle mannered, sensitive, playful and affectionate. A cheerful attitude is the hallmark of the breed and one should settle for nothing less.

7

Analysis of
the Standard

by Richard Beauchamp

THE BICHON FRISE CLUB OF AMERICA aligned its Standard to concur with the preferred format of the American Kennel Club in 1988. In doing so, the club also addressed the problem of proportions, which hitherto had been a matter of personally interpreting words like "slightly," "medium" and "moderate."

The newly written Standard gives both breeder and judge an ideal with which to compare any specimen of the breed. It is not a question of "what I like" but what is required. Personal perference can and does exist, of course, but these preferences must exist within the framework of the Standard or they constitute a disservice to the breed.

The primary clarification in the 1988 Standard Revision was in the very important height-at-shoulder to length-of-body ratio. Previously described was a body (sternum to buttocks) that was "slightly longer" than the dog's height. Obviously, "slightly longer" was interpreted in as many ways as there were interpreters.

Thus we had both long-legged, short-bodied dogs and short-legged, long-bodied dogs both taking major awards. Ridiculous but understandable under the old Standard.

Lest the reader believe the proportions called for in the 1988 Standard revision were arbitrarily conceived, it is important to note they are based upon specific proportions called for in the original French Standard of the breed, written in 1933. As this Standard endured various interpretations in the United States, specifics were reduced to generalities. The current Standard, however, represents a return to the source.

The original French Standard called for a body (sternum to buttocks) 22.5 percent longer than the dog's height at the withers. The BFCA rounded that figure off to a more easily determined 25 percent (or one-fourth) longer than tall. While the 22.5 percent figure was increased to one-fourth for ease of comparison, it should be obvious that "one-fourth longer" should be the maximum body length.

These definitive proportions should help eliminate the confusion on the part of breeders and judges who have been committed to keeping the Bichon as far from looking like a "bastardized Poodle" as possible. Their erroneous thinking is, "If a Poodle is short (measuring the same from sternum to buttocks as from withers to ground), then the Bichon must be long and low to create an obvious difference."

Not so! While the Bichon is not as short in body as the Poodle, it is only one-fourth longer. One breed is square, the other just off square.

There is one proportionate measure not directly dealt with in the current Standard—length from withers to tail (referred to as "length of back" by many). Using body length in proportion to height as the measure of correctness, the distance from withers to tail does have less significance. However, it follows that the measurement must be less than the dog's length of body and less than the height at withers in order to attain the balance that we strive for. Specifically, the ideal length from withers to tail is one fourth less than the distance from withers to ground.

Another significant proportion in the Standard is that which relates to depth of body and length of leg. In profile, half the distance from withers to ground is body, half is leg. In other words, looking at an 11-inch dog in profile, an ideal specimen would measure approximately 5½ inches from withers to lowest point of chest and 5½ inches from lowest point of chest to ground.

The Standard adds still another dimension to the breed's framework in its description of the Bichon's neck. It is long, measuring (from occiput to withers) one third the length of the body (sternum to buttocks).

It is important to interject here the relative importance of shoulder angulation. Not only does it directly affect movement, but also all the foregoing proportions. They are all dependent upon proper placement and angulation of the shoulder. It can easily be seen how steeply placed withers will not only shorten the neck but lengthen the back as well, throwing off the entire balance.

These proportions create the breed's basic framework. Anyone planning to judge this breed or embark upon a breeding program must have them committed to memory. He should know them all without thinking about it; know them well enough to recognize their absence, even in spite of a clever trim. They are a part of breed type and represent the "ideal" toward which

116

we all must aspire. One should not, however, expect all dogs measured to meet these specifications, for the perfect dog has yet to be bred. Understanding these proportions and using them as a goal will give us all, breeder, exhibitor and judge, a common goal. The requirements in a Standard are the breed's blueprint, the breeder is the builder and the judge the building inspector.

The Breed Standard of the Bichon Frise is written well enough so that the dog fancier and judge need not be subjected here to an endless rehash of its points that are already perfectly clear. I would suggest, however, that the novice begin his study of the breed with a good primer on canine anatomy. Those chapters that deal with balance, construction and movement are the basics upon which the Standard of the Bichon is built and should be clearly understood long before one attempts to commence upon a breeding program. It is hoped that the judge-to-be has already thoroughly mastered them.

While a complete understanding of the Standard's requirements is basic to both the breeder's and the judge's education, it is the "other knowledge," the bits and pieces gleaned over the years, that round out his appreciation of the breed. In what follows I will attempt to make comment on each section of the Standard; not to reiterate but to augment the reader's understanding. These comments are based upon observations I have made in my twenty-year association with this breed specifically and a lifetime with purebred dogs.

GENERAL APPEARANCE

There is a great deal about the correct Bichon Frise that will remind one of a little show pony. Both stand up over their fronts, arch their necks and thrust their rear quarters out behind them. Their attitudes are jaunty and cocky, yet there is something elegant in their stance.

SIZE AND PROPORTION

Proportion has been dealt with at great length. Remember, it remains the same for a 9½-inch Bichon as it is for one that is 12 inches. Size, so long as it falls within the acceptable limits, is absolutely immaterial.

HEAD

Three lumps of coal on a snow-white background. The look is bright, alert and sassy. It makes you expect something naughty at any moment. The Standard does provide some specific proportions here (three-eighths muzzle to five-eighths skull), but of even greater importance is what the parts of the head collectively give you in expression. Dull and stupid this breed is not, so an expression even remotely reminiscent of those attitudes is a serious departure from what we are looking for. Pigment is important. It crystalizes the expression.

NECK, TOPLINE, BODY

I'm inclined to think of the line that begins behind the skull and moves on down the neck past the shoulders to the tail as the topline. When the neck, back and body are right, they create that distinctive set of curves that characterize the Bichon. You'll only get that look if you have a long arched neck, a level back and that gentle arch over the loin. The arched loin, though concealed by the coat, gives the breed the power to thrust its rear quarter well out behind, whether on the move or standing still.

FOREQUARTERS

If the reader hasn't realized the importance of the properly laid back shoulder by this time, he is in serious trouble! Not a whole lot more can be said about its significance than already has been.

The Bichon is best described as standing well over its front, as opposed to the average Terrier front, with its short upper arm dropping the forelegs down almost directly in front of the dog.

HINDQUARTERS

The front is constructed to provide great reach. It should come as no surprise then that the rear provides the drive behind. Together they provide balanced movement.

In order to provide this drive, the rear quarter must be well angulated; that is, the upper thigh meets the lower thigh at approximately a 45-degree angle (just as the shoulder blade meets the upper arm at the same degree of angle). You'll seldom find this when the bones are short and thick. They create that straight rear quarter that is restricted in movement.

Watch for "sickle hocks." They are hocks that, from hock joint to footpad, angle forward rather than dropping down perpendicularly. Sickle hocks have no flexibility, and all the rear-quarter movement will be under the dog. It is a breed problem at the present time.

COAT

There are few if any places in the world where the Bichon is not shown in its jaunty-looking trim. The trim, by the way, was greatly instrumental in rescuing the breed from obscurity and making it one of the foremost Group and Best in Show contenders worldwide.

Of course, there are a very few who insist that the breed should still be shown in its unbrushed, ungroomed state because the first Standard written for the breed dictated that method of presentation. That first Standard was written at a time and in a place long before dog shows became as sophisticated as they are today, and long before methods of presentation were as developed as they are in this day and age. Were excessive, ungroomed coat ever a utilitarian matter in this breed, one might see the point in continuing on in this tradition. This, however, is a companion breed, developed to please the eye.

The nongrooming position leads one to ask if it is our responsibility as dog fanciers to maintain the wording of a Standard or ensure the perpetuation of a breed. One cannot deny the great impact "smartening up" the Bichon has had on its universal acceptance and popularity. Surely its future is ensured.

For those who claim trimming and brushing is a change in the Standard, I can only counter that it is one that can be quickly remedied after the show with just a simple bit of neglect.

On the other hand, West Highland White Terrier faces, necklines carried halfway down the back, the white buffalo look (twenty-pound front combined with five-pound rears) can hardly be considered trimming, "to reveal the natural outline of the body" as the Standard requires. If the reader will recall, the Standard quite clearly states under General Appearance, "Any deviation from the ideal described in the standard should be penalized to the extent of the deviation." Exaggerated and highly stylized trims are very much a deviation from the Standard.

COLOR

The whiter the better, and hopefully this is created in the whelping box rather than at the hairdresser. While bleaching may well fool the judge, it does not fool the genes. The Standard does allow minor shadings of color, but it must be watched that too much color is not perpetuated.

GAIT

Everything in the Standard makes the Bichon capable of being one of the best moving dogs in the ring today. "No gross or incapacitating exaggerations . . . no inherent reason for lack of balance or unsound movement." The judge and the breeder must keep this continually in mind, as it is vital to the future of the breed. Reach and drive and maximum ground covering with minimum effort are basic to this breed. It must be sought after.

TEMPERAMENT

"A cheerful attitude is the hallmark of the breed and one should settle for nothing less." Can it be said more simply? A shy or vicious Bichon has no place in the ring or in the whelping box. A Bichon Frise is above all a companion. He has been historically and remains so to this day. He is a treat to behold and a joy to live with.

8

Bichon Frise Standards Around the World

T HE BREED STANDARD is the nucleus of any breed. The Bichon Frise Standard, as approved by the members of the Bichon Frise Club of America, Inc., and adopted by the American Kennel Club, has been discussed in detail. The following includes: The original French Standard, as written by Madame Nizet de Lehmans and her committee and adopted in 1933, the FCI Standard, and the Standards of Canada, England and Australia. The New Zealand Kennel Club adopted virtually the same Standard as Australia. Both are similar to the English interpretation, which is clearly logical, since the original dogs came from England directly or via England from the United States. The FCI Standard is used in all other countries.

It is interesting to note that only the United States, through the American Kennel Club, allows full participation of the national or parent club in determining the contents of the Breed Standard. The American Standard was submitted to the American Kennel Club in 1973 prior to full breed recognition, modified in 1981 and again in 1988 (by request of the AKC in their efforts to standardize the format). In all instances a Standard committee was selected from the club membership. Their work was submitted to the board of directors and elected by the general membership, and the final draft was sent to the membership for a vote. A two-thirds vote of approval is necessary, not just a simple majority. It is then sent to the AKC for that body's approval and adoption.

In Canada a committee of Bichon breeders submitted a Standard to the Canadian Kennel Club and its Standard committee. While much of the projected Standard was retained, changes were made and adopted by the CKC without further approval of the Bichon Standard committee.

When the breed was introduced into England, the FCI Standard was adopted as an interim Standard. A committee was eventually organized by the breeders, and the results of their efforts submitted to the British Kennel Club, known as The Kennel Club. As in Canada, the Standard committee of The Kennel Club reviewed the draft, made their changes and adopted the results. A modification made in 1987 was accomplished entirely through the work of the Standard committee of The Kennel Club.

The Bichon is shown in the Toy Group elsewhere in the world, while the American Bichon breeders opted for the Non-Sporting Group, as discussed earlier. Interestingly enough, despite the admonition in several of these Standards that the smaller dogs bear the element of success, there is not the dramatic difference in size that one might expect, partially because American bloodlines are involved in many cases, and partially because breeders found that superior quality was more easily attained in a reasonably sized package.

There are some interesting variations, but none more striking than the descriptions of "coat." There is no discussion of grooming or presentation other than to state that the coat shall remain untrimmed. It should be obvious to the reader after viewing pictures of the Bichons around the world that this aspect of these Standards is being quietly overlooked by breeders, exhibitors and judges alike.

A letter from Madame E. Laisne, Closmyons Bichons of France, to Rudy Van Voorst of Australia states:

> Here in France for grooming the Bichon must keep all its fur and for showing you must comb the dog fully, then bathe it three days before the competition and you are not to touch it again.
>
> This is to make sure that the fur has regained its curls. You can before the show give a slight combing to the mustache, beard, tail and the ends of the paws, but you must not use a brush that goes to the roots of the fur . . . as you can see the grooming of the Bichon Frise which is a Franco-Belgian breed is not the same as the American grooming. I hope that this little advice will not upset you, in your place, you do as you please . . .

It is safe to say that if the "American grooming" had not developed, you would not be reading these words. Dog fanciers previously held little interest in a "street urchin," however enchanting his personality, an obvious truth in England and Scandinavia, as well as the United States. The breed existed in Europe for years and no serious interest had ever developed. A bit of glamour was introduced and the rest in history.

In Canada there has been some discussion to bring the Standard of that country in line with the American Standard. Since half of the judging in Canada is done by American judges, and conversely a large number of Canadians judge the Bichon in the United States, this would be a reasonable suggestion. Also noted is the fact that the majority of top producing and winning Canadian Bichons have American ancestry, which adds further credence to this idea.

122

The Havanese and the Bolognese Standards have been included as a point of interest, since they have retained their identity and have emerged in recent years in distinct fashion.

FRENCH STANDARD FOR THE BICHON FRISE

In March of 1933 the following breed standard was adopted by the Societe Centrale in France.

General Appearance

A little dog, gay and joyful, with a medium size muzzle and long hair curling loosely. Dark eyes are bright and expressive. Viewed from the side giving a slightly roached appearance.

Head

The cranium is larger than the nose and will measure approximately from two inches to three and one-half inches, the circumference of the cranium corresponding to the height of the withers, about ten and one-half inches.

Lips—Fine, somewhat dry but less than the Schipperke, never drooping and heavy, they are normally pigmented black, the lower lip should not be heavy or noticeable but should not be soft and not let the mucous membrane show when the mouth is closed.

Denture—Normal, the fore teeth of the lower jaw should be against and behind the points of the upper teeth (scissors).

Muzzle—Should not be thick and heavy but not pinched. The cheeks are flat and not muscular, the stop accentuated slightly.

Eyes—Dark, as much as possible surrounded by black, are rather round and not almond shaped. They should not be placed at an oblique angle, are lively, not too large, not showing any white when looking forward. They should not be too big and prominent like the Pekingese. The eye socket should not sag and the eye globe should not bulge in an exaggerated manner.

Cranium—Rather flat to the touch although the fur gives a round appearance.

Ears—Drooping, well covered with long wavy hair, carried rather forward when at attention, the length of the cartilage cannot reach the nose as the French Poodle but only half way the length of the muzzle. In fact they are not as large and are finer than those of the Poodle.

Crest (or neck)

Rather long. Carried highly and proudly, it is round and fine, close to the cranium, widening gradually to meet the withers. Its length is approximately one-third of the length of the body (proportion being about four and one-half inches to thirteen and one-half inches for a subject eleven inches high).

Withers

Are rather oblique, not prominent, giving the appearance of being as long as the fore arm, approximately four inches. Fore arm should not be spread out from the body and the elbow, in particular, should not point outward.

123

Legs

Are straight when looking from the front, of good standing, of fine bones, the pastern short and straight when viewed from the front, very slightly oblique from the profile view, the toe nails should be black by preference, but it is difficult to obtain.

Chest

Well developed, the sternum is pronounced, the lower ribs rather round and not ending abruptly, the chest being horizontally rather deep. The flanks are close to the belly, the skin is fine and not floating.

Loin

Large and muscular. The hock is more elbowed than the Poodle.

Tail

Is normally carried upwards and graciously curved over the dorsal spine. The hair of the tail is long and will lay on the back.

Pigmentation

Under the white hair is preferably dark. The sexual organs are also pigmented black, bluish or beige, as are the spots often found on the body.

Colour

Preferably all white, sometimes white with tan or grey on the ears and body.

Hair

Should be fine, silky and loosely curled, its length being approximately two and one-half inches to four inches long. Unlike the Maltese the Bichon Frise also has an undercoat.

Size

The height of the withers cannot be over twelve inches, the smaller dog being the element of success.

Reason for disqualification

Over and undershot, inferior prognathism, pink nose, flesh coloured lips, pale eyes, tail curled in a corkscrew manner, black spots in the fur.

FÉDÉRATION CYNOLOGIQUE INTERNATIONALE (FCI)
STANDARD: BICHON À POIL FRISÉ (CRISP-HAIRED BICHON)
FRENCH-BELGIAN BREED

General Appearance

A small dog, gay and playful, with a lively gait, a muzzle of moderate length, long hairs corkscrewed and very slack, resembling the fur of the Mongolian goat. The carriage of the head is proud and high, the dark eyes are vivid and expressive.

Head

The skull, longer than the muzzle, is in the proportion of 8 to 5 cms, the circumference of the skull corresponding to the height at withers, about 27 cms.

Nose—The nose is rounded, well black, smooth and glossy.

Lips—The lips are thin, fairly lean, less however than in the Schipperke, falling just enough for covering the lower lips, but never heavy or pendent, they are normally pigmented with black to the commissures, the lower lip cannot be either heavy or apparent, or slack and does not allow to see the mucous when the mouth is closed.

Dentition—The dentition is normal, that is to say that the lower incisors are placed just behind the teeth of the upper jaw.

Muzzle—The muzzle should not be either thick or heavy, without however being pinched; the cheeks are flat and not very muscular. The stop is hardly accentuated, the hollow between the arcades slightly apparent.

Eyes—Dark, as much as possible, edged with dark eyelids, rather rounded and not almond-shaped; they are not placed obliquely, are lively, not too large, leaving no white. They are neither big nor prominent, like those of the Griffon Bruxellois or the Pekingese; the socket should not be protruding. The globe of the eye should not come out in an exaggerated way.

Skull—The skull is rather flat at touch, though the fur makes it look round.

Ears—The ears are drooping, well furnished with hairs crisp and long, carried rather forward when on the alert, but so that the fore edge touches the skull and the length of the cartilage should not go to the nose, as in the Poodle, but stops at half-length of the muzzle. Moreover, they are much less wide and finer than in this dog.

Neck

The neck is fairly long, carried high and proudly. It is round and slim near the skull, broadening gradually and fitting smoothly into the shoulders. Its length is very approximately ⅓ of the length of the body (proportion of 11 to 33 cms for a 27 cms-high specimen; the points of the shoulder against the withers being taken as basis).

Shoulder

The shoulder is fairly slanting, not prominent, giving the appearance of being of same length that the arm, about 10 cms, this one is not out of the body, in particular the elbow.

Legs

The legs are well straight, seen from front, finely boned; the pattern is short and straight seen from front, very slightly slanting seen from profile. The claws will be preferably black, however, it is an ideal difficult to attain.

Chest

The chest is well developed, the sternum pronounced, the backs rounded and not finishing abruptly, the chest having horizontally a fairly large depth.

Flanks

The flanks are well lifted at the belly, the skin is thin and not floating, giving an appearance fairly Greyhound-like.

Loin

The loin is wide and well-muscled, slightly domed. The pelvis is wide, the rump slightly rounded, the tail is set on a little more below the back line than in the Poodle.

Thighs

The thighs are wide and well muscled, the arms well slanting, the hock is also more angulated than in the Poodle, the foot nervous.

Tail

Normally, the tail is carried lifted and gracefully curved, in the line of the spine, without being rolled up; it is not docked and cannot be close to the back; however, the hair may fall on the back.

Pigmentation

The pigmentation under the white hair is preferably dark; the sexual organs are then pigmented with black or bluish or beige, as the specks and markings one often sees on the body.

Colour

Pure white.

Hair

Fine, silky, corkscrewed, very slack, resembling that of the fur of the Mongolian goat, neither flat nor roped and reaching 7 to 10 cms.

Toilet

The dog may be presented with only the feet and muzzle clipped.

Size

The height at withers cannot go beyond 30 cms, the small size being an element of success.

Heavy faults

Disqualifications: lower or upper prognathism so developed that the incisors no longer touch each other. Pink nose, fleshcoloured lips, pale eyes, cryptorchidy, tail rolled up and turned like a helix. Black specks in the hair.

Faults to be avoided

Pigmentation extending into the hair so that to form red specks. Hair flat, wavy, roped or too short. Monorchidy. Any prognathism other than that described here above. Dog too low or too short.

THE CANADIAN STANDARD FOR THE BICHON FRISE
[Effective July 1, 1975]

Origin and Purpose

The Bichon Frise originated in the Canary Islands, and was formerly called the Tenerife after the largest of this group of islands. It has been bred as a companion dog because of its friendly and affectionate nature.

General Appearance

A small, sturdy, lively dog projecting an air of dignity and intelligence. Having a powder puff appearance with the tail carried gaily over the back.

Temperament

Stable, outgoing and alert.

Size

Not under 9 inches (22.86 cm) and not over 12 inches (30.5 cm) at the withers with preference given to dogs 10–11 inches (25.4 to 28 cm) and bitches 9½–10½ inches (24.13 to 26.67 cm).

Coat and Color

The coat should be white, with shadings of cream or apricot on the ears and/or body permissible. The coat is double with the outer hair profuse, soft, silky and loosely curled. Two inches or longer on adults. The skin pigmentation is preferably dark, nose, lips and eyerims must be black.

Head

The circumference of the skull equals the height at the withers which should be approximately 10½ inches (26.67 cm).

Skull—broad and rather flat, not coarse, covered with a top-knot of hair giving it a rounded appearance.

Muzzle—the skull is longer than the muzzle in the ratio of 8 to 5. Not heavy or snipey, with a slighly accentuated stop.

Nose—black, round and pronounced.

Mouth—lips black, fine and never drooping, scissors bite.

Eyes—black or dark brown, large round, expressive and alert, surrounded by halos which are dark grey to black pigmentation extending ¼" (6.3 mm) or more around the eye.

Ears—the ear is drooped, set level with the eyes and when alerted brought slightly forward but placed in such a way that the front edge touches the skull and does not angle away from the skull. Well covered with long, finely curled hair with the ear leather reaching the mid point of the muzzle.

Neck

Fairly long, carried high and proudly. Round and slender near the skull, broadening gradually and fitting smoothly into the shoulders. Length of neck measures one third that of body.

Forequarters

The shoulders are well laid back with upper and lower arms of equal length. The forelegs are perfectly straight, close to the body, with pasterns slightly bent.

Body

Length of body measured from sternum to pinbones longer than the height at the withers, the ideal ratio being 10 to 13. There is a gradual slant upwards from the withers to the rump. The sternum well pronounced with a good spring of ribs rather round and blending smoothly into the loin. The chest is deep, extending to the elbows. The loin is large and muscular. The tail is set level with the back.

Hindquarters

The upper thigh is well muscled with stifle well bent.

Feet

Round and tight (cats paw) pads thick.

Tail

The tail is carried upwards, elegantly curled, in line with the spine without being rolled up; the tail is not docked. The tailbone should not touch the back, however the feathering may.

Gait

Balanced and vigorous, with good reach in the forequarters and good drive in the hindquarters. The legs must move straight fore and back along the line of travel.

Faults

Cowhocks, snipey muzzle, poor pigmentation, protruding eyes, yellow eyes, undershot or overshot bite in excess of $1/16$ inch (1.6 mm), corkscrew tail, too short a coat in adult dogs.

Disqualifications

Over 12 inches (30.5 cm) or under 9 inches (22.86 cm), black hair in the coat, pink eyerims.

Gait/Movement

Balanced and effortless with an easy reach and drive maintaining a steady and level topline. Legs moving straight along line of travel, with hind pads showing.

Coat

Fine, silky, with soft corkscrew curls. Neither flat nor corded, and measuring 7–10 cm in length. The dog may be presented untrimmed or have muzzle and feet slightly tidied up.

Colour

White, but cream or apricot markings acceptable up to 18 months. Under white coat, dark pigment desirable. Black, blue or beige markings often found on skin.

Size

Ideal height 23–28 cm (9″–11″) at withers.

Faults

Any departure from the foregoing points should be considered a fault and the seriousness with which the fault should be regarded should be in exact proportion to its degree.

Note: Male animals should have two apparently normal testicles fully descended into the scrotum.

BREED STANDARD
BICHON FRISE CLUB OF GREAT BRITAIN

General Appearance

Well balanced dog of smart appearance, closely coated with handsome plume carried over the back. Natural white coat curling loosely. Head carriage proud and high.

Characteristics

Gay, happy, lively little dog.

Temperament

Friendly and outgoing.

Head and Skull

Ratio of muzzle length to skull length 3:5. On a head of the correct width and length, lines drawn between the outer corners of the eyes and nose will create a near equilateral triangle. Whole head in balance with body. Muzzle not thick, heavy nor snipey. Cheeks flat, not very strongly muscled. Stop moderate but definite, hollow between eyebrows just visible. Skull slightly rounded, not coarse, with hair accentuating rounded appearance. Nose large, round, black, soft and shiny.

Eyes—Dark, round with black eye rims, surrounded by dark haloes, consisting of well pigmented skin. Forward-looking, fairly large but not almond shaped, neither obliquely set nor protruding. Showing no white when looking forward. Alert, full of expression.

Ears—Hanging close to head, well covered with flowing hair longer than leathers, set on slightly higher than eye level and rather forward on skull. Carried forward when dog alert, forward edge touching skull. Leather reaching approximately half-way along muzzle.

Mouth—Jaws strong, with a perfect, regular and complete scissor bite, i.e. the upper teeth closely overlapping the lower teeth and set square to the jaws. Full dentition desirable. Lips fine, fairly tight and completely black.

Neck

Arched neck fairly long, about one third length of body. Carried high and proudly. Round and slim near head, gradually broadening to fit smoothly into shoulders.

Forequarters

Shoulders oblique, not prominent, equal in length to upper arm. Upper arm fits close to body. Legs straight, perpendicular, when seen from front; not too finely boned. Pasterns short and straight viewed from front, very slightly sloping viewed from side.

Body

Forechest well developed, deep brisket. Ribs well sprung, floating ribs not terminating abruptly. Loin broad, well muscled, slightly arched and well tucked up. Pelvis broad, croup slightly rounded. Length from withers to tailset should equal height from withers to ground.

Hindquarters

Thighs broad and well rounded. Stifles well bent; hocks well angulated and metatarsals perpendicular.

Feet

Tight, rounded and well knuckled up. Pads black. Nails preferably black.

Tail

Normally carried raised and curved gracefully over the back but not tightly curled. Never docked. Carried in line with backbone, only hair touching back; tail itself not in contact. Set on level with topline, neither too high nor too low. Corkscrew tail undesirable.

AUSTRALIA: THE R.A.S.K.C. STANDARD OF THE BICHON FRISE

General Appearance

Gay, happy, lively little dog, the coat falling in soft, corkscrew curls. The head carriage is proud and high; the eyes alert and full of expression.

Head and Skull

The skull longer than the muzzle, the whole head in balance with the body. The muzzle should not be thick or heavy, nor should it be snipey, the cheeks flat and not very strongly muscled; the stop should be slight and the hollow between the eyebrows just visible. Skull flat when touched, although the hair tends to make it look round. The nose should be round, black, soft and shiny.

Eyes—Dark, with dark eye rims, fairly round, never almond shaped nor obliquely set; lively, not too big; never showing any white. Neither large nor prominent. The socket should not be pronounced.

Ears—Narrow and delicate. Hanging close to the head and well covered with tightly curled, long hair. Carried forward when the dog is alert in such manner that the forward edge touched the skull and not carried obliquely away from the head. The leather should reach half-way along the muzzle.

Mouth—Scissor bite, that is to say, the incisors of the lower jaw should be placed immediately behind and in contact with those of the upper jaw. The lips should be fine, fairly tight and completely black, drooping just sufficient for the lower lips to be covered by the upper, but never heavy or hanging. The lower lip should be neither heavy, protruding nor flabby and should never show the mucous membrane when the mouth is closed.

Neck

Fairly long, carried high and proudly. Round and slim near the head, gradually broadening to fit smoothly into the shoulders. Length about one third the length of the body (proportions of 33 cm.–11 cm. for a dog of 27 cm. at the withers).

Forequarters

Shoulders oblique, not prominent, and unequal in length to the upper arm (approximately 10 cm). The upper arm should fit close to the body. Legs straight when seen from the front, perpendicular and finely boned. The pastern should be short and straight when viewed from the front, very slightly sloping when viewed from the side.

Body

Chest well developed, with deep brisket. The floating ribs well rounded and not terminating abruptly. Loin broad, well muscled, slightly arched and well tucked-up. The pelvis broad, the croup slightly rounded.

Hindquarters

Thighs broad and well-muscled, oblique. Stifles well-bent and hocks well let down.

Feet

Small, rounded and well knucked-up. Nails preferably black.

Tail

Normally carried raised and well curled gracefully over the back but never tightly curled. It should not be docked and should not touch the backbone but the hair should always fall on to the back. Slightly low set.

Coat

Fine, silky, with soft corkscrew curls. Neither flat nor corded, and measuring 7–10 cm. in length. The dog may be presented untrimmed or have muzzle and feet slightly tidied up.

Colour

Pure White. Under the coat dark pigment is preferred. Black, blue or beige markings are often found on the skin.

Height

Less than 30 cm., smallness being highly desirable.

Faults

Any departure from the foregoing points should be considered a fault and the seriousness of the fault should be in exact proportion to its degree.

Note: Male animals should have two apparently normal testicles fully descended into the scrotum.

9

Comparing the Standards

AFTER LOOKING OVER THE BREED Standards from other countries, the reader is certainly aware that the Bichon Frise Standard of the United States is far more comprehensive and detailed than the rest. The Standards of other countries leave a great deal to personal interpretation. By contrast, the American Standards have always been more inclusive, and the current Standard adopted in the fall of 1988 has narrowed these perimeters even more dramatically. Judges have responded favorably to this American Standard adopted in 1988, calling it one of the most precise and explicit they have read.

The Bichon Frise has become a breed of international scope, thus making it especially interesting to examine and compare some of the Standards in reference to major points, notably the American, Canadian and British (Australian) Standards. The British also adopted a new Standard, bringing it more in line with that of the United States. There continue to be areas of difference, however.

In the past, the Breed Standards of Australia and New Zealand followed those of Great Britain, which was logical, as their dogs came from there. When the recent British Standard was adopted, the Australians followed suit. However, in a surprising move, the New Zealanders did not.

Comments on the British Standard obviously reflect the Australian Standard also.

Int. Ch. Twinley Sailor's Hornpipe, the first documented Bichon to have earned his international championship (in France), with a visible outline and a semblance of grooming. Owned by M. De Silva of France.

GENERAL APPEARANCE

U.S.A.: A "small, sturdy, white powder puff," a merry temperament is described. *Canada:* "Small, sturdy, powder puff" but adds an air of "dignity and intelligence," a more somber approach. *Great Britain:* Our first major difference, showing the Continental influence, "well balanced . . . smart appearance . . . gay, happy, lively . . . natural white coat curling loosely." The latter phrase certainly does not conjure up the powder puff of a dog we are accustomed to seeing in the United States and Canada. This is a reflection back to the FCI and French Standards, which described "long hair curling loosely."

SIZE, PROPORTION AND SUBSTANCE

U.S.A.: Dogs and bitches 9½ to 11½ primary preference. Chest to rump one fourth longer than height at the withers. Withers to lowest point on chest is half the distance from withers to ground. Compact, medium bone. *Canada:* Not under 9 inches, not over 12, 10 to 11 inches for dogs and 9½ to 10½ for bitches preferred. Length from sternum to pinbone longer than height at the withers, 10:13 ratio ideal. *Great Britain:* ideal 9 to 11 inches for dogs and bitches, length from withers to tailset should equal height from withers to ground. Neither Canadian nor British Standards discuss substance. There are subtle differences in these proportions; the size preferences are significant. There is no doubt that the Bichon's placement in the Toy Group in these countries as opposed to the Non-Sporting Group in the United States provides their emphasis on the smaller dog. Interestingly enough, many foreign judges cannot shake this prejudice, or preference, if you will, on size when judging in the United States, despite the "primary preference" stated in the U.S. Standard.

HEAD

Eyes

U.S.A.: Black or dark brown, with halos, set to look forward. The almond-shaped or protruding eye is faulted. *Canada:* Black or dark brown eye with halo required but no mention of forward set, the almond eye or the protruding eye. *Great Britain:* Similar to U.S. description, including eye set and faulting the obliquely set, almond shaped and protruding eye.

Ears

U.S.A.: Set slightly higher than the eye and rather forward. Frame the face when alert. *Canada:* Ears are set level with the eyes, brought forward when alerted. Unfortunately, this ear set does not usually frame the face in the desired soft manner and frequently produces a "spaniel look." *Great Britain:* Set on slightly higher than eye level and rather forward on the skull. Carried forward when alert. All three Standards have the ear leather reaching halfway the length of the muzzle.

Skull and Muzzle

U.S.A.: slightly rounded skull, slightly accentuated stop, balanced head is three parts muzzle to five parts skull. Line from outside corner of eye to nose is a near equilateral triangle. Strong lower jaw, scissors bite. *Canada:* Skull is longer than muzzle in the ratio of 8:5. Slight accentuated stop and scissors bite. However, overshot and undershot bites are *not* faults unless in excess of 1.6 mm. The Canadian breeders have always been distressed over this allowance. No Bichon Standard has ever called for less than a scissors bite, thus there is no historical precedence. *Great Britain:* Jaws strong, with a perfect, regular and complete scissors bite. Ratio of muzzle length to skull length is 3:5. The equilateral triangle of line from corner of eye to nose is also included.

NECK

All three Standards call for a long, arched neck "carried proudly." *U.S.A.:* Length of neck from occiput to withers is approximately one third the distance from forechest to buttocks. *Canada* and *Great Britain* state the neck is one third the length of the body.

TOPLINE

U.S.A.: Level except for a slight muscular arch over the loin. *Canada:* A gradual slant upwards from the wither to rump; quite a different interpretation. *Great Britain:* Topline is not specifically described other than to state that correct movement produces a level topline.

BODY

The three Standards are in virtual agreement. Chest is well developed, lowest point of chest extends at least to the elbow, ribs moderately well sprung ("moderately" is eliminated in the other two Standards), with a muscular loin.

136

TAIL

U.S.A.: Tail is set on level with the topline, well plumed and carried over the back. A low tail set or the attitude that produces a drooping tail is severely penalized. *Canada:* The tail set, per se, is not described. Tail carried upwards and "elegantly curled." The tail bone may not touch the back, the feathering may. *Great Britain:* Set on level with topline, "neither too high nor too low," carried in line with the backbone, only the hair touching the back not the tail. Observation reveals that the American breeder prefers a higher tail set than his British counterpart within that stated framework of "set on level with topline." Actually, the previous British Standard called for the tail "slightly low set," but that has been modified in the recent Standard as indicated. A low tail set distorts the topline and brings the rear legs under the body with resultant constricted movement.

FOREQUARTERS

Shoulders

All three Standards describe the upper arm and forearm equal or approximately equal in length, shoulders well laid back (U.S.A. states near a forty-five-degree angle), straight legs, close to body with slight slope of pasterns.

HINDQUARTERS

Again basic agreement with well-muscled upper thigh, well-angulated rear, well-bent stifles. Canadian description very brief.

COAT

Here, certainly, is a dramatic area of difference. *U.S.A.:* soft, dense undercoat with outer coat of a coarser, curlier texture. Presentation is described in detail. *Canada:* There is a double coat with the outer hair "soft, silky and loosely curled." No description of presentation is offered. *Great Britain:* "Fine, silky, with soft corkscrew curls . . . may be presented untrimmed or have muzzle and feet slightly tidied up." The Canadian Standard contradicts itself. The second paragraph describes the dog as having a "powder-puff" appearance and sentences later describes the coat as soft, silky and "loosely curled." In Great Britain what actually appears in the show ring and what is described in the Breed Standard are not one and the same. The show presentation of the British Bichon is outstanding, and there is considerable in-depth level of talent that produces that fine presentation. One

American breeder Lois Morrow, Chamour Bichons, pictured with a new Bichon friend in Chamonix, France, April 1989. His appearance is reminiscent of the Bichon in the Ronner-Knip painting of the late 1800s.

must remember that in Great Britain, unlike the United States, professional handlers are virtually nonexistent, and the Bichons are groomed and shown by their owners. Australia has the same Standard as Great Britain, and also has some very stylized grooming, so the restrictions are obviously being disregarded. Without question the American Bichon has influenced grooming and presentation throughout the world.

COLOR

The U.S. and Canadian Standards allow for shading of cream or apricot on ears and body, with the U.S.A. limiting it to 10 percent of the entire coat of an adult. The British allows no color in the coat after eighteen months of age.

GAIT

U.S.A.: "Free, precise and effortless . . . with an easy reach and drive that maintain a steady topline." *Canada:* "Balanced and vigorous . . . good reach . . . good drive." *Great Britain:* "Balanced and effortless with an easy reach and drive maintaining a steady and level topline." This is an area of basic agreement.

TEMPERAMENT

U.S.A.: "Sensitive, playful and affectionate." *Canada:* "Stable, outgoing and alert." *Great Britain:* "Friendly and outgoing. . . . Gay, happy, lively." Whatever the adjective might be, it is obvious that all agree the Bichon has a delightful temperament. As the final sentence of the American Standard states: "A cheerful attitude is the hallmark of the breed and one should settle for nothing less."

Now a brief look at the Standard of New Zealand.

Once again coat—i.e., presentation—is vastly different, for this Standard calls for a coat that is "fine, silky with soft corkscrew curls." Once again this detail is being ignored and the dogs are groomed. Also a "slightly low" tail set is called for, which produces the problems described earlier. While this Standard is not dramatically different, the lack of detail again allows for personal interpretation, which seldom favors the breed.

An interesting phenomenon appears to be taking place. Admittedly, most of the countries who operate under Standards that denounce grooming and suggest that only the muzzle and the feet be "slightly tidied up" quietly disregard this admonition. However, on the Continent, especially in France, the ungroomed Bichon has reigned supreme. Now, however, there may be a breakthrough!

Int. Ch. Twinley Sailor's Hornpipe, bred by Pauline Block of England and owned by M. De Silva of France, completed his championship with the following wins: October 1987, Belgium; March 1988, Spain; January 1989, Paris, France; and February 1989, Reims, France. Unremarkable, you say. Not so. Look at the picture on page 134 and be amazed. Granted, the presentation is not ready for Westminster and Madison Square Garden. But this dog looks clean and he has been scissored at some juncture. There is definitely the beginning of a pattern, and the head has been rounded and the eyes cleared. That this Bichon was allowed to remain in the ring, let alone win Best of Breed and his third CACIB, is but a miracle. Perhaps this represents the beginning of changing attitudes. The differences in Bichon Frise Standards around the world have narrowed through the years. Today the major area of disagreement lies in presentation, and it is hoped that gatherings of Bichon breeders such as the International Bichon Frise Congress can eventually affect international unity.

10

Choosing a Puppy

Is THE BICHON FRISE FOR YOU? Do the traits and idio-
syncrasies of this breed suit the life-style and environment of you as an
individual or you as a family? Everyone must resist the temptation of being
overcome by the cuddly white puppy, for acquiring a Bichon on impulse is
rarely successful.

With proper care the Bichon is a hardy, healthy breed and can be
expected to live a long and happy life. Unlike many breeds, especially the
larger ones, life expectancy for a Bichon can be fourteen to fifteen years,
while sixteen to seventeen years is not uncommon. So barring the unforeseeable, you and your family are making a long-term commitment, and this
should be carefully considered.

As a white, double-coated breed, the Bichon presents some obvious
limitations. First he will require more basic grooming and coat care than
many breeds. Unless you have both time and extraordinary talent, this will
require professional assistance. Does this suit your budget and family
schedule? Secondly, if your life-style includes backpacking in the High Si-
erras or similar outdoor high-energy-level activities, you might want to re-
appraise your choice of a Bichon as a companion.

The Bichon is an outgoing, friendly breed that thrives on companion-
ship, both human and canine. When properly introduced, they also get along
very well with kittens and adult cats. Being left alone for long periods of time
is not a high-priority item with a Bichon and can result in behavior problems.
Sadly, this is not unique to this breed.

The Animal Health Newsletter, published by the Cornell University
College of Veterinary Medicine (November 1988) states:

"Bijou," an original drawing by Bernice Richardson.

Nearly one quarter of all dogs and cats in a community with a well-organized animal care and control network will pass through the shelter annually. Every year some 13 million unwanted and unclaimed former pets will have to be destroyed . . . a good pet is by nature one socialized to humans, requiring, in turn, daily attention and affection. Long absences of the owner can create serious behavior problems and behavior problems are the most common reason that pets are abandoned or consigned to animal shelters.

The Bichon Frise is gregarious by nature; thus he is particularly despondent when the door closes behind you or family members and he is left alone.

Having balanced these warnings and limitations with your life-style and family needs, you make the decision—you WANT A BICHON FRISE! He is playful, giving and affectionate, his size is perfect, he is so incredibly appealing, he appears to be nonallergic, the high maintenance will not be a problem and you will anticipate his flea sensitivity by appropriate measures in house and yard. Yes, indeed, the Bichon is for you!

Simple enough, but there are more decisions—male or female, show puppy or pet?

Many people put on mental brakes at the suggestion of "showing" a dog through simple lack of information, so let's explore this idea. First there is the strata of the Best in Show– and Group-winning dog, which is far beyond the level of interest and commitment for the average person. But there is also the dog that is deserving of a championship by virtue of his quality. Responsible breeders like "to finish" their dogs (complete a championship) as a means of evaluating a line for present and future breeding programs.

An owner can have the pleasure of watching his dog compete, while enjoying the rapport of breeders, exhibitors and other owners. The decision to acquire a "show dog" often leads to new friends and activities. Do some investigating. Attend an all-breed show or a Specialty show (for Bichons only) in your area. The American Kennel Club can put you in touch with the appropriate club secretaries for show dates and locations.

To pursue the concept of a show puppy, you will want to choose a breeder who will work with you regarding the selection of a show prospect and his eventual career. Beware of the individual that guarantees that a very young puppy will grow and become a top show specimen. Long-time knowledgeable breeders with generations of champions behind their lines can better predict a possible show prospect than a breeder with limited background and experience. However, show *potential* is all that can be honestly said of the very young.

Because prospective owners so often desire a *young* puppy, many breeders offer a contractual arrangement for compensation to owners whose show-potential puppy does not mature as anticipated. Obviously an older puppy or adult offers the best guarantee to the individual with high expectations for the show ring.

Along with the Conformation ring there is also the arena of Performance Events described elsewhere. These can be enormously satisfying activities for both owner and Bichons, on a one-to-one level, while offering a new arena for

Bichon puppy,
nine days old.

Bichon puppies,
four weeks old.

Littermates,
eight weeks old.

Male puppy,
sixteen weeks old.
Photo by Missy.

friendships and activities. Obedience clubs are active throughout the United States, and once again the American Kennel Club can help you find organizations in your area.

Perhaps actual competition in Obedience is not your strong suit. Then consider basic obedience classes for a well-mannered Bichon that you and everyone else will enjoy.

Make no mistake, the Bichon Frise as a "pet" is quite simply *wonderful!* All the endearing qualities that attracted you to this breed are part and parcel of his personality, and with your care and concern there will be happy years ahead.

Male or female? People often have stereotyped ideas on this subject, but many of these can be tossed aside when considering the Bichon. Males generally get along with each other, as do the females, and the adults in turn are very tolerant of the youngsters. It is not at all uncommon for numbers of both sexes to live together quite amicably. Many believe the female of a breed to be more affectionate than the male. Not so with Bichons, as owners find them equally loving; so don't bypass the male Bichon on this count. The semiannual estrus makes the female a concern; however, you will find that breeders normally require neutering of pet Bichons, both male and female.

Male versus female is ultimately a matter of choice, but since both are delightful, don't be too rigid in your decision.

The increasing popularity of the Bichon Frise in recent years strikes fear in the heart of the dedicated Bichon owner and breeder who truly cares about the future of the breed. Indiscriminate breeding by unknowledgeable people will indeed destroy the character, nature and essence of the breed.

Occasionally a caller states he wants a female Bichon—no, no, not to show, "just something to breed." Sometimes this caller is simply uninformed and is apologetic once he is educated. However, too often there is little concern for the Bichon and a large concern for profit; hence the apprehension felt by the conscientious breeder in the placement of a puppy.

Whether you opt for the fun and experience of the show or obedience Bichon or decide a pet will be a sufficient challenge, the choice of a breeder is of utmost importance.

Look for the cooperative individual who takes the time to answer your questions freely and comprehensively, who offers the details of all available information—i.e., books, magazines, clubs, videos—that will give you additional background on the breed and, incidentally, an opportunity to document any claims.

Look for the person who encourages your visits to see the litter, the mother and other relatives. This enables you to evaluate temperament, type and the development within the line while seeing the environment in which the puppy was raised. Be concerned if you are not allowed to see the facilities and other Bichons.

If a show puppy is involved and you are a novice, expect the breeder to explain in detail the procedure involved in acquiring a championship, the training and conditioning necessary and the financial commitment. Handling

Littermates, nine weeks old.

Photos by Missy.

Record-breaking litter of eleven puppies . . . count them! Dam, Ch. Ladywood's Chi Chi Beene, Ladywood Bichons, Linda Lewis.

146

should be discussed, whether the amateur wishes to try his hand or should a professional be involved. Sometimes a combination of the two is appropriate.

Whether pet or show, does the breeder offer a "support system," with full instruction, complete medical records and hopefully a "hotline" for help and questions along the way? Of course you will be given a pedigree and registration papers or an appropriate guarantee thereof.

In recent years written contracts have become common to protect all parties concerned, most especially the puppy. Breeders want a written commitment that the buyer will love and care for the puppy properly. They want assurance the puppy has not been bought for resale (to puppy mills, perhaps). The breeder often wants the puppy returned for placement if the unforeseeable should arise and the buyer cannot retain possession. The buyer, of course, wants a guarantee of a sound, healthy Bichon, with an accurate pedigree and verifiable medical records.

Show contracts are more varied and comprehensive. Understandably, a breeder does not want to place a puppy who has show potential with owners who agree to show and then fail to honor that agreement when the youngster reaches maturity and is judged worthy of championship. All aspects of any contracts should be discussed freely and in detail. This ensures there will be no misunderstandings in the future.

You have decided to acquire a Bichon. He will be a member of your family for many years to come. Take care in your selection. Find the breeder who has done the utmost to breed to the Standard, to place puppies with love and compassion and who really cares about the future of the breed. Don't settle for anything less.

THE PUPPY

Nothing is more captivating than a Bichon Frise puppy. The period between six and twelve weeks is especially important, as the littermates interact and the mother becomes more than the "dinner table" as she instructs, disciplines and plays with her offspring.

Occasionally a Bichon finds motherhood more than she bargained for, and after the early weeks decides maternal duties are not for her. Fortunately, this is not the rule. Quite the contrary, for often other female Bichons in a household enjoy the "baby-sitting" role when mother takes a break—a delight to watch and beneficial for the litter.

An important part of socialization comes from the human element—old, young, male, female. Touching, stroking, lifting, playing—all handling and fondling by humans is important in the development of warm, sunny temperaments in puppies whose self-confidence and sense of security will allow them to bond well in future environments.

Growth patterns in Bichons are not entirely predictable. For example, the smallest puppy at birth can become the largest adult. Bichon breeders who have been involved in other breeds claim the Bichon can be a real challenge,

What more can you say? The essence of the Bichon puppy is caught in this photo by Geraldine Paolillo of an eight-week-old Bichon owned by Doris Hyde, Dove-Cote Bichons.

as it is frequently prone to erratic phases of development that can turn the not-so-promising puppy into a stylish adult. Unfortunately, the reverse is also true. The Bichon matures more slowly than many breeds and generally does not reach its peak until three years old or better.

Bichon litters vary in size, but three to five is most common. There is an extraordinary Bichon who deserves mention at this juncture: Ch. Lady-wood's Chi Chi Beene (Ch. Alridge Romeo de Beau Monde ex Ch. Mel-Mar's Sweet Shadow Sue), owned and bred by Linda Lewis (Ladywood) and Marvel Brown (Mel-Mar). This little lady had two litters. Each litter had eleven—yes, *eleven*—puppies, and all of them survived. This certainly must be a record. The first litter was sired by Enroh's Bonhomne de Neige and the second by Ch. Ladywood's Motor City Cobra. Both were sons of Ch. Val-Va Don's Guiser. Three champion sons are Best of Breed winners, and two have Group placements. Three other children are pointed and en route to championships. Chi Chi Beene herself was a multiple Best of Breed winner over top Specials and loved the show ring—a special little lady.

A Bichon mom's thoughts: "Come on, kids, it takes some effort to look this good."
Drawing by Geraldine Paolillo.

11

Grooming the Bichon Frise

THE BREED STANDARD calls the Bichon Frise a "white powder puff of a dog," and it is often this aspect of the breed, the coat, that first captivates the fancier.

The beauty and quality of this coat are dependent upon heredity and coat care, plus the general health and well-being of the dog. While still a consideration, genetically poor coats are less common today, which leaves the emphasis on internal factors (a proper, well-balanced diet and freedom from internal parasites) and external factors (proper brushing, washing, scissoring and freedom from external parasites).

While puppies have a soft, single coat, the mature Bichon has a double coat made up of both coarse guard hairs *and* a softer undercoat. It is a combination of the two that produces the "bodied" fluffy coat that stands out from the body as opposed to the soft, silky coat that lies down and often parts and separates. The mature coat, with the coarser guard hairs, generally starts to come in about one year of age. A fully mature coat may take until the age of two or even three. When going through coat change, extra care and brushing will be necessary to fight the tangles caused by loosening puppy hairs.

Proper equipment is essential. Even if the Bichon is groomed professionally, the owner must have the following items to keep the coat free of mats and tangles between shop appointments.

One "pin brush," 8½ inches long with 1-inch teeth.

Two "slicker" brushes, one 4½ x 2 inches, the other 2½ x 1¾ inches. The latter is excellent for puppies and for adult ears, beards, tails, etc.

One Belgian-type comb, 7½ inches long, teeth at least 1 inch.

Look for brushes with rubber backing; this will have more "give" and will not rip the coat. Running brushes through a piece of carpeting eliminates initial stiffness.

The objective when brushing or combing is to leave the hair on the dog and not have it end up on brush or comb. Dirt is a villain. No matter how carefully you brush if the hairs are coated with dirt they can be needlessly pulled out. Hose outside areas and keep inside areas and bedding clean. Get rid of dirt and dust *before* they get into the coat. An apartment dog that must be walked on city sidewalks will need bathing more often than the house dog that has his own special clean area to use. Check fences, doggy doors, beds, etc., for rough areas that can catch the coat and pull it out.

Now we come to the *Great Coat Destroyers*—ticks, lice and, especially, *the flea*. These are the scourge of Bichon coats. Some Bichons are more allergic to fleas than others, but the breed in general seems to have a very high sensitivity. If your Bichon is scratching, licking or chewing, fleas are probably the cause. It takes only a flea or two to destroy a beautiful coat in record-breaking time.

If a flea bite is not attended to, reddened areas of hair brought about by licking or "hot spots" can result. The latter are caused by the dog literally chewing at its skin or scratching hard enough to break the skin in an effort to relieve the itching. If unattended, painful, oozing spots appear, one-half to two inches in diameter, and veterinary help is needed.

A large percentage of veterinary office calls involve skin problems, and the majority of those are flea related. How frequently the dog appears with scratched-out coat, tangled hair, hot spots and areas of reddened hair and the veterinarian hears, "My dog doesn't have fleas." Yes it *does* have fleas, and it is time for all-out war. If you see two fleas there are probably two hundred in house and yard. Simply bathing the dog with a flea shampoo will not eliminate the problem; the total environment must be treated. Commercial pest control services may be used, inside and out, or you may use the flea bombs that are on the market while spraying your yard with malathion- or diazanon-type spray. Whichever method you choose, the dog must get rid of its fleas at the same time; it is a three-part program—house, yard and dog, all at the same time. It goes without saying that all other pets in the household must be treated also. To be effective, treatment must be repeated in two weeks in accordance with the flea reproductive cycle.

Remember, the dog who goes for daily walks can easily pick up new fleas and keep the cycle going. Households with outdoor cats are fair game for another bout with fleas, and even the neighbor's cat that "passes through" can bring unwelcome guests. Fleas can be controlled, but it takes work. An added note: fleas bring tapeworm, a debilitating internal parasite.

BRUSHING

The beautiful fluffy coat that every Bichon should wear can only be achieved with regular care. Coat wise, acquiring a Bichon as a puppy is a blessing. A new owner, unaccustomed to caring for an adult coat, would be unprepared for what is in store. By learning to maintain the easy puppy coat and progressing in proficiency as the coat matures, the owners adapt to the changes.

Since brushing an adult Bichon is more than a five-minute job, teach your puppy at an early age to lie down and enjoy the attention. Start it in your lap with kind, but firm words of ''down'' and ''stay'' plus words of praise. A little scratching on tummy or chest may placate the one who objects. As it gets older, accustom it to lying on a table top and standing quietly. Whether groomed at home or professionally, there will be less trauma if the dog is accustomed to being groomed in both positions.

Find a table that is a comfortable height. Kitchen counters work well, with a piece of rubber-backed carpet or a rubber mat covered with a towel to keep feet from slipping. Needless to say, no dog should be left unattended.

Brushing must be done thoroughly but gently. The most efficient method is called ''line-brushing.'' With the dog lying on its side, take your left hand and push a section of hair on the top side away from you and hold it down. With the pin brush, gently brush through the hair that is not held down, brushing toward you.

If the hair looks tangle free, release the pressure of your left hand, pull a line of hair along the part toward you and brush that. Working gently, get the teeth of the brush to the skin. The mats form close to the skin, so brushing only the *ends* of the hair will accomplish very little. Continue the process, moving up the side to the backbone, as far as you can comfortably reach. Repeat, using the slicker brush this time. While the dog is on his side, line-brush the hind and foreleg on that side. This is easiest if you hold the leg in the left hand and work from the top of the leg to the foot, brushing the hair *away* from you rather than toward you. The important thing is to reach the skin, gently covering every square inch.

Turn the dog over and repeat the procedure on the other side. Next, starting on the head, above the eyes, line-brush the hair on top of the skull, brushing the hair in the direction of the dog's nose, and work softly, for this skin is delicate. Go down the back of the neck and the top of the body to the tail, then do the sides of the neck, the front of the chest, the ears and beard. Last but not least we have the tail. Here use special care, for on many Bichons the tail plume is very fragile. We want a full, flowing tail, not a wispy little bottle-brush.

Now we "foof." The Belgian comb is used for his. "Foofing" is a descriptive verb invented by Bichon owners to describe the motion that puts the lift in the Bichon coat, making it rise and stand away from the body. Starting at the hindquarter, work forward, going from left to right, with light, uplifting strokes. Teeth into coat, lift, teeth into coat, lift. Properly done, it may take twenty strokes to cover four inches of body, for you will be using overlapping strokes. This is used on the body, neck, top of the head and as much of the legs as possible. The ears and beard are gently combed through. Use of the comb will tell you how good your brushing was, for if the comb doesn't go through easily, you did not do a thorough job.

This may sound long and tedious. Not so if done often enough to prevent mats and tangles. Except in extraordinary cases, mats should not be cut out. Brushing them out can be time consuming, but it is possible and worth the effort. A bit of baby powder worked in with the fingers permits the brush to work through without removing too much hair. Patience is a virtue.

Reference has been made primarily to the adult coat, but puppy owners should be prepared for what is ahead. Keep that puppy well brushed and free of mats and coat care for the adult will not be difficult. The puppy coat doesn't need the pin brush, as the coat lacks density, but line-brushing with the slicker will be the same as with the adult. Accustom your puppy to being combed from head to tail.

THE BATH

Bichon exhibitors at shows are frequently asked, "How do you keep your dog so white?" The answer, of course, is frequent bathing. If a Bichon is shown every weekend, you can be sure it will be washed twenty-four to forty-eight hours before the show, and its legs and beard may be rewashed and dried on the day.

There are many dog shampoos on the market, several with bluing agents especially for white dogs. Most are concentrated. Using an empty pint-size bottle with a squirt top, fill with warm water and concentrate according to the dilution chart on the bottle.

For a dog whose coat is a bit dry, and for ease in brushing out the coat, a conditioner can be used as a final rinse. Because of the nature of the Bichon coat, these must not be used too heavily or the coat will appear oily and won't stand up properly. Before bathing, assemble the necessary equipment: spray attachment for the sink, cotton for the ears, shampoo, conditioner if needed, towels, dryer and brushes and combs.

A word of caution about hair dryers. Whether using one designed especially for dogs or the smaller type for human hair, do not use excessive heat too close to the dog's skin. It is painful for the dog and unnecessary. If using a hand dryer, try and have someone assist you, for drying is done by the line-brushing method, and two hands are needed for that.

There are three last items before the bath: nails, ears and anal glands. If nails are trimmed regularly from puppyhood, you normally avoid a scene when the clippers appear. Long nails can force the pads to spread, which is dangerous as well as unsightly. Remember there is a "quick" that will bleed if cut, so work with care.

The ear canal should be kept free of hair. The Bichon's "drop ear" prevents air reaching the inner ear, thus encouraging moisture and possible infection. Antibiotic ointment or powder is recommended in the ear after bathing and drying. An ear with excessive brown wax and offensive odor needs veterinary care.

The anal glands located below and at the sides of the anus secrete a fluid during defecation that serves as a territorial marker. Occasionally this fluid becomes impacted and must be expressed with thumb and forefinger in the "eight and four o'clock" position. If you have doubts about accomplishing any of these procedures, ask for veterinarian assistance or instruction.

Our equipment is ready. Our dog is brushed out. There are no mats, for mats become "felted" and almost impossible to remove if they become wet. So into the sink the dog goes. Now it is up to you to be firm but gentle. A puppy's experience with its early baths can determine its attitude for the rest of its life. Since the Bichon is a breed that requires frequent bathing, it makes sense to take the extra time and effort to develop positive attitudes in the early stages.

Using warm water, wet the dog down *thoroughly*. First apply the shampoo to beard and any areas that are especially dirty or stained. This allows the bluing agent to work while you wash and scrub the rest of the dog. A mature dog will use a pint of the diluted shampoo-water mixture. Wash thoroughly, for it is pointless to reach this stage and not get the maximum benefits. When well scrubbed, rinse. Then rinse some more. Working from front to back is most effective. The importance of rinsing cannot be emphasized too strongly. Soap residue in the coat acts as a magnet to dirt, making it virtually impossible to scissor and gives an overall, dull, lifeless appearance. When you think all the soap has been removed, *rinse once more!*

DRYING

The drying process is the secret to successful scissoring. If each hair is not pulled straight and dry, it will curl up, and curly hair cannot be scissored smoothly. Careful drying of a mature dog in preparation for scissoring will take at least one hour.

As the dryer is warming, we towel-dry the dog and give it a quick brushing through with the pin brush as a preliminary straightening. We start drying with the head and neck, so lay the dog down on its stomach and chest and cover the rest of it with a towel. With the dryer blowing warm air from the back to the front, start drying just above the eyes, working back over the skull and down the neck to the shoulders. On each area use the pin brush first to dry and separate and then the slicker brush to totally dry and straighten. The

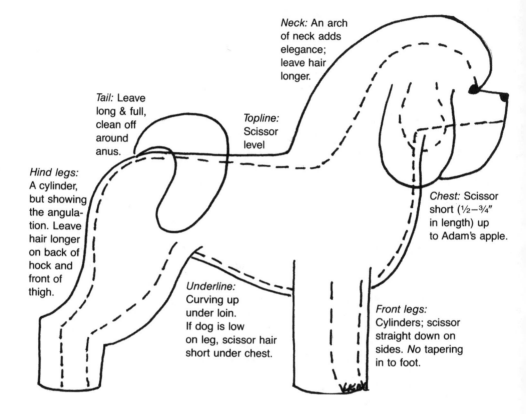

Neck: An arch of neck adds elegance; leave hair longer.

Tail: Leave long & full, clean off around anus.

Topline: Scissor level

Hind legs: A cylinder, but showing the angulation. Leave hair longer on back of hock and front of thigh.

Chest: Scissor short (½–¾" in length) up to Adam's apple.

Underline: Curving up under loin. If dog is low on leg, scissor hair short under chest.

Front legs: Cylinders; scissor straight down on sides. *No* tapering in to foot.

156

warm air flow must be directed at the exact point at which you are brushing, and you should brush in the same direction as the air flow. Use the slicker brush to pull the hair straight, from the skin to the end of the hair strand. And work gently.

When the head and the back of the neck are finished, do the sides of the neck and work around to the front, drying ears and beard. The very small slicker brush is especially helpful in this area. Be sure the ear area is completely dry. Dampness in the ears can be a source of bacterial infection. People often dry the top of the ear but neglect the underside, a dangerous omission.

Next do the front legs and chest, then move down the side of the dog, keeping your towel over the area yet to be dried. If an area has dried before you reach it, dampen it again with a spray bottle. Hair that has dried and curled cannot be properly straightened. Remove the towel underneath the dog, as it will now be damp, then turn the dog over and repeat the process on the other side. Once dry, we "set the hair by turning our dryer to the cool setting and "foofing" through the entire coat with our Belgian comb.

SCISSORING

If you have just finished drying a young puppy, scissor him now while he is likely to be a bit tired. If you wait until he has had a nap, you will be trying to scissor a bouncing ball.

There is controversy over the best kind of scissors to use. A pair of household scissors simply will not do the job. They will not be as sharp as you need, and their action will be so stiff you will soon have a tired hand. A nice pair of scissors, made especially for cutting hair, can be bought for about $25.00. Ask your breeder for recommendations.

Repeated scissoring on the coats of puppies and young dogs, done every two to three weeks, helps produce a better coat. Regular "tipping" of the coat allows the finer undercoat to grow and develop sooner.

Whether a show dog or a pet, every Bichon owner wants his dog to look its best. In actuality, the only difference should be in the length of the coat. Every Bichon should be trimmed in a pattern that will enhance its best qualities and minimize the lesser ones. With short-haired dogs, there are no illusions, with coated breeds you have the opportunity of *visually* changing the structure.

Elsewhere in this book the breed Standard has been discussed. Review the drawings and descriptions, then plant a picture in your mind of what the ideal should be. Now look at your Bichon, both standing still and in motion. Where does he fall short of the ideal, and how can you improve it? Example: If your dog is overly long, excess hair on the chest and rear quarter will only accentuate this.

Note the drawings on page 158. Figure A depicts a dog close to that called for in the Standard. Figure B shows a long-bodied dog with insufficient

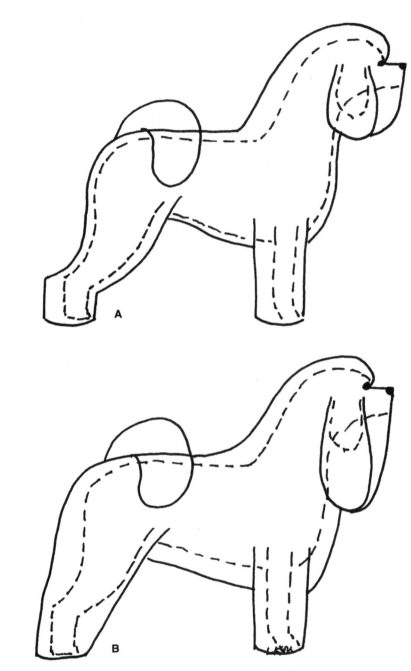

A. Note how proper grooming enhances good conformation.
B. Excess coat can cause the same dog to appear out of balance.

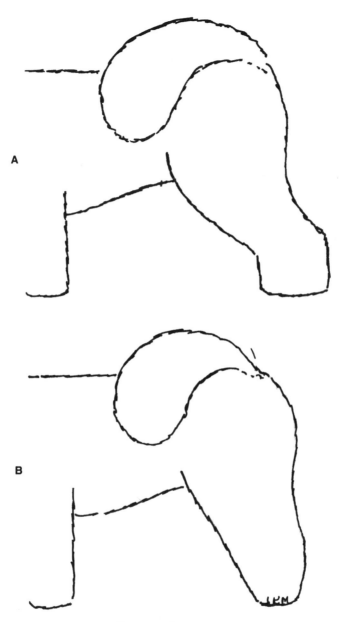

SHOW THE ANGULATION.
A. These hindquarters are beautifully groomed to highlight the dog's natural contours.
B. Here, an overabundant coat obscures the dog's actual outline.

neck and straight hindquarters. Please note that the trims in both drawings were drawn over the *same* body. Obviously, improper trimming can make a structurally good dog look bad. Fortunately, the reverse is also true. Review figure A, then examine your dog and see what changes can be made to make it visually more correct.

If possible, work with a mirror three to four feet from your grooming surface. It will give you a true picture of your progress. Don't be afraid to be creative; the hair will grow back if you make a mistake. Needless to say, if you are going go show your Bichon, you will want to find your ideal pattern several months in advance.

A prominent judge of Bichons was asked what point he would stress in a discussion on grooming. He answered with one word: "Outline!" A good outline or pattern is not achieved in one session. It usually evolves over a period of time as you watch your dog move and evaluate possible improvements. If your Bichon reaches the show ring, make that first impression count; the "outline" should make the dog look as close to the Standard as possible.

Our dog is bathed, dried with coat combed and "lifted." The lifting with the comb continues throughout the scissoring process to produce a smooth, plush look.

Start on the chest and scissor from the Adam's apple to the top of the front legs and continue under the chest between the legs. On the average dog, this hair will be ¾ inch long or less, if you wish to visually shorten body length.

Hindquarters next, in order to establish our "outline." Scissor from the tail, down over the buttocks to the top of the hock, following the curve of the dog's leg. Cut the hair ½ to ¾ inches, leaving the hair on the back of the hock 1½ inches long to emphasize angulation.

After watching your dog move away from you once or twice, you are ready to scissor the hind legs. Is there sufficient width? Eliminate hair, if necessary. Scissor a straight line down, no bowed legs. On the front of the leg, show the curve in the thigh and stifle area, then a straight vertical line down to the foot. The hind legs are scissored as in figure A. No heart shapes; an inverted U, please.

Now we move to the body. Start under the chest, combing the hair straight down. The line will be a curve, from the loin to the front legs, following the natural curve of the body. If the dog has short legs, leave only ½ inch of hair underneath. If the legs are long, leave up to 1½ inches of hair. Gradually work up the side of the dog toward the backbone. If you left only ½ inch of hair under the chest, gradually increase the hair length as you come up the sides.

Scissor the top of the back in a straight, level line. Bring this line to approximately 2 inches behind the point of shoulder. The front legs are next. They should resemble cylinders with straight sides. Now go up over the sides of the shoulders and blend in with the chest.

The hair on the back of the neck and the top of the head should be considerably longer than that on the rest of the body. We want to achieve an

160

Head: Basically a circle. No indentation at top of ears. Nose midpoint between hair on top of head and bottom of beard.

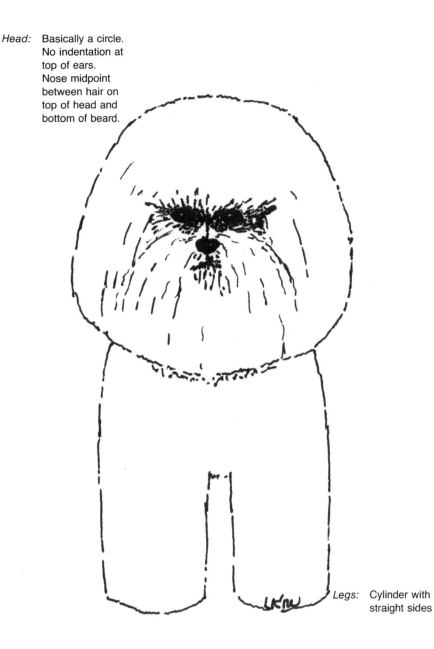

Legs: Cylinder with straight sides

161

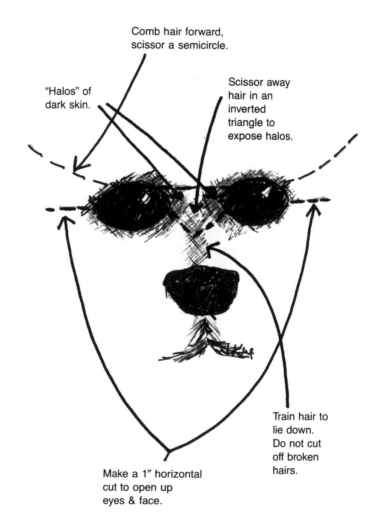

Comb hair forward, scissor a semicircle.

Scissor away hair in an inverted triangle to expose halos.

"Halos" of dark skin.

Train hair to lie down. Do not cut off broken hairs.

Make a 1″ horizontal cut to open up eyes & face.

162

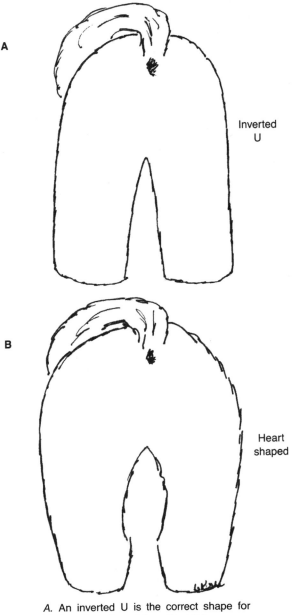

A

Inverted
U

B

Heart
shaped

A. An inverted U is the correct shape for
hindquarters viewed from the seat.
B. Heart-shaped hindquarters are incorrect.

163

"arch of neck" like that of the show pony to give the elegance our Bichon deserves. Blend the sides of the neck with the shoulders.

On the head, the black nose should be considered the center of a circle. Scissor the hair between the eyes in an inverted triangle, taking the hair down almost to the skin. This exposes the black "halos" and accentuates the beautiful Bichon expression. (No halos? Twenty minutes of sun a day is often all that is needed unless a genetic pigmentation problem is involved.) The hair above the eyes should be combed forward. Scissor in a curve. Then blend into the top of the head and the back of the neck. At the outer corner of each eye make a 1-inch scissor cut. This "opens up" the face.

Comb hair of ears, beard and mustache downward. There should be no indentation at the top of the ears, in the manner of a pet Poodle trim. Starting at the back, trim to produce a soft, rounded effect, continuing to the back of the other ear.

There you have it, the results of your efforts—an immaculate Bichon wearing its "goin' to meetin' " coat. You may rest assured your Bichon loves being beautiful and the attention that comes its way as a result, for you will see a little air of confidence, a little strut, that wasn't there before.

There is no question about it. The Bichon Frise is a high-maintenance breed. There is also no question that they are worth every bit of effort and time spent on their behalf.

12

Medical Notes

_____

THE EXTERNAL CARE of the Bichon Frise has been discussed in detail. It is now appropriate to examine some areas of concern that will aid in producing a healthy puppy as well as a beautiful one, and your assistant in this endeavor is your veterinarian. Seek an individual who will cooperate with you and is willing to add to his knowledge of what, for many, is a new breed.

DIET

A well-balanced diet is the first priority. When acquiring a puppy or an older dog, most people rely on the advice of the breeder regarding diet. He will often have preferences that have produced satisfying results for him and is always willing to share this information. The American people's love affair with pets has brought on a surge of companies producing superior food products, which makes proper nutrition for the puppy, the adult and the geriatric dog a much simpler task.

Quality dry food ("kibble") is the foundation of the breeders' food plan. In addition, many add beef, lamb, chicken and turkey (usually ground), cooked vegetables and rice in various combinations. Organ meats are added occasionally. Cottage cheese and yogurt are popular suggestions, especially for young dogs; however, on occasion the oldster likes this "garni" also.

Allergies are not unheard of in the Bichon Frise. A number of dogs with recurring "hot spots" (and no fleas) have found relief on a veterinary-recommended regimen of ground lamb, rice and, strange as it may seem, carrots and green beans, finely chopped and well cooked.

Dietary supplements are normally used, especially for the show dog, who may be undergoing more stress than life at home with its pillow and bone might provide. Supplements are highly recommended for the young and old and considered mandatory for the pregnant or lactating bitch. Oil added to the diet is frequently suggested for dogs with chronically dry skin. Your veterinarian should advise you in this area.

INOCULATIONS

When you acquire your new Bichon, your breeder will give you the schedule of inoculations. There is, however, a recommendation that is *strongly* advised. The DHLP shot (canine distemper, infectious canine hepatitis, canine leptospirosis and the kennel cough complex) is normally administered in combination. In recent years, with the advent of Parvo (canine parvovirus), the vaccine was added to the above and administered as a "five in one" shot.

Unfortunately, in some cases with the Bichon Frise, and with many other breeds, there has been a reaction to this procedure that often takes the form of neurological impairment, a problem that has been substantiated in published material. As a result, a large number of breeders now give puppies the DHLP and the Parvo vaccine separately at two-week intervals. A number of Bichon owners continue the separate inoculations into adulthood. A few veterinarians are uncooperative and deny this problem exists. Bichon breeders and owners who have had affected dogs in the past are impatient with these closed minds and prefer the individual who is interested in working with them in dealing with any problems that might exist in the breed. The small effort involved is worthwhile.

CARE OF THE TEETH

Dental disease is a major problem in all veterinary medicine today, and the Bichon has not escaped it. The problem is not confined to the mouth alone, as the bacteria produced by infected teeth are carried through the blood stream. When the bacteria enter one of the body's filtering systems they tend to lodge there, contributing directly to heart, liver, joint and kidney disease.

Periodontal disease is the primary cause of tooth loss and is a major concern in smaller breeds such as the Bichon. It is the familiar story of plaque, which infects the area around the gums, causing the gums, the bone and supporting structure around the tooth to dissolve and recede from the roots. This produces looseness of the teeth and eventual loss.

Professional cleaning is the first step toward controlling the problem.

This should include scaling, root planing or gingival curettage and polishing. Any deep pockets must be removed. Home care is then essential:

1. Brush the teeth two to three times a week with a soft brush and water, more often if possible. Starting at a young age makes it easier. Scratch the muzzle, handle the mouth and soon you will be able to rub teeth and gums with your finger. Garlic water may make the whole project more palatable for your puppy or older dog. Make it a game with lots of praise.
2. If your Bichon won't allow the brush, rub the teeth with a dry cloth. (If you work with patience, almost all Bichons will allow you to use the brush.)
3. Provide some hard, dry food, plus safe chew toys and large bones that cannot be broken up and swallowed.
4. Repeat professional cleaning as needed to avoid future problems.

BLADDER STONES

Canine bladder stones is another disease known in Bichons and other small breeds, which seem to be more often affected than large breeds. It is important that you recognize some of the symptoms of this disease. If they appear, seek immediate veterinary care, for if the bladder stones cause urinary blockage, the results could be permanent kidney damage or death. The symptoms are frequent urination, bloody urine, straining, weakness, depression and loss of appetite.

Bladder stones form when excess minerals and waste products accumulate in the bladder and form crystals. There is no single cause; however, excessive indoor confinement or any situation that forces a dog to hold its urine increase the likelihood that bladder stones will form. High dietary levels of phosphorus and magnesium have been directly linked, as has excessive protein in the diet.

Certain types of bladder stones must be surgically removed, but today most stones can be dissolved by feeding a special diet restricted in protein and certain minerals. Your veterinarian will recommend the proper treatment and dietary management if necessary.

HIP DYSPLASIA

Canine hip dysplasia is a developmental abnormality of the hip joint that appears to have a pattern of genetic predisposition. While it is not common in the Bichon Frise, it is known to exist. Fortunately, a number of the early foundation Bichons were X-rayed and certified clear by OFA (Orthopedic Foundation for Animals). Today many breeders routinely X-ray their Bichons and especially those that are used for breeding. Ever more frequently, stud dog owners require certification or screening of a bitch being sent for breeding. Conversely, many would not think of breeding their bitches to a dog that is not certified. Because the Bichon is a small breed, it is not as likely to have the acute discomfort and the compensating movement often associated with hip dysplasia in larger breeds. The absence of these does not prove a dog is free of dysplasia, however; only X-ray can accomplish that.

On the whole, the Bichon Frise is a sound little dog with few of the problems that habitually plague many breeds. The Bichon is strong of heart, both literally and figuratively speaking. The first Bichon Frise to win a Best in Show, Ch. Chaminade Syncopation, lived to the age of eighteen!

Now that's *heart!*

13

Performance Events

<hr>

PERFORMANCE EVENTS are those events wherein a specific activity of a dog is judged, as opposed to classes where the conformation of a dog is judged against a breed Standard.

Performance Events include American Kennel Club Obedience Trials, Tracking Tests and Field Trials. Recently, the American Kennel Club recognized Agility as a separate special event for exhibition and viewing at either Obedience or Conformation events. In addition, the parent clubs of several Working breeds offer certificates in recognition of achievements in Weight Pulling and other ''original function'' events. Remarkable as it may seem, the Bichon has successfully competed in all but one of the above events.

OBEDIENCE TRIALS

Obedience Trials provided the Bichon its first opportunity for title competition in 1971, when the Bichon was accepted into the Miscellaneous Class. Helen Temmel (Rivage d'Ami), formerly of New York and now a Florida resident, was an early breeder and the original advocate of obedience training for the Bichon Frise. Ch. Sandra de la Lande de Belleville, U.D., Bda. C.D. (Omer de Frimoussettes ex Ondine de la Lande de Belleville), achieved her Champion Dog (C.D.) title in October 1971. She earned the title of Utility Dog (U.D.) in 1974 and was the first Bichon to do so. This was also the year she earned her Bermuda C.D. A conformation champion, she reached the pinnacle at the 1977 Bichon Frise Club of America National Specialty, where she won both Best of Opposite Sex (from the Veterans Class) and High in

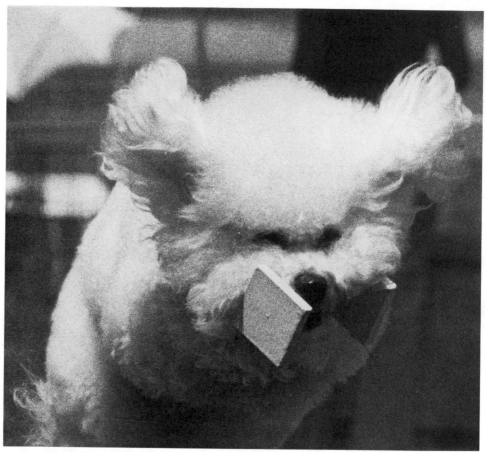

Ch. Primo's Prima Tana, C.D.X., the irrepressible Bichon of Joan and Frank Cresci, Primo Bichons. Tana was the highest-scoring Bichon in Obedience, 1978-79.

Trial. Her grandson, Ch. Roger-Bontemp de Stonehedge (Ch. Chaminade Syncopation ex Landine chez Rivage d'Ami), won the 1974 National Specialty B Match, then teamed with his granddam to win Best Brace in Show at the Bronx County Kennel Club show in 1975. Ch. Chateau's Idealbo Rivage d'Ami (Kalon of Goldysdale ex Qulici of Goldysdale) was the first Bichon to attain both his conformation championship and Companion Dog titles.

Sally B'S It's About Time (Niki of Craighill, C.D., ex Madam Muffin), owned by Duane and Sally Boyle of Minnesota, was the ninth and most recent Bichon to earn a Utility title and the first in four years. This U.D. was earned in five shows, an outstanding accomplishment.

The highest achievement at an Obedience Trial is "High in Trial." In 1981 the first Bichon reached that goal, Am. and Can. Ch. West-wynd's Legacy de Lucie, Am. U.D., Can. C.D.X. (Ch. Teeny Tepee's Chief of Diandee ex Qulici of Goldysdale), owned by Dolores Greening of Michigan. Lucie has a long list of accomplishments. She was first in Open, first in Utility and High in Trial at the 1981 Bichon Frise Club of America National Specialty. Two days after the Specialty she went High in Trial at the Ann Arbor Kennel Club show, the first Bichon Frise ever to win this honor at an all-breed event. She also has a Canadian High in Trial, Brantford Kennel Club in 1981.

Another Bichon successful in both Conformation and Obedience was Am. and Mex. Ch. Cali-Col's Scalawag, C.D. (Dapper Dan Gascoigne ex Cali-Col's Our Daphne), winner of three Bests in Show, eighteen Group firsts and two Mexican Bests in Show. Scalawag was trained and shown to his Companion Dog title by Betty Ribble (California), who later became an AKC licensed Obedience judge, and he won High in Trial at the first Bichon Frise Club of America Specialty in 1976.

Frank and Joan Cresci of California (Primo Bichons) began their Bichon involvement with Ch. Primo's Prima Tana, C.D.X. (Ch. Chaminade Mr. Beau Monde ex Ch. Tres Beau Affaire). Mr. Cresci trained and showed Tana to her C.D. title, then her Conformation title, and while midway to the latter she earned her C.D.X. Not long after producing a litter she was High in Trial at the Bichon Frise Club of San Diego Specialty in 1978, a feat she repeated again the following year. This foundation bitch was the dam of four champions, an obvious success in the Obedience ring, the Conformation ring and the whelping box. Mr. Cresci pursued his interest and became a successful handler of all breeds, with emphasis on the Bichon.

While the Bichon Frise is not generally thought of as a highly competitive breed in Obedience work, it has proven to be very successful. Obedience trainers consider the Bichon to be quick and readily adaptable. Could this be a reflection back to the Bichon's earlier days as a "trick dog" or "circus dog"?

TRACKING TESTS

Tracking is a sport readily enjoyed with your dog. Eventually there are AKC trials to be entered and titles to be earned—Tracking Dog (T.D.) and

C and D's B A Watson, C.D.X. Owner: Billyjo Porter.

Watson negotiates the tire hoop, adjustable from a 30-inch center down to a 12-inch center.

Watson takes the A-frame, six feet high.

Watson learning to hurdle the A-frame, with owner Billyjo Porter.

Learning the "dog walk" with owner.

The "spread jump"—two poles eighteen inches apart; the Bichon flies!

Tracking Dog Excellent (T.D.X.). For the T.D. test the dog must work a track about 450 yards long, laid half an hour to two hours before by a person unknown to the dog. There will be three or four turns in the track and a glove to find at the end. For the T.D.X. test the dog must follow a track of 800 to 1,000 yards, usually with five or more turns; in addition to the glove at the end, three other articles are dropped along the track that the dog must find. The track must be three to five hours old, and two other people will walk across the track to create a scent distraction the dog must ignore.

To many individuals the mention of "Bichon Frise" and "tracking" in the same breath would constitute a conflict in terms. But to Dibett's Kiss Me Kate (Am. and Can. Ch. Blue Dover Dayelean's Tinka ex Ee's R Impulsive Rachel) and her owner, Priscilla Roper of Washington, it is all in a day's work.

Kate earned her C.D. in 1981 at the age of four, and in 1987 she became the first Bichon Frise to earn her Tracking Dog title and later that same year earned her C.D.X. The title was earned at the Richland Kennel Club Tracking Test held in the desert outside Pasco, Washington.

Priscilla feels you and your dog develop a special relationship as you work together out in the country away from distractions. You will be encouraging your dog to use his natural scenting abilities. Any breed of dog, but not every dog, can be taught to track. You must start with a dog that has a certain amount of independence, and spirit, as eventually it will be expected to move out on its own and plunge into whatever terrain is presented. Your local kennel club can put you into touch with tracking enthusiasts, and excellent books on tracking training are available should you wish to pursue this novel but satisfying way of time shared with your Bichon.

AGILITY

Agility is a fast-paced event in which dogs race individually with their handlers over a 100-yard course of obstacles in less than a minute. It got its start as a specialty event at the International Horse Show in England. The equipment used then mainly consisted of hurdles, the tire hoop, weaving poles and stay table. The spectators loved it, and many dog owners wanted to participate. The sport grew and other obstacles were introduced, and now complete regulation equipment includes the A-frame, dog walk, two types of tunnels, a seesaw, plus the hoop, weave poles, table and any number and type of hurdles.

In 1979 the British Kennel Club sanctioned Agility Tests as "a form of competition where the animal's fitness and the handler's ability to train and direct the dog over and through certain obstacles is tested." The American Kennel Club has acknowledged Agility for special exhibition at AKC events since July 1988.

A Bichon in Agility? Meet C and D's B A Watson, C.D.X. (Ch. C and D's Freedom Call ex Ch. C and D's Bit of Spring), owned and trained by

Ch. Chateau's Idealbo Rivage d'Ami, C.D.X. (*left*), and Ch. Jeannine Chez Rivage d'Ami, C.D., in this classic photo of Bichons in action. Owned by Helen Temmel.

Am. and Can. Ch. Westwynd's Legacy de Lucie, Amer. U.D. and Can. C.D.X. Owner-handler: Dolores Greening.

Dibett's Kiss Me Kate, C.D.X., T.D., the first Bichon to win a Tracking Dog title. Owner-handler: Priscilla Roper.

Billyjo Porter of Texas. Watson obtained his C.D. and was High in Trial at the El Paso Kennel Club in 1984. In August 1985 he participated in the Gaines Western Regional, a non-AKC competition, with Team ADEPT (Agility Dogs of El Paso Texas). This was probably the first Agility demonstration in the United States with a sizable audience. In 1986 Watson completed his C.D.X. with a score of 199 (out of a possible 200) and was in a runoff for High in Trial. He will debut in Utility and continue his Agility demonstrations.

Agility training is yet another area of activity that can be shared by dog and owner. The training is not complex, and the rewards are an enormous builder of confidence for the Bichon and great fun for the dog and owner alike.

WEIGHT PULLING

Weight Pulling is not an American Kennel Club event but is offered by the parent club of several Working breeds who award a Working Dog Certificate after the completion of three qualifying "legs." The story of Magic adds the final word to the presence of the Bichon in Performance Events.

Ch. Beau Monde Mar-Jon's Magic (Ch. Mar-Jon's Drummer Boy ex Ch. C and D's Beau Monde Moonmist), whelped in June of 1976, spent the first two years of her life with two Malamutes and owner Carol Crane (Michigan). Carol had a small freight sled and occasionally harnessed up the Malamutes in winter to take neighborhood children for rides—all witnessed by Magic. In the winter of 1978 Magic was measured, and a harness was made for her. She was hooked up to her show dolly and off she went, never balking, acting as though she had watched the Malamutes often enough to know just what to do.

She began on kitchen linoleum and progressed to carpeting in the dining room, living room and hallway. Gradually things were added—a book, two books, a purse. Each time something was added she would pull for a week or more before any additional weight was added, so it was a very slow, gradual process.

The first time Magic pulled in competition was at the Detroit Kennel Club in March 1979. At that time the distance from starting point to finish line was 20 feet—since changed to 16 feet. Competition is determined by ratio of dog's body weight to amount of weight pulled in sixty seconds' time. No bait is allowed to entice the dog. She ended up beating many of the Malamutes at Detroit and in succeeding weight pulls. During all the Weight Pulling competition she weighed ten pounds. She never hesitated from start to finish and even had the proper technique, dipping her head down and pulling strictly from the shoulders and chest in a straight line to the finish.

In the beginning the crowds would laugh and assume it was all a joke until they saw how well she did and how serious she was. At this point they applauded and cheered each time a weight was added and she was able to pull it. A few complained that it was cruel, not understanding how hard they had

Ch. Beau Monde Mar-Jon's Magic, the weight-pulling Bichon. A story of patience, training, conditioning—and a Bichon who happened to love pulling. Owner: Carol A. Crane.

Magic takes a friend for a ride.

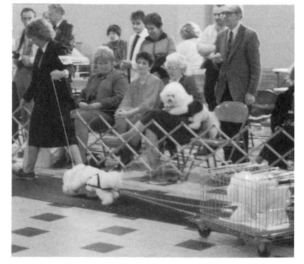

Magic in the show ring completing her championship. Owned and handled by Carol Crane.

worked and how well conditioned Magic was. Henceforth, it was always announced to the public beforehand the training time and the long process involved.

At Wonderland in Michigan, in October 1979, Magic pulled a weight of 133 pounds in seven seconds and at Oakland County Kennel Club (in Michigan), in November 1979, she pulled a weight of 138 pounds in fifteen seconds. She was stopped at 138 pounds and withdrawn from competition.

Two of Magic's offspring, Ch. Karoluck's Do U Believe 'N Magic and Ch. Karoluck's Magic Moment, have been trained as their mother had been. They have pulled separately in demonstration and as a brace (which the Malamutes do not do unless in a sled race). They each have their own custom-made harnesses to ensure proper fit so they will pull correctly, which is absolutely essential.

The story of Magic is offered from the standpoint of human interest and to point out the surprising and often novel characteristics of the Bichon Frise. We do not suggest that anyone should attempt this sort of training. Magic's background was unique, as was the knowledge and patience of her owner.

The Bichon is adaptable to many of the Performance Events described. It is hoped that new and prospective owners will become involved and find additional enjoyment of their Bichons through such activities.

A lovely senior citizen with her visitor and new friend, a Bichon Frise. The warmth and love seen here says it all. The Bichon is indeed a successful "therapist."

Esther Loveridge in 1989 celebrating her 107th birthday with Lindy, age seven months. An obviously remarkable lady who has her annual birthday photograph taken with one of the Bichons. *Langdale Nursing Home, Sussex, England.*

14

The Therapy Dog

THE PREVIOUS CHAPTER discussed Performance Events as those events wherein a specific activity of the dog is judged. There are other facets of performance, no judging involved, in which the Bichon has begun to participate with great success. One arena in which the multifaceted talents of our Bichon Frise are displayed is that of dogs for the hearing impaired. It is a new sphere of activity and little information is available but there are two documented cases of Bichons currently working in this capacity with great success.

On a much larger scale, a great deal has been written about the role of animals in caring for the sick, the handicapped and the elderly. Dogs appear to be especially adaptable because of their variation in size, the ease of handling and their special relationship with Man.

Within this framework the Bichons are finding a special niche. They are small enough to sit on a lap or beside a patient, and the soft white coat is wonderful for stroking. Experiments have been carried out that indicate there is a sense of deprivation if we are not able to experience the sensation of touch. We are also familiar with the professional journals that show well-publicized tests wherein the stroking of a dog reduces stress and lowers blood pressure.

In addition, there is often the factor of loneliness, which seems to be made more bearable when holding and fondling a dog. Ours is an aging society, and senior citizens alone, isolated and often with little or minimal family support are becoming increasingly common. The emotionally disturbed and physically handicapped benefit in a similar manner. It has been clearly established that the visit of a dog can bring happiness—the kind of happiness that results when other methods of therapy have failed.

In 1979 an organization called Therapy Dogs International was founded for the purpose of registering temperamentally stable dogs to visit facilities for children, the aged and the handicapped. The organization registers individual dogs who have been approved by a licensed obedience trainer. An annual fee is paid for membership, which provides insurance while the dog is in the facility. In May of 1989 there were two thousand dogs registered, with interest and participation soaring on the national level.

Northern California has a representative group of TDI dogs who, with their owners, regularly visit acute hospital rehabilitation units, convalescent hospitals (nursing homes), facilities for the developmentally disabled, schools for the retarded and facilities that specialize in the treatment of Alzheimer's Disease.

This group is called Lend a Hand—Lend a Heart, and there are three active Bichon owners, Rosmarie Blood, Dorothy Hottle and Sally Mitchell, who regularly participate with one or more of their five Bichons, Ch. Primos Miss Abbe V Crockerly, C.D.; Torab's Katie the Imp; Ch. Chaminade Chamour Snowbird; and the two Australian imports, Ch. Azara Crockerly Rose and the newest arrival, Azara's Christina. Most of the members of this particular group belong to the Sacramento Dog Training Club, and therefore the dogs involved have had some obedience training.

While formal obedience training is helpful, it is not absolutely imperative. However, a dog must be calm, friendly, adaptable and responsive to basic commands in order to be successful as a Therapy Dog, for obviously these circumstances can involve both unusual equipment and behavior unfamiliar to the dog. This can range from the exuberance of children to the fragility of the elderly. The stories told by this group are at once tender, heartrending and often exhilarating; it is doubtful that any member has been left unaffected.

Lend a Hand—Lend a Heart suggests that the owners make three visits, without their dogs, in order to observe the procedure and routine and see if they indeed would like to become involved. It is also an opportunity to learn what is expected of the dogs and what they might encounter. Three additional visits are made to facilities with the dog, where his behavior is witnessed and approved by an accredited trainer based on Therapy Dogs International criteria.

Betty Blake, an obedience trainer of Citrus Heights, California, with twenty years experience, has certified a number of Therapy Dogs. She looks for a steady, secure dog that relates as well to its owner as it does to the circumstances its environment offers. Its ability to adapt and react positively to the unpredictable is of utmost importance. Naturally she expects the dogs to be immaculate and well presented. If the dog passes his "test," it may be registered as a TDI dog and can wear the yellow tag identifying him as a trained Therapy Dog.

The Sacramento group is wholly voluntary, and it normally meets once a week. Dorothy Hottle describes the typical pattern of a visit:

> The facilities usually prefer midafternoon visits. So we arrive and meet outside and let the dogs get reacquainted before we enter the visiting areas or day rooms. The nursing staff have the residents in this room awaiting our arrival.

Some are in wheelchairs, others on chairs and couches arranged in a circle. We enter the room in single file and each dog is introduced by his name, his breed and his handler. The dogs are brought to the center of the room so the people can get a good look, and the reaction is immediate with lots of "ohs" and "ahs." We start our program with a brief obedience demonstration, from the very basic exercises through the most difficult ones. Some have been altered in order to include audience participation. In addition, some of the dogs and their owners have put a lot of time and energy into special tricks, and the residents seem to especially enjoy this. Rosmarie Blood's Ch. Azara Crockerly Rose has really taken to the entertainment portion, as she quickly learned to dance, jump through a hoop and all the while is the ultimate socialite as she goes from person to person in greeting.

Part of the group makes room visits to give patients who were unable to come to the day room an opportunity to see the dogs and spend time with them. We always stop at the doorway on these occasions and ask if they are interested, never going in if they seem hesitant, although most of them are so surprised and delighted to see the dogs they can hardly wait to get their hands on them! Polaroid pictures are taken of people with their favorite dogs to have as a memento of our visit.

It is interesting to watch the reaction of the people to our presence. The first visit is met with questioning looks and curiosity. The second is met with eagerness and the anticipation of holding "their" dog again. We never fail to hear about the beloved pet someone once had; they want to talk to you about them and recall the happy times they had shared. Perhaps those who touch us most are the ones who respond to our dogs when nothing else has reached them . . . the motionless stroke victim who moved her fingers through the Bichon coat, the withdrawn lady, fearful at first, who ended with the Bichon in her arms and her cheek against his head, or the little boy who crawled because he could not walk to touch his favorite dog. You must experience it to know the thrill of watching your pet make someone happy as these Bichons do. It is worth any effort that goes into it.

Lend a Hand—Lend a Heart is a well-organized and productive group. There are similar groups around the country that are equally energetic and ambitious, and that will always welcome new owners with qualified dogs. This will enable many of them to eventually expand their programs to include such things as nurseries and day care centers. There are also smaller groups that function with great success. Whatever your area has to offer, investigate and participate. Remember that Therapy Dog programs require commitment. There will be no regrets.

In all of the stories we hear involving Bichons in therapy work, a major emphasis has been on their sensitivity to individual needs. The following anecdotes told about the grand veteran dog, Ch. Miri-Cal's Motet, by his owner, Anne Jones of Virginia, puts it all in heartwarming perspective:

Teddy became a therapy dog through his Obedience Training Club. His therapy co-workers all seem to have lots of letters before or after their names; O.T.C.H., C.D., C.D.X., U.D. Teddy has a Ch. in front of his name, indicating that he is an AKC champion. He has done lots of wonderful things as a show dog. As an obedience dog his career was not so successful. On his first (and only)

183

appearance in the Obedience ring, he did a ''long sit'' at the feet of his handler, the ''long down'' at the feet of the judge and upon recall command he ran out of the ring and jumped into the lap of his human ''sister.'' These are not considered proper responses to the commands! The only letters that Teddy will ever have after his name are C.L.O.W.N. After nine years of intermittent obedience training we are resigned to this.

But Teddy is a wonder to behold in a nursing home or among disabled children. His intelligence allows him to sense who gets a kiss, who needs to cuddle up and who needs just to pat his head.

I have seen my Bichon work his way around a room full of elderly women, greeting each one in turn. For the prim and proper lady a ''sit'' and a hand-shake. The exuberant and effusive lady gets a wet ''kiss.'' If asked he is most willing to jump into a warm lap. Every lady there receives *her* kind of ''hello'' with no instruction from me.

With the very old and the very young, a dog becomes what the heart wants him to be. A small child may see his stuffed animal ''come to life.'' A blind child feels with his hands the beauty that his eyes will never see. The deformed and disabled sense instant acceptance. Therapy dogs fill these needs and ease the hurts.

I remember the gentleman in the wheelchair who declared Teddy to be ''just like Sam''—a German Shepherd, as it turned out. Never mind. The heart sees something that is within.

One day by request I went to visit an elderly lady in a nursing home. She had told one and all that Teddy was coming. As it turned out it was not Teddy I took but a litter of pups along with their mother. The staff asked that I not take them into this lady's room, as her roommate did not like dogs. As we waited in the lounge both women came in, and it was the roommate who held each pup and who cuddled them close. She was so thrilled by these babies, and thanked me profusely that I had shared them with her. As the ladies were wheeled back to their room, each person they met was told to ''go see the puppies. They are Teddy's babies, you know.'' And they were! Little Therapy dogs waiting to grow up.

Therapy Dogs International has members around the country. Your local obedience club is a good place to start. The American Kennel Club is an additional source of information. The corresponding secretary of the Bichon Frise Club of America will have Therapy Dog information pertaining specifically to the Bichon. It is interesting to note that the Bichon is also being used successfully as a Therapy Dog in England, so his talents are being recognized internationally. Without doubt the Bichon's size, sensitivity and basic love of people make him a versatile and responsive ''therapist.'' This is an extraordinarily rewarding activity for owner and Bichon to share.

15

Top Producing
Sires and Dams

THE STUDY OF PEDIGREES is an ever-engrossing
project. The long-time Bichon fancier is always fascinated by the often surprising interrelationships that occur along with the simple, basic marvel of the
breed's historical progress. The newcomer delights in discovering the ancestors of his new acquisition. The prospective exhibitor and possible breeder
may delve more into aspects of heredity and the emergence and subsequent
progress of individual bloodlines.

Upon reviewing the early history of the Bichon Frise in the United
States, one can understand why the gene pool was limited for a number of
years. It therefore follows that a number of common ancestors appear and
reappear throughout these pedigrees, firmly establishing the influence, and in
some cases the dominance, of certain early Bichons. It is interesting to note
where these dogs appear and how they interrelate as the individual breeders
develop their own lines, their own interpretation of the breed, in ensuing
years.

It is not likely that the impressive records of some of these top producers
will be equaled soon. Several factors are called into play.

You will note, for example, that seven of the eleven sires and six of the
dams are now deceased. Their careers as producing sires and dams occurred
during the 1970s and the early 1980s. The kennel names that are familiar
today were in the evolutionary process at this time. Breeders began by acquiring a female or possibly two and of necessity had to seek a stud dog

elsewhere to initiate or complement a projected breeding program. As time progressed and lines developed, breeders were able to use males within their own lines, and the need or desire to use males outside these lines occurred less frequently.

In addition, there has been an important socioeconomic factor, that of increased complications regarding air travel. The increase in the cost of shipping animals in recent years has been staggering. Deregulation brought with it a loss of confidence due to flight delays and cancellations, while mergers have resulted in several carriers that simply do not accept animals. A decade ago shipping the female to the stud dog of choice was a common procedure—the rule, not the exception. Today the reverse is true, and the shipping of an unattended animal is a decision made with care, planning and considerable funds.

A reminder to the novice at this juncture: the producing record of the female Bichon will seldom equal the male, as she is likely to produce a limited number of litters in her career, while a given male may possibly sire innumerable litters.

Notice the interrelation that occurs in this limited collection of twenty-five pedigrees. Also interesting is the fact that not only have these Bichons themselves proved influential, but in many instances their sires and dams have often been equally so, perhaps not in the number of champions produced but in influence down the line.

There are a number of family combinations on the list. Ch. Chaminade Mr. Beau Monde has a son, Ch. Vogelflight's Music Man, and two daughters, Braymar's Bali Hai and Ch. C and D's Beau Monde Moonshine. Ch. Teeny Tepee's Chief of Diandee has a son, Ch. Beau Monde Huckster, while Reenroy's Riot Act has both a son and a daughter, Ch. Winmar's Magnificent Scamp and Reenroy's Image of Ami. Scamp has a daughter, Ch. Jalwin's Panache of Win-Mar, who in turn has a son, Ch. Jalwin Just a Jiffy. This "family affair" goes one step further, for Jiffy also has a son, Ch. Paw Mark Talk of the Town. Ch. Parfait Coming Home has a daughter, Ch. Parfait Ebony and Ivory. Ch. C and D's Count Kristopher completes the father-daughter sequence with Ch. Beau Monde the Firecracker. There is but one brother-and-sister combination in the twenty-five, but what a combination it was, for Count Kristopher and Countess Becky accounted for forty-five champion offspring between them.

The following pedigrees are of Bichon Frise sires with nineteen or more champion offspring and Bichon Frise dams with nine or more champions.

Further investigation reveals a number of common ancestors and firmly establishes the dominance of specific dogs since breed recognition.

It is a rare Bichon that does not have one or more of these outstanding producers somewhere in his pedigree. They have played a special role in the history of this wonderful breed.

Top Producing Bichon Sires

Name	No. of Champions Produced
Ch. Chaminade Mr. Beau Monde	65
Ch. Vogelflight's Music Man	47
Ch. Teeny Tepee's Chief of Diandee	37
Ch. Beau Monde the Huckster	35
Ch. Leander Snow Star	33
Ch. C and D's Count Kristopher	29
Ch. Loftiss Reenie	27
Ch. Parfait Coming Home	21
Ch. Paw Mark's Talk of the Town	21
Reenroy's Riot Act	21
Ch. Jalwin Just a Jiffy	20
Ch. Win-Mar's Magnificent Scamp	19

Top Producing Bichon Dams

Ch. Beau Monde the Firecracker	17
Ch. C and D's Countess Becky	16
Ch. Jalwin Panache of Win-Mar	14
Ch. Vogelflight's Fantasia	13
Braymar's Bali Hai	11
Ch. Barbra Gatlock of Druid	10
Ch. Shabob's Nice Girl Missy	10
Ch. Tomaura's Touch of Elegance	10
Ch. Norvic's Alpine Sparkler	10
Ch. Cali-Col's Shalimar of Reenroy	9
Ch. C and D's Beau Monde Moonshine	9
Ch. Parfait Ebony and Ivory	9
Ch. Reenroy's Image of Amy	9

CH. CHAMINADE MR. BEAU MONDE (1970–1984)

Owned by Richard G. Beauchamp and Pauline Waterman;
bred by Barbara B. Stubbs

Ch. Chaminade Mr. Beau Monde is the all-time top producing Bichon sire with sixty-five champions to his credit, thirty-three females and thirty-two males. These offspring have in turn produced an astounding 205 champions! Fifty-one of these sixty-five produced at least one champion. Thirty-five produced two or more champions. Twenty-four produced three or more champions and an amazing nineteen produced four or more.

Mr. Beau Monde's sire, Ch. Cali-Col's Robspierre, produced eleven champions, and his dam, Ch. Reenroy's Ami du Kilkanny, five. His double grandsire, Mex. Ch. Dapper Dan de Gascoigne, holds a special place in Bichon history, having sired seventeen champions that included many Bichons destined to influence breeders across the country. These have become familiar names in the pedigrees of latter-day champions.

Mr. Beau Monde sired several outstanding litters. One of the most famous was the renowned "Brothers Four" bred by Mary Vogel. Ch. Vogelflight's Music Man was not only the top winning Bichon for two years, but succeeds his father as the number two all-time top producing sire. All four brothers were champion producers, although Choir Boy produced his champions in England.

The three litters out of Ch. C. and D's Countess Becky produced eleven champions and provided several breeders with foundation bitches. Five of these champion daughters were the dams of Best in Show Bichons, which included the top winning Bichon of all time, Ch. Devon Puff and Stuff, bred and owned by Nancy Shapland.

Another daughter, Ch. Petit Four Beaucoup was also the dam of a Best in Show Bichon, Ch. Petit Four Xmas Bonus, bred by Judith Hilmer.

Mr. Beau Monde sired the first owner-bred and handled Best in Show Bichon, Ch. Lambo of Loch Vale, bred and owned by Diane Ayres, and the first Best in Show Bichon bitch, Ch. C and D's Beau Monde Sunbeam, owned by George Ann Slocum. Ch. Vogelflight's Music Man and Ch. Vogelflight's Choir Master bring to four the total of Best in Show offspring.

A son and a daughter, Ch. Beau Monde the Actor and Ch. Keystone Christine, produced Ch. Beau Monde the Stripper. She was dam of Ch. Beau Monde the Huckster, who became the number four all-time top producing sire.

It is fitting that the sixty-fifth and last champion sired by Mr. Beau Monde was named Ch. Chamour Finale, and that she should carry on the tradition of her famous father by producing a multiple Best in Show– and Specialty Best in Show–winning son in her first litter, Am. Mex. Int. Ch. Chaminade Le Blanc Chamour. The legacy of Mr. Beau Monde continues.

Photo by Missy.

Andre de Gascoigne
Dapper Dan de Gascoigne
Lady des Frimoussettes
Ch. Cali-Col's Robspierre
Helly of Milton
Lyne of Milton
Hanette of Milton
Ch. Chaminade Mr. Beau Monde
Andre de Gascoigne
Dapper Dan de Gascoigne
Lady des Frimoussettes
Ch. Reenroy's Ami du Kilkanny
Eddy White de Steren Vor
Little Nell of Cali-Col
Nelly of Cali-Col

CH. VOGELFLIGHT'S MUSIC MAN (1975-1987)

Owned by Victoria A. and Burton L. Busk;
bred by Mary M. Vogel

Ch. Vogelflight's Music Man was not only the second all-time top producing Bichon sire, but he was also one of the breed's top competitors, with eight all-breed Bests in Show and eighty Groups to his credit, and he remains the only Bichon to be a three-time winner of the Bichon Frise Club of America National Specialty.

Music Man produced forty-seven champions, twenty-four males and twenty-three females. Twenty-four of these offspring became champion producers themselves, for a total of seventy-nine champions.

His daughters have proven to be successful additions to several lines: litter sisters Ch. Bella Angeline of Deja Vu and Ch. Bella Graziella of Deja Vu have produced six and five champions respectively for Deja Vu Bichons of Karla Matlock. Ch. J'Con's Leading Lady has produced four champions for J'Con and Connie Armitage, including a multiple Group winner, Ch. J'Con's Peenaw Weenaw. Ch. Sheramour Showtime Lady is the dam of five champions for Sheramour and Sherry and Charles Watts, with a multiple Group-winning daughter, Ch. Sheramour's Roxanne.

Ch. Wicked Music by Craigdale, a daughter bred in Canada by Dale Hunter, the dam of four champions, produced Ch. Craigdale's Ole Rhondi. This Music Man grandson became the sire of eighteen, including two all-breed Best in Show winners and a National Specialty winner.

Eleven of the Music Man champions were by another result of Vogelflight breeding, Ch. Vogelflight's Fantasia, the fourth all-time top producing dam.

Two Music Man sons produced well for their owners: Ch. Windstar's Minstrel Singer with nine champions for Windstar and Estelle and Wendy Kellerman and also Ch. C and D's Tarzan with six champions including the owner-handled Best in Show winner, Ch. C and D's Xmas Knight, who joined his sire and grandsire as a successful producer with eighteen champions to his credit.

Andre de Gascoigne
Dapper Dan de Gascoigne
Lady des Frimoussettes
Ch. Cali-Col's Robspierre
Helly of Milton
Lyne of Milton
Hanette of Milton
Ch. Chaminade Mr. Beau Monde
Andre de Gascoigne
Dapper Dan de Gascoigne
Lady des Frimoussettes
Ch. Reenroy's Ami du Kilkanny
Eddy White de Steren Vor
Little Nell of Cali-Col
Nelly of Cali-Col
Ch. Vogelflight's Music Man
Dapper Dan de Gascoigne
Ch. Reenroy's Royal Flush de Noel
Little Nell of Cali-Col
Ch. Teeny Tepee's Chief of Diandee
Teeny Tepee's Sparkling Jewel
Teeny Tepee's Mauri Julene
Goldysdale Princess of Tinytown
Ch. Vogelflight's Diandee Ami Pouf
Tinker II of Rich-Lo
Vogelflight's Diandee Pouf
Vogelflight's Bebe Zwingalee

CH. TEENY TEPEE'S CHIEF OF DIANDEE (1972-1986)

Owned by Clover Allen; bred by Elizabeth Shehab

Ch. Teeny Tepee's Chief of Diandee is the number three all-time top producing sire. He has thirty-seven champions to his credit, nineteen females and eighteen males. These offspring have in turn produced seventy-six champions.

It is not surprising that he has such an outstanding record when one delves into his pedigree. His sire, Ch. Reenroy's Royal Flush de Noel, is a brother to Ch. Reenroy's Ami du Kilkanny. Ami, you will remember, is the dam of top producer Ch. Chaminade Mr. Beau Monde and a second influential son, Ch. Chaminade Tempo. Chief's dam is Teeny Tepee's Mauri Julene. A second son of hers, Ch. Teeny Tepee's Cherokee Prince, is the sire of sixteen champions. This includes a trio of Bichons influential in the Norvic line of Alice Vicha; the Group winners Ch. Norvic Nautical Noah and Ch. Norvic's Easy Does It; and Ch. Norvic Nebuchadnessar, grandsire of multiple Best in Show winner and top producer Ch. Jalwin Just a Jiffy. It also includes the now famous bitch, Ch. Vogelflight's Diandee Amy Pouf, dam of another top producer, Ch. Vogelflight's Music Man and his noted brothers. These half brothers, Chief and Prince, have indeed made outstanding contributions.

Ch. Teeny Tepee's Chief of Diandee has three champion daughters that have been a credit to their sire. Ch. Jadeles January Frost is the dam of three champions, including Ch. Jadeles October Gobblin, who is the sire of nine champions for Jadeles and Judith Thayer. Ch. Beau Monde the Hooker produced four champions for Tondia and Victoria Busk. Ch. C and D's Bit of Spring produced four champions for C and D, including Ch. C. and D Petit Four White Xmas, sire of ten champions, and Ch. C and D's Xmas Knight. This Bichon was not only a successful sire of fourteen champions but was also an owner-handled Best in Show winner for his breeder, Dolores Wolske.

It was the breeding to Ee R's Royal Trinquette that would produce another record breaker. Ch. Beau Monde the Huckster was the third in a trio of champions from that breeding, Ch. Beau Monde the Hooker, discussed above, and Ch. Beau Monde the Hustler, with four champions to his credit. Huckster would follow in his father's footsteps, and we thus have the second of the great father-son producing combinations that would manifest such an impact on the breed.

Andre de Gascoigne
Dapper Dan de Gascoigne
Lady des Frimoussettes
Ch. Reenroy's Royal Flush de Noel
Eddy White de Steren Vor
Little Nell of Cali-Col
Nelly of Cali-Col
Ch. Teeny Tepee's Chief of Diandee
Ombre de la Roche Posay
Teeny Tepee's Sparkling Jewel
Oranda de la Roche Posay
Teeny Tepee's Mauri Julene
Izor Prince des Frimoussette
Ombre de la Roche Posay
Iona II de la Roche Posay
Goldysdale Princess of Tinytown
Natchen of Cali-Col

CH. BEAU MONDE THE HUCKSTER (1977–   )

*Owned by Nancy Shapland; bred by Richard Beauchamp
and Pauline Waterman*

Ch. Beau Monde the Huckster, the number four all-time top producing sire, has thirty-five champions to his credit, twenty-one females and fourteen males. These thirty-five have in turn produced forty-six champions. In addition to his producing record, Huckster was a multiple Group winner.

The Huckster daughters as a group were more dominant than the sons. Perhaps the most successful litter of Huckster's career was the breeding to Ch. C and D's Beau Monde Moonshine. Five champion offspring resulted, and these five in turn produced eleven champions. The best known of these was Best in Show and Best in Show Specialty winner Ch. Crockerly Beau Monde Eclipse, who was the number one Bichon in 1980.

Ch. Diamant's Dominique, whose dam was Ch. Ardezz Juliette Diamant, produced three champions. One of these was Ch. Diamant Le Magnifique, who became a multiple Best in Show and a Best in Show Specialty winner and is proving to be a successful producer in his own right, with six champions to his credit to date.

A third daughter was Ch. Avalanche Lily of Loch Vale out of Ch. Muguet of Loch Vale. Lily produced son Ch. Tres Jolie Mr. Vagabond, who became a Best in Show and Best in Show Specialty winner.

A fourth daughter, Ch. Larkshire Paper Doll, was from the breeding to Ch. Braymar's Chaminade Pavanne. She produced six champions. Two of her daughters have produced three and four champions to date and are making a good showing for a continuation of the strong bitch line initiated by Huckster.

A final daughter to be mentioned is Ch. Chaminade Cantata, whose dam, Braymar's Bali Hai, is a top producer in her own right. Cantata produced five champions. Most notable are two daughters, who have each produced a champion litter that boasted a multiple Best in Show and Best in Show Specialty winner.

It should be noted that the males, Ch. Crockerly Beau Monde Moonglo and Ch. Crockerly Beau Monde Man in the Moon, have each produced four champions.

Thus we have the second of our father-son combinations of top producers.

Andre de Gascoigne
Dapper Dan de Gascoigne
Lady des Frimoussettes
Ch. Reenroy's Royal Flush de Noel
Eddy White de Steren Vor
Little Nell of Cali-Col
Nelly of Cali-Col
Ch. Teeny Tepee's Chief of Diandee
Ombre de la Roche Posay
Teeny Tepee's Sparkling Jewel
Oranda de la Roche Posay
Teeny Tepee's Mauri Julene
Ombre de la Roche Posay
Goldysdale Princess of Tinytown
Natchen of Cali-Col
Ch. Beau Monde the Huckster
Ch. Cali-Col's Robspierre
Ch. Chaminade Mr. Beau Monde
Ch. Reenroy's Ami du Kilkanny
Ch. Beau Monde the Actor
Petit Galant de St. George
Ee's R Royale Trinquette
Ee's R Cali-Col Ritzy Ruffles
Ch. Beau Monde the Stripper
Ch. Cali-Col's Robspierre
Ch. Chaminade Mr. Beau Monde
Ch. Reenroy's Ami du Kilkanny
Ch. Keystone's Christine
Mister Tinker of Thur-Em
Bijou of Thur-Em
Robley's Angel of Rockin-R

AUST. AND AM. CH. LEANDER SNOW STAR (1976–   )

Owned by Laura Purnell; bred by Wendy Streatfield

Ch. Leander Snow Star is currently the fifth all-time top producing Bichon Frise sire. He was bred in England by Leander Bichons and Wendy Streatfield and was subsequently sent to Australia, where he garnered an outstanding show record. At the age of six years he came to the United States and his current owner, Laura Purnell and the Tomaura Bichons, where once again he proved to be a multiple Best in Show and Group winner and Specialty Best in Show winner. He established himself as an outstanding producer bred to bitches from a variety of bloodlines, such as Jalwin, Chaminade, Balverne, Keleb, Sarkis and others, as well as the Tomaura bitches of his owner.

He is the sire of thirty-three champions, twenty males and thirteen females. Ch. Tomaura's Mor Bounce to the Oz, a multiple Group winner, has produced seven champions for the Sumarco Bichons of Roy Copelin. Ch. Balverne Applause Applause produced four champions for her owner, Mary Ann Pichel of Balverne Bichons. Ch. Leander Snow Star's champion children in turn have produced twenty-six champions.

His top winning offspring to date is Ch. Westoak Wizard of Pawz, a multiple all-breed Best in Show, Specialty Best in Show and Group winner for owners Susan and Peter Barron.

196

Peppe de Barnette
Ch. C & D's Count Kristopher
Quentia of Goldysdale
Ch. C & D's Beau Monde Blizzard
Ch. Chaminade Mr. Beau Monde
Ch. C & D's Sunbonnet
Ch. C & D's Countess Becky
Leander Snow Venture
Ch. Chaminade Mr. Beau Monde
Ch. C & D's Beau Monde Sunflower
Peppe de Barnette
Ch. C & D's Countess Becky
Quentia of Goldysdale

Ch. Leander Snow Star
Dapper Dan de Gascoigne
Ch. Cali-Col's Robspierre
Lyne of Milton
Ch. Chaminade Mr. Beau Monde
Dapper Dan de Gascoigne
Ch. Reenroy's Ami du Kilkanny
Little Nell of Cali-Col
Ch. C & D's Beau Monde Sunflower
Quintal de Warnabry
Peppe de Barnette
Romance de Bourbiel
Ch. C & D's Countess Becky
Ombre de la Roche Posay
Quentia of Goldysdale
Oree de la Roche Posay

CH. C AND D'S COUNT KRISTOPHER (1971–1985)

Owned by Charles and Dolores Wolske;
bred by Roberta Barnette Houser

Ch. C and D's Count Kristopher is the first member of our brother-sister combination to make an appearance. These littermates have made an extraordinary impact on the development of the Bichon; indeed, no other duo can lay claim to their combined influence.

In Count Kristopher we have our sixth all-time top producing sire, with twenty-nine champion offspring to his credit, seventeen males and twelve females. They in turn produced an impressive total of sixty-three champions.

A son, Ch. C and D's Beau Monde Blizzard was a Best in Show and multiple Group winner and the sire of ten champions. Blizzard would ultimately become influential in his own right. He produced a Best in Show– and National Specialty–winning son, Ch. Beau Monde the Iceman. A second son, Group and Specialty winner Ch. Cali-Col's Conquistador, was also sire of six champions.

When bred to Ch. C and D's Katie Did, Count Kristopher produced four champions. One of these was a Specialty Best in Show son, Ch. Bunnyrun the Heartbreaker, who in turn would sire fourteen champions and an all-breed Best in Show son of his own, Ch. Bunnyrun the Quarterback, another successful producer with nine champions to his credit.

On the distaff side the Count Kristopher daughter, Ch. Beau Monde the Fawn, produced five champions. Her daughter, Ch. Beau Monde Regal Rose, produced four champions and was a multiple Group winner.

In addition to having a sister included in this group of top producing Bichons, it is the Ch. C and D's Count Kristopher daughter, Ch. Beau Monde the Firecracker, who is the all-time top producing dam. The interrelationship of our top producers continues to unfold.

Photo by Martin Booth.

Int. Ch. Jimbo de Steren Vor

Quintal de Warnabry

Int. Ch. Janitzia de Steren Vor

Peppe De Barnette

Int. Ch. Jimbo de Steren Vor

Romance de Bourbiel

Int. Ch. Kitoune de Steren Vor

Ch. C & D's Count Kristopher

Izor Prince des Frimoussette

Ombre de la Roche Posay

Iona II de la Roche Posay

Quentia of Goldysdale

Izor Prince des Frimoussette

Oree de la Roche Posay

Forne de Dierstein

199

CH. LOFTISS REENIE (1971–1985)

Owned by Laura Purnell; bred by J. Loftiss

Ch. Loftiss Reenie is a second top producing sire from the Tomaura Bichons of Laura Purnell and is the sire of twenty-seven champion offspring, eighteen females and nine males, who in turn have produced a total of thirty-eight champions.

Ch. Keleb Snowbear O Tomaura was the sire of five champions, while Ch. Keleb's Kricquette of Tomaura was the dam of five champions, for the Keleb Bichons of Judy Fausset. Ch. L'Etoile Brillante was the dam of six champions for Sophia Yanculeff. Ch. Tomaura's Symphony of Sumarco produced four champions for Roy Copelin's Sumarco Bichons.

Nine of the champion progeny of Ch. Loftiss Reenie were by Ch. Tomaura's Touch of Elegance. While several from this combination produced a number of champions, none had more impact or influence than Ch. Tomaura's Moonlite Sonata, for he was destined to become the sire of the top winning Bichon in the history of the breed, Ch. Devon Puff and Stuff. Her winning record puts her in a class by herself; thus it follows that Bichons appearing in the pedigree behind her have a special place in the annals of Bichon history.

Andre de Gascoigne
Dapper Dan de Gascoigne
Lady des Frimoussettes
Cali-Col's Only Sam of Reenroy
Helly of Milton
Lyne of Milton
Hanette of Milton
Reenroy's Torro
Quintal de Wanarbry
G.W. Chere Rose
Goldysdale Nada
Ch. Loftiss Reenie
Andre de Gascoigne
Dapper Dan de Gascoigne
Lady des Frimoussettes
Reenroy's Tanya
Lochinvar du Pic Four
Rank's Merilee of Reenroy
Rank's Gay

CH. PARFAIT COMING HOME (1980–   )

Owned and bred by Joanne Spilman

Ch. Parfait Coming Home is the first of three Bichon sires to be dis cussed here that has twenty-one champions to his credit. These champion offspring, thirteen females and eight males, have to date produced thirty-two champions of their own.

The dam of Ch. Parfait Coming Home, Ch. Parfait Apple Crunch, produced Ch. Chamour Finale. Finale in turn produced a multiple Best in Show and National Specialty winner whose sister took the Best of Opposite Sex award, Ch. Chaminade Le Blanc Chamour and Ch. Chamour Sable du Chaminade respectively.

The uncle of Ch. Parfait Coming Home is Ch. Parfait Apple Crisp. He is the sire of another National Specialty winner, Ch. Hellsapoppin of Druid, one of only three bitches to garner that title.

Through the sire, Ch. L'Havre Joyeux Desi, we see the de la Roche Posay line emerge again. With this outstanding background it is not surprising that Ch. Parfait Coming Home has been a successful producer.

Ch. Parfait Ebony and Ivory is the top producing daughter of Coming Home, and her nine champions rate her a place on the all-time list. Her sister, Ch. Parfait Heaven Scent, is the dam of three champions, while a third daughter, Ch. Win-Mar's Lillian of Druid, has produced five champions.

The top producing sons are Ch. Littlecreek Skol of FoxLaur with six champions, Ch. Pere Jacque Samson D'Parfait with five and Ch. Ivy Todd Gatlock of Druid with four at this writing.

Ch. Paw Paw Punjab
L'Havre Joyeux Mr. Majestic
L'Havre Shady Lady
Ch. L'Havre Joyeux Desi
Ch. Rickel du G.W.
L'Havre Joyeux Tina Tart
Richelle du G.W.
Ch. Parfait Coming Home
Ch. Chaminade Tempo
Ch. Cameo Temptation Chaminade
Ch. Kahil's Color Me White
Parfait Apple Crunch
Ch. Cali-Col's Robspierre
Ch. Chaminade Mr. Beau Mode
Ch. Reenroy's Ami du Kilkanny
Joanne's Elke of Chansom
Ch. Chansom Gift of Sunny Knoll

CH. PAW MARK'S TALK OF THE TOWN (1981–   )

Owned and bred by Pauline Schultz

Ch. Paw Mark's Talk of the Town had an illustrious show career with his breeder-owner-handler. He is the third of our all-time top producing sires with twenty-one champions to his credit, thirteen males and eight females.

This pedigree is particularly interesting as it contains four of the top producing sires and two of the top producing dams, which is a record.

Talk of the Town has produced successfully when bred to Bichons from Alefar, Angelic, Brereton, Seastar and of course from his own Paw Mark kennel. His daughter, Ch. Paw Mark's PS I Love You, is the dam of the 1987 National Sweepstakes winner, Ch. Paw Mark's Jet Parade Ex Cel, who was also Best of Winners at the same show. The champion children have in turn produced four champions at this writing.

Ch. Norvic's Nebuchadnessar
Ch. Diandee Masterpiece
Diandee Sweet Pollyanna
Ch. Jalwin Just a Jiffy
Ch. Win-mar's Magnificent Scamp
Ch. Jalwin Panache of Win-Mar
Ch. Nerak's Sweet Stuff of Charda
Ch. Paw Mark's Talk of the Town
Ch. Ee's R King George of Kriskanu
Ch. Beau Monde Ee's R Express
Ee's R Cali-Col's Ritzy Ruffles
Ch. Tres Beau Impeccable Imp
Ch Cali-Col's Robspierre
Ch. Chaminade Mr. Beau Monde
Ch. Reenroy's Ami du Kilkanny
Ch. C & D's Beau Monde Moondust
Peppe de Barnette
Ch. C & D's Countess Becky
Quentia of Goldysdale

REENROY'S RIOT ACT (1970–1982)

Owned by Mayree Butler and Stella Raabe;
bred by Mayree Butler

Reenroy's Riot Act is the second of our all-time top producing sires with twenty-one champions to his credit, eleven females and ten males. Note once again the interrelationship of these top producers. The sire of Riot Act, Ch. Stardom's Odin Rex, and the sire of Ch. Chaminade Mr. Beau Monde, Ch. Cali-Col's Robspierre, are brothers.

Certainly Riot Act's most prestigious offspring is his son, Ch. Win-Mar's Magnificent Scamp, who with nineteen champions of his own is also on the top producer list and gives us an additional father-son combination.

A second son, Ch. Wynchin Vive La Revolution, produced nine champions, including Ch. Shangrila's Youngblood Hawk, a multiple Group winner in the early 1980s. A third son, Ch. Reenroy's Riot Squad, produced four champions.

Several Riot Act daughters make an equally impressive appearance. Ch. Reenroy's Image of Ami, with nine champions, is on the list of top producing dams, giving us another father-daughter combination. A second daughter, Ch. Kahil's Color Me White, produced the all-breed Best in Show and Specialty Best of Breed winner, Ch. Cameo Temptation Chaminade, who figures in the pedigree of Ch. Parfait Coming Home.

A third daughter, Ch. Reenroy's Tera Tiki, is the dam of Ch. Reenroy's Double Trouble, a Specialty Best of Breed winner and the sire of seven champions.

Two Riot Act sons, Ch. Seascape the Tidal Wave and the previously mentioned Ch. Win-Mar's Magnificent Scamp, are prominent in the pedigree of yet another top producer, the dam Ch. Jalwin's Panche of Win-Mar, and ultimately her progeny, who also appear on the list of top producers, which at this juncture should come as no surprise. The champion offspring of Reenroy's Riot Act produced thirty-eight champion children of their own.

Andre de Gascoigne
Dapper Dan de Gascoigne
Lady des Frimoussettes
Ch. Stardom's Odin Rex, Jr.
Helly of Milton
Lyne of Milton
Hanette of Milton
Reenroy's Riot Act
Andre de Gascoigne
Dapper Dan de Gascoigne
Lady des Frimoussettes
Reenroy's Ruffles
Lochinvar du Pic Four
Rank's Merrilee of Reenroy
Rank's Gaye

CH. JALWIN JUST A JIFFY (1978–   )

Owned by Pauline Schultz; bred by Ann D. Hearn

Ch. Jalwin Just a Jiffy is another of our all-time top producing sires, with nineteen champion children, twelve females and seven males. His pedigree contains a bevy of our top producing Bichons, so it is not surprising that he has followed in their footsteps. Jiffy is the second of our top producing sires to win a National Specialty in addition to his multiple all-breed Best in Show and Group wins.

Jiffy's most renowned offspring is, of course, his son, Ch. Paw Mark's Talk of the Town, who precedes his father on the top producer list and also followed his success in the show ring. A second son, Ch. Paw Mark's Triple Threat, has a Group win and placements. A third son, Ch. Brereton's B B Cody, is the sire of four champion bitches, including the Group winner Ch. Paw Mark's September Song and her sister, Ch. Paw Mark's Lollipop Labow, who has a Specialty win to her credit and a Best of Opposite Sex win at the 1987 National Specialty.

A daughter, Ch. Brereton's Happy Hour, produced three champions, including Ch. Brereton's Stonewall Jackson, who sired a litter with five champions by Ch. Win-Mar's Lillian of Druid. A second daughter, Ch. Paw Mark's Pebbles of Brereton, was the National Sweepstakes winner in 1983. Jiffy is also the grandsire of Ch. Sandcastle Bikini, a Specialty and Group winner who is currently producing champions of her own.

At this writing the champion offspring of Ch. Jalwin Just a Jiffy have in turn produced forty champion children.

Photo by Missy.

Ch. Teeny Tepee's Cherokee Prince
Ch. Norvic's Nebuchadnessar
Reenroy's Riot Act
Ch. Reenroy's Image of Ami
Reenroy's Babette
Ch. Diandee Masterpiece
Ch. Reenroy's Royal Flush de Noel
Ch. Teeny Tepee's Chief of Diandee
Teeny Tepee's Mauri Julene
Diandee Sweet Pollyanna
Chateau's Miss Lucy of Diamonds
Ch. Jalwin Just a Jiffy
Ch. Stardom's Odin Rex, Jr.
Reenroy's Riot Act
Reenroy's Ruffles
Ch. Win-mar's Magnificent Scamp
Int. Ch. Jimbo de Steren Vor
Scille de Warnabry
Int. Ch. Janitzia de Frimoussettes
Ch. Jalwin Panache of Win-Mar
Reenroy's Riot Act
Ch. Seascape the Tidal Wave
Vintage Year Rubion
Ch. Nerak's Sweet Stuff of Charda
Gabby de Gascoigne
Nerak's Love Dove
Nerak's Baby Birdie

CH. WIN-MAR'S MAGNIFICENT SCAMP (1972–1988)

Owned and bred by Marie Winslow

Ch. Win-Mar's Magnificent Scamp is another of the outstanding producers from the pivotal era of the early 1970s. As the son of one top producer, Reenroy's Riot Act, and the sire of another, Ch. Jalwin Panache of Win-Mar, Scamp was destined to influence future pedigrees.

It is interesting that he is one of but three of our top producers whose dam is an import and not American bred, in this case from the De Warnabry Kennels of France.

Scamp is the sire of nineteen champions, ten females and nine males. He had notable success when bred into the Druid line as well as the kennel-mates from Win-Mar. These nineteen have in turn produced a total of forty-one champions.

Most impressive is the daughter Ch. Jalwin Panache of Win-Mar, who is the third all-time top producing dam, with fourteen champions to her credit. Her sister, Ch. Win-Mar's Windsong de Sumarco, produced four champions, while Ch. Belle Coeurs Scoven Magnific and Ch. Druid Bianca Jen Jul produced two each.

Scamp was bred to Ch. C and D's Dragon Lady, who was then sent to Japan. The litter was whelped and a male puppy returned to the United States and C and D Bichons. This was Ch. C and D's Taro the Great, the only known Bichon to have been bred in Japan and later achieve his American championship title.

A champion son, Ch. Scamper Gatlock of Druid, was a Specialty Best of Breed and Group winner and the sire of seven champions. Ch. Win-Mar's Little Elf was yet another Group-winning son, with six champions to his credit.

```
                              Dapper Dan de Gascoigne
              Ch. Stardom's Odin Rex, Jr.
                              Lyne of Milton
      Reenroy's Riot Act
                              Dapper Dan de Gascoigne
              Reenroy's Ruffles
                              Rank's Merrilee of Reenroy
Ch. Win-Mar's Magnificent Scamp
                              Gift de Steren Vor
              Jimbo de Steren Vor
                              Cate de Steren Vor
      Scille de Wanarbry
                              Amigo Mio d'Egriselles
              Int. Ch. Janitzia des Frimoussettes
                              Bouclette des Frimoussettes
```

CH. BEAU MONDE THE FIRECRACKER (1976–)

Owned by Sherry Fry; bred by Richard Beauchamp
and Pauline Waterman

Ch. Beau Monde the Firecracker was originally co-owned by Mr. Beauchamp and Sherry Fry and later by Mrs. Fry alone.

Firecracker is one of the father-daughter producing combinations. Her sire, Ch. C and D's Count Kristopher, has been notably influential. Her dam, Ch. C and D's Sunbeam, is another of the Mr. Beau Monde–Countess Becky daughters, and is the breed's first Best in Show bitch.

Of twenty-four puppies born to Firecracker, seventeen completed their championships, eight males and nine females, an extraordinary record and the most by any Bichon dam.

The first of two litters sired by Ch. Vogelflight's Music Man produced seven puppies, six became champions. Am. Ch. Beau Monde the Kobold Kaddie went to Sweden to Lars and Inger Adehemier (Inghedens). He attained his Swedish championship and sired a champion son and a daughter who was a successful producer.

Ch. Beau Monde the Kobold Klown, a multiple Group winner, sired five champions for Scott Johnson (Woodway) while Ch. Beau Monde the Kobold Kosmos produced four champions for Fanfare Bichons of Burke Asher.

The second Firecracker litter, also sired by Ch. Vogelflight's Music Man, produced seven puppies, of which five became champions. Ch. Kobold Daybreak was the dam of four champions for Roger Davis (Polisson). Ch. Kobold Dayglow O Kingscross produced a champion for Kingscross Bichons of Judy McNamara and Jody Collier. Ch. Kobold Daytona went to Mr. and Mrs. Satoki Hayashi of Japan, where his son became the first Bichon to be sent to Taiwan.

Firecracker produced two champion bitches by Ch. D'Shar's Rendezvous du Chamour. The final four champions were sired by Ch. Kobold's Windjammer. The most notable is Ch. Kobold's Skyrocket, the sire of seventeen champions to date, eleven females and six males, for owners Berne and Linda Thorpe (Alexsun). Eight of these were produced when bred to his grandam, Ch. Vogelflight's Fantasia, and four produced when bred to Ch. Sheramour Showtime Lady for Charles and Sherry Watts (Sheramour). In the second litter, bred to Fantasia, six puppies were produced and all six became champions.

Int. Ch. Jimbo de Steren Vor

Quintal de Warnabry

Int. Ch. Janitzia de Steren Vor

Peppe de Barnette

Int. Ch. Jimbo de Steren Vor

Romance de Bourbiel

Int. Ch. Kitoune de Steren Vor

Ch. C & D's Count Kristopher

Izor Prince des Frimoussettes

Ombre de la Roche Posay

Iona II de la Roche Posay

Quentia of Goldysdale

Izor Prince des Frimoussettes

Oree de la Roche Posay

Forne de Dierstein

Ch. Beau Monde the Firecracker

Dapper Dan de Gascoigne

Ch. Cali-Col's Robspierre

Lyne of Milton

Ch. Chaminade Mr. Beau Monde

Dapper Dan de Gascoigne

Ch. Reenroy's Ami du Kilkanny

Little Nell of Cali-Col

Ch. C & D Beau Monde Sunbeam

Quintal de Warnabry

Peppe de Barnette

Romance de Bourbiel

Ch. C & D's Countess Becky

Ombre de la Roche Posay

Quentia of Goldysdale

Oree de la Roche Posay

CH. C AND D'S COUNTESS BECKY (1971–1984)

Owned by Charles and Dolores Wolske;
bred by Roberta Barnette Houser

Ch. C and D's Countess Becky is one of the most influential bitches of all time, adding luster to the producing reputation already established by her brother, Ch. C and D's Count Kristopher. Becky produced sixteen champion offspring, twelve females and four males. This makes the producing record of these sixteen all the more extraordinary. The male may sire many offspring while the female produces relatively few in her lifetime. But in their turn, Becky's sixteen champions produced an astounding fifty-five champions of their own!

Thirteen of these champions were sired by Ch. Chaminade Mr. Beau Monde. Without question this proved to be one of the most remarkable combinations in the development of the breed in the United States and ultimately in other countries, notably England and Australia.

The "Sun" litter produced five champions, who in turn produced seventeen of their own. Ch. C and D's Beau Monde Sunbeam was the first Best in Show Bichon bitch and dam of Ch. Beau Monde the Firecracker, all-time top producing dam. Ch. C and D's Sunbonnet produced eight champions including a Best in Show son, Ch. C and D's Beau Monde Blizzard. Ch. C and D's Sunburst sired Ch. C and D's Stargazer, multiple Group winner and sire of nine champions. Ch. C and D's Sunflower was the dam of the international Best in Show winner and top producer Ch. Leander Snow Star. An impressive list for one litter.

The "Moon" litter produced five champions who were responsible for twenty-four more champions. Ch. C and D's Beau Monde Moonshine is an all-time top producer in her own right. Ch. C and D's Beau Monde Moondust was the dam of six champions for Laura Keator (Tres Beau). The Moondust son, Ch. Tres Beau Decor, began a four-generation dynasty of Best in Show winners. Moonglory and Moonfire produced five and three champions respectively, while Moonmist produced one, Ch. Beau Monde Mar-Jon Magic, noted for her participation in Performance Events and being the dam of five champions.

The third Mr. Beau Monde–Becky litter produced three champions. The most significant of these was Ch. C and D's Devon Hell's Lil Angel, who was the dam of Ch. Devon Puff and Stuff, the top winning Bichon in breed history. One cannot ask for more: top winners, top producers and top foundation dogs for other lines. The Mr. Beau Monde–Countess Becky offspring offered it all.

Ch. C and D's Tarzan, sired by Ch. Vogelflight's Music Man, produced seven champions to date including a Best in Show son. The overall record of this outstanding bitch is truly phenomenal.

Photo by Missy.

                              Int. Ch. Jimbo de Steren Vor
              Quintal de Warnabry
                              Int. Ch. Janitzia de Steren Vor
      Peppe de Barnette
                              Int. Ch. Jimbo de Steren Vor
              Romance de Bourbiel
                              Int. Ch. Kitoune de Steren Vor
Ch. C and D's Countess Becky
                              Izor Prince des Frimoussettes
              Ombre de la Roche Posay
                              Iona II de la Roche Posay
      Quentia of Goldysdale
                              Izor Prince des Frimoussettes
              Oree de la Roche Posay
                              Forne de Dierstein

CH. JALWIN PANACHE OF WIN-MAR (1976–1989)

Owned by Ann D. Hearn; bred by Marie Winslow

Ch. Jalwin Panache of Win-Mar is the number three all-time top producing dam, with fourteen champions to her credit, nine males and five females, who in turn produced thirty-four champions. Six were sired by Ch. Diandee Masterpiece, six by Ch. Leander Snow Star and two by Ch. C and D's Xmas Knight, showing in-depth quality from the three pedigrees. This is not surprising, since her sire and grandsire are both top producers.

Without question her most prominent offspring was Ch. Jalwin Just a Jiffy, who became a top producer of twenty-one champions for Paw Mark Bichons, in addition to being a multiple Best in Show and Specialty winner.

Ch. Jalwin Justice, a sister to Jiffy, is the dam of eight champions and has been another successful producer for Paw Mark. Her champions have included a Specialty winner, Ch. Paw Mark's Lollipop Labow, and Group winner Ch. Paw Mark September Song.

Dapper Dan de Gascoigne
Ch. Stardom's Odin Rex, Jr.
Lyne of Milton
Reenroy's Riot Act
Dapper Dan de Gascoigne
Reenroy's Ruffles
Rank's Merrilee of Reenroy
Ch. Win-mar's Magnificent Scamp
Int. Ch. Jimbo de Steren Vor
Scille de Warnabry
Int. Ch. Janitzia de Frimoussettes
Ch. Jalwin Panache of Win-Mar
Ch. Stardom's Odin Rex
Reenroy's Riot Act
Reenroy's Ruffles
Ch. Seascape the Tidal Wave
Vintage Year Rubion
Ch. Nerak's Sweet Stuff of Charda
Gabby de Gascoigne
Nerak's Love Dove
Nerak's Baby Birdie

CH. VOGELFLIGHT'S FANTASIA (197?–   )

Owned by Sherry Fry and Jim Taylor;
bred by Mary M. Vogel

Ch. Vogelflight's Fantasia, with thirteen champion offspring, is the fourth top producing bitch in the breed to date. Fantasia's sire, Ch. Vogelflight's Choir Master, was a litter brother to the now-famous Ch. Vogelflight's Music Man. Choir Master was a successful sire in his own right, with eleven champions to his credit and a successful show career behind him.

Fantasia produced four of her champion children bred to Ch. Kobold's Kilimanjaro, one of the first winners and producers to carry the Kobold prefix. A son, Ch. Kobold's Windjammer, was bred to the top producer, Ch. Beau Monde the Firecracker. This breeding produced Ch. Kobold's Skyrocket. Skyrocket was then bred back to his grandam, Fantasia. This breeding produced an amazing eight of her twelve champion offspring. In one litter six puppies produced six champions, four females and two males. Ch. Taylored Alexsun Thor had multiple Group placements, while Ch. Taylored Alexsun Callisto finished with a Group Three. Ch. Kobold's Superstition produced two champions and Ch. Kobold's Taylored Siren produced one.

Dapper Dan de Gascoigne
Ch. Cali-Col's Robspierre
Lyne of Milton
Ch. Chaminade Mr. Beau Monde
Dapper Dan de Gascoigne
Ch. Reenroy's Ami du Kilkanny
Little Nell of Cali-Col
Ch. Vogelflight's Choir Master
Ch. Reenroy's Royal Flush de Noel
Ch. Teeny Tepee's Chief of Diandee
Teeny Tepee's Mauri Julene
Ch. Vogelflight's Diandee Amy Pouf
Tinker II of Rich-Lo
Vogelflight's Diandee Pouf
Vogelflight's Bebe Zwingalee
Ch. Vogelflight's Fantasia
Tinker II of Rich-Lo
Vogelflight's Beesch Swingales
Little Angel of Thur-Em
Ch. Vogelflight's Kara Pouf
Kalon of Goldysdale
Chateau's Kara Rivage d'Ami
Bui-Lici of Goldysdale

BRAYMAR'S BALI HAI (1974–1988)

Owned by Barbara Stubbs and Roberta Kuester;
bred by Martin Rothman

Braymar's Bali Hai is another progeny of Ch. Chaminade Mr. Beau Monde to become a top producer. Bali Hai whelped eleven champion offspring

Ch. Braymar Chaminade Pavanne was the Best of Opposite Sex winner at three National Specialties, the third time from the Veteran class. Her daughter, Ch. Larkshire's Paper Doll, became the dam of six champions. Pavanne's littermate, Ch. Braymar Caprice du Chaminade, was the dam of Ch. D'Shar's Rendezvous du Chamour, sire of thirteen champions, including the 1983 top Bichon, Ch. Craigdale's Ole Rhondi.

Ch. Chaminade Cantata, whose sire was another of the all-time top producers, Ch. Beau Monde the Huckster, produced five champions, including a Group-winning son, Ch. Chaminade Le Jazz Hot, and two daughters who each produced multiple Best in Show–winning sons in their first litter: Ch. Chaminade Sugar Baby and son Ch. Westoaks Wizard of Pawz, and Ch. Chaminade Blue Velvet and son Ch. Alpenglow Ashley du Chamour, top Non-Sporting dog for 1988. Ashley was a member of an all-champion litter of four.

Andre de Gascoigne
Dapper Dan de Gascoigne
Lady des Frimoussettes
Ch. Cali-Col's Robspierre
Helly of Milton
Lyne of Milton
Hanette of Milton
Ch. Chaminade Mr. Beau Monde
Andre de Gascoigne
Dapper Dan de Gascoigne
Lady des Frimoussettes
Ch. Reenroy's Ami du Kilkanny
Eddy White de Steren Vor
Little Nell of Cali-Col
Nelly of Cali-Col
Braymar's Bali Hai
Ch. Dapper Dan de Gascoigne
Ch. Cali-Col's Octavius Caesar
Lynn of Milton
Ch. Braymar's Nicole
Iull Insha de Steren Vor
Mistoufle du Roi des Loutins
Ines de Warnabry
Quirikette de Steren Vor
Ch. IB&B Canaro Bleu de Steren Vor
Laite de Steren Vor
Altesse d'Egriselles

CH. BARBRA GATLOCK OF DRUID (1978–   )

Ch. Barbra Gatlock of Druid became the dam of ten champions for the Druid Bichon kennels of Betty Keatley and Betsy Schley.

A top producer himself, having sired a total of nineteen champions to date, Ch. Win-Mar's Magnificent Scamp sired four of those out of Ch. Barbra Gatlock of Druid. The combination worked so well that Barbra Gatlock was subsequently bred to Magnificent Scamp's son, Ch. Win-Mar's Little Elf. This union produced three champions.

When bred to Ch. Barkley's Fancy Me Winston, Barbra Gatlock produced two champions, with still another champion being sired by Ch. Parfait Coming Home.

The Specialty and Group winner Ch. Scamper Gatlock of Druid is the sire of seven champions, and the top producing offspring of Barbra Gatlock.

<pre>
                    Ch. Seascape the Seafarer
        Ch. Legacy's Diplomat
                    Ch. Gabby's Angel of Willow
    Ch. Druid's Diplomacy
                    Ch. Keathy Gatlock
        Ch. Ava Gatlock of Druid
                    Ch. Luty P.W.
Ch. Barbra Gatlock of Druid
                    Ch. Win-Mar's Magnificent Scamp
        Ch. Win-Mar's I'ma Big Wheel
                    Win-Mar's Suzette
    Win-Mar's Three Coins of Druid
                    Reenroy's Riot Act
        Win-Mar's Dinah-Mite
                    Little de Warnabry
</pre>

CH. SHABOB'S NICE GIRL MISSY (1969–1980)

Owned by Gertrude Fournier; bred by Mrs. George A. Roberts

Ch. Shabob's Nice Girl Missy is one of the early top producing dams, having been born in the late 1960s. She was the dam of ten champion offspring, seven by Mex. Ch. Cali-Col's Shadrack, two by Cali-Col's Winston de Noel and one by Ch. Cali-Col's Ulysses.

Ch. Cali-Col's Alouette, the Ulysses-Missy daughter, was the dam of three champions when bred to Ch. Chaminade Mr. Beau Monde. The best known of these champion offspring in the show ring was the owner-handled Best in Show Ch. Lambo of Loch Vale.

As a producer, the best-known of Missy's children was Ch. Cali-Col's Haley's Comet, the sire of eight champions, four of whom were champion producers.

Missy's offspring in turn produced fifteen champions, proving once again that quality does indeed beget quality.

Photo by Missy.

          Andre de Gascoigne
       Dapper Dan de Gascoigne
         Lady des Frimoussettes
  Rank's Ronnie
         Eddy White de Steren Vor
      Cali-Col's Mynette
            Helly of Milton
        Lyne of Milton
            Hanette of Milton
Ch. Shabob's Nice Girl Missy
            Andre de Gascoigne
         Dapper Dan de Gascoigne
            Lady des Frimoussettes
      Ch. Stardom's Odin Rex, Jr.
            Helly of Milton
        Lyne of Milton
            Hanette of Milton
    Shabob's Sugar Girl
         Lochinvar du Pic-Four
      Jean Rank's Crystal
           Eddy White de Steren Vor
        Cali-Col's Mynette
           Lyne of Milton

CH. TOMAURA'S TOUCH OF ELEGANCE (1978–   )

Owned and bred by Laura Purnell

Ch. Tomaura's Touch of Elegance is the third of our all-time top producing dams with ten champion offspring, seven males and three females. Nine of these ten champions were sired by Ch. Loftiss Reenie and the tenth by Ch. Leander Snow Star, both of whom were top producers also.

An outstanding son was Ch. Tomaura's Moonlite Sonata, who produced eight champions. A daughter, Ch. Devon Puff and Stuff, the top winning Bichon in breed history, is now the dam of a champion litter of four. A son and litter brother to Puff, Ch. Devon Vive Poncho, has been an extremely successful sire of fifteen champions. A second son, Ch. Tomaura's Bear Fax O'Achlyne, has produced well for Achlyne Bichons of Forrest and Barbara MacNab and is the sire of six champions at this writing.

A second son, Ch. Tomaura's Mor Bounce to the Oz, the Snow Star offspring, is the sire of seven champions. He and his half sister, Ch. Tomaura's Symphony of Sumarco, a Reenie daughter and dam of four champions, have been an effective addition to Sumarco Bichons.

Peppe de Barnette
Ch. C & D's Count Kristopher
Quentia of Goldysdale
Ch. C & D's Beau Monde Blizzard
Ch. C & D's Sunbonnet
Ch. Tomaura's Frosty Snowman
Ch. Cali-Col's Haley's Comet
Tomaura's Bundle of Joy
Petite Monique Cherri
Ch. Tomaura's Touch of Elegance
Petit Galant de St. George
Ch. Chanson's Clouds of Mainbrace
Starlette de la Persaliere
Ch. Mainbrace Betsy of Tomaura
Dapper Dan de Gascoigne
Ch. Cali-Col's Robspierre
Lyne of Milton
Chaminade's Fantasia
Chaminade Mazurka

227

CH. NORVIC'S ALPINE SPARKLER

Owned by Anne Freeman; bred by Norman and Alice Vicka

Ch. Norvic's Alpine Sparkler, whelped in 1981, is the most recent of the select group of top producing dams with ten champion offspring. Five of these were by Ch. Ivy Todd Gatlock of Druid, two each by Ch. Parfait Coming Home and Ch. Little Creek Skol of FoxLaur and one by Ch. Jadeles March Freddy.

A son, Ch. Alpine Perfect Impressions, has been a Specialty and multiple Group winner. Two other offspring have scored successes in the Specials ring as well as in the Group ring, as Ch. Alpine's Charmin du Bain and Ch. Alpine's Off N Running already have Group placements.

Alpine Sparkler has proven that her children can be successful in more than one area. Her daughter, Ch. Alpine's Baby Sister, is following in her mother's footsteps. At the time of this writing, she is already the dam of two champions.

Ch. Norvic's Pal Joey
Norvic's Razzle Dazzle
Ch. Norvic's Nice N Easy
Norvic's Dazzle Me
Ch. Rank's Smile Awhile
Norvic's Heres Chrissy
Ch. Norvic's Nice N Easy
Ch. Norvic's Alpine Sparkler
Dapper Dan de Gascoigne
Ch. Cali-Col's Robspierre
Lyne of Milton
Ch. Chaminade Mr. Beau Monde
Dapper Dan de Gascoigne
Ch. Reenroy's Ami du Kilkanny
Little Nell of Cali-Col
Norvic's Sweet Stuff
Ch. Stardom's Odin Rex, Jr.
Reenroy's Riot Act
Reenroy's Ruffles
Ch. Reenroy's Image of Ami
Dapper Dan de Gascoigne
Reenroy's Babette
Nina la Douce of Reenroy

CH. CALI-COL'S SHALIMAR OF REENROY (1969–1980)

Owned and bred by Gertrude Fournier

Ch. Cali-Col's Shalimar of Reenroy is the dam of nine champion off-spring, six males and three females, who in turn produced twenty champions. Four were sired by Ch. Chaminade Mr. Beau Monde, three by Seascape the Captain's Choice and one each by Ch. C and D's Beau Monde Blizzard and Cali-Col's Shadrack.

The Blizzard son, Ch. Cali-Col's Conquistador, was a Specialty and multiple Group winner and the sire of six champions. Ch. Cali-Col's Ulysses was another multiple Group winner and the sire of seven champions. The Ulysses son, Ch. Jandee Argus, was a Best in Show winner. His daughter, Ch. Jalwin Illumine de Noel, produced five champions. A second daughter, Ch. Cali-Col's Alouette, produced three champions, including a Best in Show winner, Ch. Lambo of Loch Vale.

A third son, Ch. Cali-Col's Anchor Man, produced two champions, including Ch. Norvic's Newscaster, sire of five champions.

Andre de Gascoigne
Dapper Dan de Gascoigne
Lady des Frimoussettes
Cali-Col's Only Sam of Reenroy
Helly of Milton
Lyne of Milton
Hanette of Milton
Ch. Cali-Col's Shalimar of Reenroy
Andre de Gascoigne
Dapper Dan de Gascoigne
Lady des Frimoussettes
Cali-Col's Rhapsody of Reenroy
Eddy White de Steren Vor
Cali-Col's Our Daphne
Gipsie de Warnabry

CH. C AND D'S BEAU MONDE MOONSHINE (1974–   )

Owned by Rosmarie Blood; bred by Dolores Wolske

Ch. C and D's Beau Monde Moonshine is one of the now-famous daughters of top producers Mr. Beau Monde and Countess Becky. As the dam of nine champions, six males and three females, she too has joined the ranks of top producers. Six were sired by Ch. Beau Monde the Huckster and three by Ch. Vogelflight's Music Man and they in turn produced eighteen champion children of their own.

The best known of the Moonshine offspring was undoubtedly Ch. Crockerly Beau Monde Eclipse. She was a multiple Best in Show winner, and the National Specialty Winner and number one Bichon in 1980. She in turn produced Ch. Beau Monde the Magic Crystal, the National Sweepstakes winner in 1985.

Ch. Crockerly's Man in the Moon and Ch. Crockerly's Beau Monde Moonglo were both sires of four champions for Primo and Vale Park, while Ch. C and D's Blue Moon of Crockerly was the sire of five for Legacy Bichons.

Andre de Gascoigne
Dapper Dan de Gascoigne
Lady des Frimoussettes
Ch. Cali-Col's Robspierre
Helly of Milton
Lyne of Milton
Hanette of Milton
Ch. Chaminade Mr. Beau Monde
Andre de Gascoigne
Dapper Dan de Gascoigne
Lady des Frimoussettes
Ch. Reenroy's Ami du Kilkanny
Eddy White de Steren Vor
Little Nell of Cali-Col
Nelly of Cali-Col
Ch. C & D's Beau Monde Moonshine
Int. Ch. Jimbo de Steren Vor
Quintal de Warnabry
Int. Ch. Janitzia de Steren Vor
Peppe de Barnette
Int. Ch. Jimbo de Steren Vor
Romance de Bourbiel
Int. Ch. Kitoune de Steren Vor
Ch. C & D's Countess Becky
Izor Prince des Frimoussettes
Ombre de la Roche Posay
Iona II de la Roche Posay
Quentia of Goldysdale
Izor Prince des Frimoussettes
Oree de la Roche Posay
Forne de Dierstein

CH. PARFAIT EBONY AND IVORY (1982–   )

Owned by Joanne and Jane Lageman;
bred by Joanne Spilman and M. F. Grant

The Bichon Frise breed has several father-daughter pairs that have proven to be great producers, as witnessed by numbers of champion offspring and, in turn, the accomplishments of those offspring.

Ch. Parfait Ebony and Ivory was bred by Joanne Spilman and M. F. Grant. Owned by Joanne and Jane Lageman, she carved her niche as the distaff side of a father-daughter team of all-time top producers. She was sired by Ch. Parfait Coming Home, who has produced twenty-one champions, currently making him number eight all-time top sire.

Ebony and Ivory is the dam of nine champions. Her most successful litter was sired by Ch. Pere Jacque Samson d'Parfait, producing four champions. Two subsequent breedings, one to Ch. Pennywise the Challenger and one to Ch. Drewlaine Beau Monde Domino, each produced two champions. A fourth litter, by Ch. Pere Jacque Merry Maker, produced one champion.

L'Havre Joyeux Mr. Majestic
Ch. L'Havre Joyeux Desi
L'Havre Joyeux Tina Tart
Ch. Parfait Coming Home
Ch. Cameo Temptation Chaminade
Parfait Apple Crunch
Joanne's Elke of Chausom
Ch. Parfait Ebony and Ivory
Ch. Cameo Temptation Chaminade
Ch. Parfait Apple Crisp
Joanne's Elke of Chausom
Parfait Candy Apple
Ch. Chaminade Mr. Beau Monde
Ch. Vogelflight's Music Man
Ch. Vogelflight's Diandee Amy Pouf
Cotton R Nell
Hundred Per Cent Cotton

CH. REENROY'S IMAGE OF AMI (1972–1980)

Ch. Reenroy's Image of Ami, dam of nine champions, is the last of our father-daughter top producing combinations. Image of Ami produced well when bred to the half brothers Ch. Teeny Tepee's Cherokee Prince and Ch. Teeny Tepee's Chief of Diandee.

A daughter, Ch. Norvic's Sweet Stuff, produced five champions, including another all-time top producer, Ch. Norvic's Alpine Sparkler, the dam of ten champions.

A second daughter, Ch. Norvic's Nice N Easy, is the dam of Ch. Norvic's Razzle Dazzle, a multiple Best in Show winner and the sire of six champions of his own.

A son, Ch. Norvic's Nebuchadnessar, was the sire of Ch. Diandee Masterpiece, who in turn sired eight champions. A second son, Ch. Norvic's Newscaster, is the sire of five champions. Image of Ami's offspring produced a total of eighteen champions. She became an integral part of the Norvic line.

Andre de Gascoigne
Dapper Dan de Gascoigne
Lady des Frimoussettes
Ch. Stardom's Odin Rex, Jr.
Helly of Milton
Lyne of Milton
Hanette of Milton
Reenroy's Riot Act
Andre de Gascoigne
Dapper Dan de Gascoigne
Lady des Frimoussettes
Reenroy's Ruffles
Rank's Merrilee of Reenroy
Ch. Reenroy's Image of Ami
Andre de Gascoigne
Dapper Dan de Gascoigne
Lady des Frimoussettes
Reenroy's Babette
Mon Ami du Pic Four
Nina la Douce of Reenroy
Keepsake du Pic Four

Ch. Chaminade Syncopation, the first Bichon Frise to win a Best in Show, May 1973, and the top Bichon in 1973 and 1974. Owner: Mrs. William B. Tabler. Handler: Ted Young, Jr.

16

The Winners' Circle

THE ALL-TIME TOP PRODUCERS left their mark and are indeed responsible for the quality that ensued. The real proof of that quality came in the show ring when the Bichon Frise achieved full breed recognition in April of 1973, entered the Non-Sporting Group and began competing on the all-breed level. The following statistics show that the Bichon has succeeded beyond all expectations. Listed are Bests in Show, Group Firsts and the combined totals of second, third and fourth Group placements. Placements on the list are based on the number of dogs defeated.

1973

1. Ch. Chaminade Syncopation: No. 3 Non-Sporting Dog, 4 BIS, 13 Group 1, 13 Group placements. Owner: Mrs. Wm. Tabler.
2. Ch. Cali-Col's Scalawag: 1 BIS, 4 Group 1, 16 Group placements. Owner: Mrs. C. Pillsbury.
3. Ch. C and D's Count Kristopher: 1 Group 1, 12 Group placements. Owners: C. and D. Wolske.
4. Ch. Reenroy's Ritzie Doll: 6 Group placements. Owner: D. Goodwin.
5. Ch. Cali-Col's Ulysses: 4 Group placements. Owners: G. Fournier and M. Gunter.

1974

1. Ch. Chaminade Syncopation: No. 6 Non-Sporting Dog, 2 BIS, 20 Group 1, 28 Group placements. Owner: Mrs. Wm. Tabler.

Ch. C and D's Beau Monde Sunbeam, the first Best in Show Bichon bitch, 1974, owned by Mrs. Jonathan Slocum.

2. Ch. Cali-Col's Scalawag: No. 8 Non-Sporting Dog, 3 BIS, 8 Group 1, 18 Group placements. Owners: M. Dougherty and Estate of Mrs. C. Pillsbury.

3. Ch. C and D's Beau Monde Sunbeam: 4 BIS, 8 Group 1, 23 Group placements. Owner: Mrs. G. Slocum.

4. Ch. Flogan's Clique: 1 BIS, 6 Group 1, 12 Group placements. Owners: G. and M. Houghton and A. Sheimo.

5. Ch. Rank's Eddie: 3 Group 1, 14 Group placements. Owners: Calandra Kennels and R. Koeppel.

1975

1. Ch. Keystone Christine: 3 Group 1, 30 Group placements. Owner: Mrs. G. Slocum.

2. Ch. Chaminade's Syncopation: 8 Group 1, 18 Group placements. Owner: Mrs. Wm. Tabler.

3. Ch. Beau Monde Ee's R Encore: 1 BIS, 7 Group 1, 6 Group placements. Owner: P. Klinkhardt.

4. Ch. Cali-Col's Scalawag: 4 Group 1, 5 Group placements. Owners: C. N. and Estate of Mrs. C. Pillsbury.

5. Ch. Chaminade Tempo: 3 Group 1, 4 Group placements. Owner: Mrs. Wm. Morrow.

1976

1. Ch. C and D's Beau Monde Blizzard. 2 BIS, 11 Group 1, 20 Group placements. Owners: Dr. and Mrs. D. DiNardo and V. Busk.

2. Ch. C and D's Stargazer: 8 Group 1, 35 Group placements. Owner: N. Shapland.

3. Ch. Chaminade Syncopation: 5 Group 1, 18 Group placements. Owner: Mrs. Wm. Tabler.

4. Ch. Chaminade Tempo: 5 Group 1, 14 Group placements. Owners: Mrs. Wm. Morrow and Mrs. Wm. Tabler.

5. Ch. Jadeles the Kid H H Pride: 1 BIS, 9 Group 1, 11 Group placements. Owner: N. Makowiec.

1977

1. Ch. Vogelflight's Music Man: No. 3 Non-Sporting Dog, 3 BIS, 21 Group 1, 54 Group placements. Owners: Mr. and Mrs. B. Busk.

2. Ch. Chaminade Tempo: 9 Group 1, 23 Group placements. Owners: Mrs. Wm. Morrow and Mrs. Wm. Tabler.

3. Ch. Kobold's Kilimanjaro: 5 Group 1, 32 Group placements. Owner: S. Fry.

4. Ch. Paw Paw Knickerbocker: 3 Group 1, 24 Group placements. Owner: R. Koeppel

5. Ch. Jadeles the Kid H H Pride: 3 Group 1, 21 Group placements. Owner: N. Makowiec.

1978

1. Ch. Vogelflight's Music Man: No. 3 Non-Sporting Dog, 3 BIS, 46 Group 1, 35 Group placements. Owners: Mr. and Mrs. B. Busk.
2. Ch. Beau Monde the Iceman: 1 BIS, 14 Group 1, 36 Group placements. Owners: Dr. A. D. and S. M. DiNardo.
3. Ch. Kobold's Kilimanjaro: 11 Group 1, 36 Group placements. Owner: S. Fry.
4. Ch. Beau Monde Regal Rose: 6 Group 1, 17 Group placements. Owner: E. M. Iverson.
5. Ch. Norvic's Easy Does It. 2 Group 1, 19 Group placements. Owners: R. and L. Kendal.

1979

1. Ch. Vogelflight's Choir Master: No. 9 Non-Sporting Dog, 2 BIS, 7 Group 1, 25 Group placements. Owner: E. M. Iverson.
2. Ch. Vogelflight's Music Man: 2 BIS, 10 Group 1, 12 Group placements. Owners: Mr. and Mrs. B. Busk.
3. Ch. Beau Monde the Huckster: 8 Group 1, 28 Group placements. Owner: N. Shapland.
4. Ch. Beau Monde the Iceman: 1 BIS, 4 Group 1, 39 Group placements. Owner: Mrs. C. Porter.
5. Ch. C and D's Blue Moon of Crockerly: 25 Group placements. Owner: D. Siebert.

1980

1. Ch. Crockerly Beau Monde Eclipse: No. 7 Non-Sporting Dog, 1 BIS, 10 Group 1, 42 Group placements. Owner: N. Shapland.
2. Ch. Teakas Erbin Einar: No. 10 Non-Sporting Dog, 2 BIS, 40 Group placements. Owners: J. Boston and L. Payne.
3. Ch. Cameo Temptation Chaminade: 1 BIS, 2 Group 1, 18 Group placements. Owners: J. and C. Denney and Mrs. Wm. Morrow.
4. Ch. Norvic's Razzle Dazzle: 1 BIS, 4 Group 1, 17 Group placements. Owner: Mrs. R. O'Keefe.
5. Ch. Jalwin Just a Jiffy: 1 BIS, 7 Group 1, 21 Group placements. Owners: P. and M. Schultz.
6. Ch. Tres Beau Decor: 8 Group 1, 21 Group placements. Owner: G. Iverson.
7. Ch. Beau Monde the Iceman: 2 Group 1, 23 Group placements. Owner: Mrs. C. Porter.
8. Ch. Rank's Raggedy Andy: 3 Group 1, 16 Group placements. Owners: N. Makowiec and L. Brandman.
9. Ch. Gay Meadows Gage D'Amour: 1 Group 1, 12 Group placements. Owner: D. Moggack.

10. Ch. Lambo of Loch Vale: 1 BIS, 1 Group 1, 7 Group placements. Owner: D. Ayres.

1981

1. Ch. Teakas Erbin Einar: No. 1 Non-Sporting Dog, 11 BIS, 50 Group 1, 18 Group placements. Owners: J. Boston and L. Payne.
2. Ch. Jalwin Just a Jiffy. No. 3 Non-Sporting Dog, 6 BIS, 24 Group 1, 37 Group placements. Owners: P. and M. Schultz.
3. Ch. Norvic's Razzle Dazzle: Number 10 Non-Sporting Dog, 3 BIS, 11 Group 1, 27 Group placements. Owner: R. Koeppel.
4. Ch. Tres Beau Decor: No. 13 Non-Sporting Dog, 2 BIS, 10 Group 1, 26 Group placements. Owner: E. MacNeille.
5. Ch. Rank's Raggedy Andy: 6 Group 1, 16 Group placements. Owners: N. Makowiec and L. Brandman.
6. Ch. Crockerly Beau Monde Eclipse: 3 Group 1, 3 Group placements. Owner: N. Shapland.
7. Ch. D'Shar Rendezvous du Chamour: 1 Group 1, 10 Group placements. Owner: Mrs. Wm. Morrow.
8. Ch. Win-Mar's Little Elf: 2 Group 1, 10 Group placements. Owner: J. Hoglund.
9. Ch. Tennerifes Artful Dodger: 2 Group 1, 12 Group placements. Owner: E. Herman.
10. Ch. Lily Gatlock of Druid: 2 Group 1, 6 Group placements. Owners: B. Keatley and B. Schley.

1982

1. Ch. Teakas Erbin Einar: No. 1 Non-Sporting Dog, 18 BIS, 48 Group 1, 28 Group placements. Owner: J. Boston.
2. Ch. Hillwood Brass Band: No. 9 Non-Sporting Dog, 2 BIS, 11 Group 1, 31 Group placements. Owner: E. MacNeille.
3. Ch. D'Shar's Rendezvous du Chamour: No. 20 Non-Sporting Dog, 4 Group 1, 30 Group placements. Owner: Mrs. Wm. Morrow.
4. Ch. Leander Snow Star: 2 BIS, 6 Group 1, 19 Group placements. Owner: L. Purnell.
5. Ch. Craigdale's Ole Rhondi: 1 BIS, 8 Group 1, 9 Group placements. Owners: L. Morrow and B. Stubbs.
6. Ch. Rank's Raggedy Andy: 2 Group 1, 21 Group placements. Owner: L. Carlton.
7. Ch. Shangrila's Youngblood Hawk: 2 Group 1, 15 Group placements. Owner: B. Baker.
8. Ch. C and D's Xmas Knight: 1 BIS, 2 Group 1, 4 Group placements. Owner: D. Wolske.
9. Ch. Lily Gatlock of Druid: 2 Group 1, 10 Group placements. Owners: B. Keatley and B. Schley.

Number two Bichon of all time, Ch. Teakas Erbin Einar, with thirty-three Bests in Show and 121 Group Firsts; Top Non-Sporting Dog, 1981–82. Breeder: Allen Sheimo. Owner: Judy Boston.

Ch. C and D's Xmas Knight, breeder-owner handled to a Best in Show win by Dolores Wolske, C and D Bichons, 1982.

10. Ch. Jalwin Just a Jiffy: 5 Group 1, 9 Group placements. Owners: P. and M. Schultz.

1983

1. Ch. Craigdale's Ole Rhondi: No. 3 Non-Sporting Dog, 7 BIS, 29 Group 1, 46 Group placements. Owners: L. Morrow and B. Stubbs.
2. Ch. Paw Mark's Talk of the Town: 10 Group 1, 26 Group placements. Owners: P. and M. Schultz.
3. Ch. Hillwood Brass Band: 6 Group 1, 20 Group placements. Owner: E. MacNeille.
4. Ch. Teakas Erbin Einar: 2 BIS, 8 Group 1, 7 Group placements. Owners: J. Boston and L. Payne.
5. Ch. Leander Snow Star: 1 BIS, 7 Group 1, 15 Group placements. Owner: L. Purnell.
6. Ch. Camelot's Brassy Nickel: 2 Group 1, 17 Group placements. Owner: P. Goldman.
7. Ch. Rank's Raggedy Andy: 4 Group 1, 11 Group placements. Owner: L. Carlton.
8. Ch. Shangrila's Youngblood Hawk: 2 Group 1, 8 Group placements. Owner: B. Baker.
9. Ch. Scamper Gatlock of Druid: 8 Group placements. Owners: B. Keatley, L. Fox and B. Schley.
10. Ch. Miri-Cal's All That Jazz: 4 Group placements. Owner: M. Barnhart.

1984

1. Ch. Paw Mark's Talk of the Town: No. 2 Non-Sporting Dog, 9 BIS, 35 Group 1, 52 Group placements. Owner: P. Schultz.
2. Ch. Craigdale's Ole Rhondi: No. 7 Non-Sporting Dog, 22 Group 1, 40 Group placements. Owners: L. Morrow and B. Stubbs.
3. Ch. Camelot's Brassy Nickel: No. 15 Non-Sporting Dog, 2 BIS, 15 Group 1, 29 Group placements. Owner: P. Goldman.
4. Ch. Miri-Cal's All That Jazz: 1 BIS, 9 Group 1, 26 Group placements. Owner: M. Barnhart.
5. Ch. Devon Puff and Stuff: 2 Group 1, 19 Group placements. Owner: N. Shapland.
6. Ch. Diandee Solitare: 2 Group 1, 13 Group placements. Owners: C. Allen and V. and C. Boudreau.
7. Ch. Glen Elfred's Fire Fly: 2 Group 1, 12 Group placements. Owner: E. Grassick.
8. Ch. Bunnyrun the Quarterback: 1 BIS, 3 Group 1, 7 Group placements. Owners: K. and B. James.
9. Ch. Craigdale's Primo: 1 Group 1, 9 Group placements. Owners: F. and J. Cresci.

10. Ch. Scamper Gatlock of Druid: 1 Group 1, 13 Group placements. Owners: B. Keatley. L. Fox and B. Schley.

1985

1. Ch. Devon Puff and Stuff: No. 1 Non-Sporting Dog, 20 BIS, 51 Group 1, 37 Group placements. Owner: N. Shapland.
2. Ch. Camelot's Brassy Nickel: No. 5 Non-Sporting Dog, 6 BIS, 24 Group 1, 34 Group placements. Owner: P. Goldman.
3. Ch. Tres Jolie Mr. Vagabond: No. 10 Non-Sporting Dog, 1 BIS, 14 Group 1, 35 Group placements. Owner: L. Aronberg.
4. Ch. Ivy Todd Gatlock of Druid: 1 BIS, 6 Group 1, 30 Group placements. Owner: A. Freeman.
5. Ch. San Don's Friendly Legacy: 2 Group 1, 20 Group placements. Owners: C. Arnold and S. Orr.
6. Ch. Paw Mark's Talk of the Town: 3 Group 1, 13 Group placements. Owner: P. Schultz.
7. Ch. Miri-Cal's All That Jazz: 6 Group 1, 7 Group placements. Owner: M. Barnhart.
8. Ch. Petit Four Super Trouper: 2 Group 1, 6 Group placements. Owner: J. Hilmer.
9. Ch. Chaminade Le Jazz Hot: 2 Group 1, 6 Group placements. Owners: L. Morrow and P. Tabler.
10. Ch. Craigdale's Ole Rhondi: 2 Group 1, 8 Group placements. Owners: L. Morrow and B. Stubbs.

1986

1. Ch. Devon Puff and Stuff: No. 1 Non-Sporting Dog, 33 BIS, 95 Group 1, 23 Group placements. Owner: N. Shapland.
2. Ch. Tres Jolie Mr. Vagabond: No. 8 Non-Sporting Dog, 1 BIS, 33 Group placements. Owner. L. Aronberg.
3. Ch. Unicorn's Nickolas Nickelbee: 9 Group 1, 25 Group placements. Owner: J. Failla.
4. Ch. San Don's Friendly Legacy: 6 Group 1, 16 Group placements. Owners: C. Arnold and S. Orr.
5. Ch. Ivy Todd Gatlock of Druid: 16 Group placements. Owner: A. Freeman.
6. Ch. J'Con's Peanaw Weanaw: 4 Group 1, 14 Group placements. Owner: P. Ryan.
7. Ch. Petit Four Super Trouper: 1 Group 1, 19 Group placements. Owner: J. Hilmer.
8. Ch. Tuta M's Baby Doll Hazel: 2 Group 1, 10 Group placements. Owners: T. and W. Strawson.
9. Ch. Paw Mark's Triple Threat: 1 Group 1, 8 Group placements. Owners: D. Rentz and P. Schultz.
10. Ch. Paw Mark's September Song: 1 Group 1, 9 Group placements. Owners: B. and P. Lee and P. Schultz.

246

Top Bichon, 1987: Ch. Unicorn Nickolas Nickelbee, son of Brassy Nickel. Breeder and owner: JoAnn Failla, Unicorn Bichons.

Specialty BOB and multiple Group winner Ch. Sandcastle Bikini, bred by Linda Dickens, handled by Deedy Pierce.

BIS Winner Ch. Sumarco Allafee Top Gun. Breeders: Roy Copelin and Cathy Jones. Owner: Mrs. William Tabler.

1987

1. Ch. Unicorn's Nickolas Nickelbee: No. 4 Non-Sporting Dog, 7 BIS, 26 Group 1, 65 Group placements. Owner: J. Failla.

2. Ch. Devon Puff and Stuff: No. 8 Non-Sporting Dog, 7 BIS, 19 Group 1, 10 Group placements. Owner: N. Shapland.

3. Ch. Diamant's Le Magnifique: No. 10 Non-Sporting Dog, 2 BIS, 25 Group 1, 28 Group placements. Owner. J. Cohen.

4. Ch. Tres Jolie Mr. Vagabond: No. 10 Non-Sporting Dog, 1 BIS, 6 Group 1, 12 Group placements. Owner: L. Aronberg.

5. Ch. Ivy Todd Gatlock of Druid: 2 BIS, 7 Group 1, 18 Group placements. Owner: A. Freeman.

6. Ch. Alpenglow Ashley du Chamour: 2 BIS, 12 Group 1, 14 Group placements. Owners: L. Morrow and J. McClaran.

7. Ch. San Don's Friendly Legacy: 2 Group 1, 32 Group placements. Owners: C. Arnold and S. Orr.

8. Ch. Bella's Mega Force: 5 Group 1, 9 Group placements. Owners: A. and L. Fitch.

9. Ch. Cullford's My One and Only: 1 Group 1, 9 Group placements. Owners: J. Cullen, L. Ford and E. MacNeille.

10. Ch. Paw Mark's September Song: 2 Group 1, 6 Group placements. Owners: B. and P. Lee and P. Schultz.

All-time top winning Bichon Frise, Ch. Devon Puff and Stuff, with sixty Bests in Show and 165 Group firsts. Best of Breed at two consecutive BFCA Nationals, 1985 and 1986. Owned and bred by Nancy Shapland, handled by Michael Kemp.

17

The Specialty Show

T HERE IS SOMETHING UNIQUE about Bichon Frise Specialty shows. A group of long-time breeders, many who have been active since the late 1960s and early 1970s, have discussed this subject and they have decided that the emphasis placed on the Specialty show by the Bichon Frise Club of America, Inc., and subsequent local clubs was a result of the initial struggle for breed recognition.

The early breeders and owners resented the fact that the Bichon Frise was not being taken seriously. There was a need to prove themselves as professional, competent, knowledgeable and quite ready to take their place as discerning members of the dog Fancy.

Continued efforts to improve the in-depth quality of the breed and its presentation were obvious priorities. But there was also a need to work together on something immediate and visible. It started with small "fun matches" around the country and grew to the Las Vegas spectacular of 1973. From that point on there was an ambiance, a distinctive mood, that became associated with the Bichon Frise National Specialty and made it that singular, not-to-be-missed annual "happening." At the same time, the events themselves drew the attention of the Fancy for their originality, attention to detail and efficient operation. The point had been made.

The American Kennel Club defines the Specialty show as "a show given by a club or association formed for the improvement of any one breed of pure-bred dogs, at which championship points may be awarded to said breed." From this succinct definition emerged the Annual National Specialty Events, four days of Bichon activities followed by all-breed shows on Saturday and Sunday, a schedule that is not for the faint of heart.

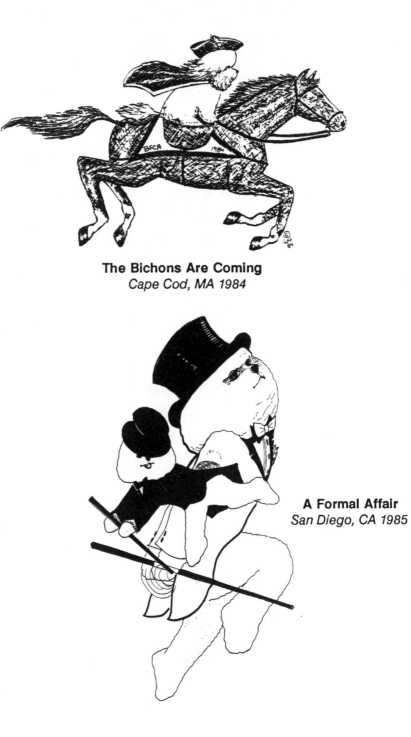

The Bichons Are Coming
Cape Cod, MA 1984

A Formal Affair
San Diego, CA 1985

Heart of America
Kansas City, KS 1986

Seattle,WA 1987

Bichons and You – Perfect Together
Allentown, PA 1988

Recent years has our Bichon enthusiast arriving in time for a Tuesday evening hospitality event arranged by the hosting club, usually involving sightseeing within the area. Wednesday morning brings a seminar with guest speakers and of course subject matter directly relating to the breed. The afternoon holds the annual meeting for members of the national parent club and Wednesday evening is on-site hospitality offered by the hosting club, which presents a special opportunity to see old friends and make new ones.

On Thursday morning the judging begins with the Breeders' Competition. In this event an individual offers a trio of dogs for judging of which she or he is the breeder of record. Three judges (usually a breeder, a handler and perhaps an AKC judge) individually evaluate each trio by means of a point system. The breeder whose trio earns the highest number of points wins the competition and a trip to the following Kennel Review Tournament of Champions, where the winning trio will compete in the Breeders' Competition on that stellar occasion.

The Breeders' Competition is a relatively new event at BFCA Specialties and was offered for the first time in 1986. Five noted Bichon breeders and fanciers were silent benefactors who subsidized the expenses of the winners for the first three years, after which time the parent club assumed that responsibility. Only a small number of breed clubs offer this opportunity for their breeders to "make a statement," and it presents fascinating competition.

The final event of the morning is the Obedience competition, which is a pleasure to watch and always well received.

The afternoon brings the Sweepstakes Judging of puppies over six and under twelve months. This event is not a point competition and has been traditionally judged by breeders. During the first three years of licensed Specialty shows—1978, 1977 and 1978—there was initial reluctance to invite Bichon breeders to judge, so AKC judges were asked: Frank Sabella, Dr. Samuel Draper and Ann Stevenson. It is interesting to note that all three of these individuals were invited back at later dates to judge the Specialty Conformation Classes, with Mr. Sabella appearing twice, 1979 and 1987.

Ten of the past eleven years have seen breeder-judges for Sweepstakes: Richard Beauchamp, Mary Vogel, Clover Allen, Judy Anderson, Gertrude Fournier, Ann Hearn, Rolande Lloyd, Lois Morrow, Barbara Stubbs and Sandra Orr. The breeder-judge is a popular precedent that will certainly continue.

The first day of judging is capped by the Thursday night awards banquet, where the top breeders, owners, handlers and dogs are honored for their successes during the previous year. This is also the occasion of the annual auction, presided over by the irrepressible Stella Raabe, one of the earliest Bichon breeders and the quintessential auctioneer.

Friday begins with Junior Showmanship competition and then the main event! The conformation classes are always exciting and suspenseful, and they continue to be the best vehicle possible for seeing the top Bichons in the country in optimum conditions and at their best, while often witnessing the debut of outstanding winners and producers of the future. Whether sitting at

1980 BFCA winner, Ch. Crockerly Beau Monde Eclipse, bred by Rosmarie Blood, owned by Nancy Shapland, Devon Bichons. Handler, Joe Waterman.

Winner of the 1978 BFCA National Specialty, Ch. Beau Monde the Iceman, bred by R. G. Beauchamp and P. Craige; owned by Dr. A. Di-Nardo.

A historic grouping from the first BFCA National Specialty, 1976. *Left to right*: Veteran Dog Ch. Cali-Col's Robspierre; his son, Stud Dog winner Ch. Chaminade Mr. Beau Monde; his grandson and BOB winner, Ch. Vogelflight's Music Man; and his granddaughter and Winners Bitch, Ch. C and D's Beau Monde Moonshine. *Photo by Missy.*

255

Michelle Konic, Best Junior Handler, 1984 BFCA National Specialty. Michelle was BFCA's Top Junior in 1984, 1985 and 1987.

Julie DeGregorio, BFCA's Top Junior Handler for 1986.

Sacha Farnsworth, Best Junior Handler at BFCA National Specialty for 1986, 1987, 1988 and 1989.

Photo by Missy.

Bruce Stubbs, of Chaminade, showing Ch. Reenroy's Ami du Kilkanny, 1972, foundation bitch for Chaminade.

Photo by Missy.

Teena Sarkissian (Runyon), of Sarkis, showing Ch. Chaminade Phoenicia, 1971, foundation bitch for Sarkis Bichons.

Photo by Missy.

Wendy Kellerman, of Windstar, showing Ch. Beau Monde Works D'Arte Witty, foundation bitch for Windstar. Wendy won third place at the Westminster KC finals, 1975.

257

ringside or wandering through the grooming areas, watching, talking, questioning, this can offer a day of education and learning that is difficult to surpass. It matters not if you are a novice just beginning or a seasoned breeder ever adding to the store, the Specialty experience is indeed unique.

A final dinner event and the good-byes begin. New friends, old friends, good memories and for the long-time breeder the quiet satisfaction of another year of achievement for the Bichon Frise.

While the Sweepstakes and conformation classes are highlights of any Specialty week, Obedience and Junior Showmanship classes are given their well deserved recognition.

OBEDIENCE AND AGILITY COMPETITION

Many of the outstanding Obedience dogs and their exhibitors have been covered in more detail in the chapter on Performance Events. There have been fine representatives of the breed competing on the all-breed level, and it is especially enjoyable to watch Obedience work at the Specialty shows. Additional excitement will enter the scene when Agility exhibitions become more frequent, for the Bichon is proving to be extremely adept at Agility work, and this is a breed that thoroughly enjoys the process. Agility workshops are becoming increasingly popular around the United States, and while the American Kennel Club has not yet added Agility to the list of approved competition classes, Bichon owners should certainly investigate Agility at the exhibition level or merely from the standpoint of basic pleasure and enjoyment for you and your dog.

JUNIOR SHOWMANSHIP

Youngsters have been involved in Junior Showmanship since the early days of recognition. This competition is judged solely on the ability and talent of the juniors as they handle their dogs in the breed ring. The quality of the dog is not to be considered, only the skill of the handler. The first highly successful junior was Wendy Kellerman of New York, who qualified for Junior Showmanship at Westminster Kennel Club in 1976 and earned a third place in that top competition. She was the Bichons' Top Junior for three years and has subsequently became a successful professional handler.

The first Bichon Frise Club of America licensed Specialty show was held in 1976. Junior Showmanship was included at this and every Specialty thereafter with the exception of 1983, when there were no entries. The first winner was Suzi Crane (California), winning in San Diego. In 1977 another Californian, Camille Jacobs, won in Maryland. In San Francisco in 1978, Suzi Crane won her second title.

Tracy Hilmer (Pennsylvania) won the 1979 show in New York, which was not a surprise, as Tracy was the Bichon Frise Club of America Top Junior for the year. San Diego, 1980, was won by Lisa Jones (Pennsylvania), who was the BFCA Top Junior for that year and the second junior to qualify for Westminster. John Nekic won at the Michigan Specialty in 1981. Atlanta hosted the show in 1982 which was won by Ruthellen Viall (New York). Michelle Konic (New York) won in Boston in 1984 and went on to be BFCA's Top Junior for 1984, 1985 and 1987. Michelle also qualified in two different years for the Westminster show. The 1985 Specialty in San Diego was won by Kim Kaufman of Canada, who also showed the Winners Bitch that day. The awards for 1986 (Kansas City), 1987 (Seattle), 1988 (Allentown, Pennsylvania) and 1989 (Houston) were all won by Sacha Farnsworth (South Carolina), quite a record for that young lady. Julie DeGregorio (Connecticut) was the BFCA Top Junior in the interim year of 1986, and Jennifer Fox (Illinois) took the honors in 1988.

Michelle Konic, who still shows in the breed ring but no longer in Junior Showmanship, says she thoroughly enjoyed her years as a Junior Handler and would recommend it to youngsters involved in dogs who are willing to put forth the necessary time and effort.

Aside from the fact that handling gave her self-confidence and increased her ability to deal with people and situations, Michelle has found some benefits from her junior handling that she had not anticipated. Recently she made both job and college applications and listed the Junior Showmanship as an outside project. She says the response to this has been amazing, as everyone has asked for details and wants to know more about the activity. Their interest has proven to be an unexpected dividend in a competitive arena.

The annual National Specialty events continue to offer a broad spectrum of activity for the Bichon owner. For the novice or the individual considering involvement in the breed, it is highly recommended. These shows continue in geographical rotation around the United States and are normally held in May. The exact date and location may be obtained from the American Kennel Club or the corresponding secretary of the Bichon Frise Club of America. The latter can see that you are placed on the mailing list for information regarding upcoming shows.

Remember also that local Bichon Frise clubs also hold Specialty shows. While the local club activities are not on such a large scale, their Specialties are highly endorsed for any Bichon fancier. The BFCA corresponding secretary also has the information regarding these dates and events.

The Bichon Frise Specialty show . . . an exceptional event. Don't miss it.

National Specialty Winners

1976

BOB: Ch. Vogelflight's Music Man. Breeder: M. Vogel. Owner: V. Busk

BOS: Ch. Cali-Col's Villanelle. Breeder: R. Warman. Owner: A. G. Mills.

BW: C and D's Beau Monde Moonshine. Breeder: C. and D. Wolske. Owner: R. Blood.

WD: Tres Beau Barbon. Breeder: T. Keator. Owner: L. Keator.

Highest Scoring Dog in Regular Classes: Ch. Cali-Col's Scalawag. Score: 194. Owners: C. N. and Estate of Mrs. C. Pillsbury.

1977

BOB: Ch. Vogelflight's Music Man. Breeder: M. Vogel. Owner: V. Busk.

BOS: Ch. Sandra de la Lande de Belleville, U.D. Breeder: M. Darolt. Owner: H. Temmel.

BW: Sundance of Keystone. Breeder: H. Kehoe. Owner: S. Palmer.

WD: Petit Four Sparkle Plenty. Breeder-owner: J. Hilmer.

Highest Scoring Dog in Regular Classes: Ch. Sandra de la Lande de Belleville, U.D., Bda. C.D. Breeder: M. Darlot. Owner: H. Temmel.

1978

BOB: Ch.Vogelflight's Music Man. Breeder: M. Vogel. Owner: V. and B. Busk.

BOS: Ch. Braymar's Pavanne du Chaminade. Breeder: M. and R. Rothman. Owner: N. and D. Morgan.

BW: Bluedover Daylean's Tinka. Breeder: T. and J. Heffner. Owner: L. and M. Daye.

WB: Drewlaine's Eau de Love. Breeder-owner: R. Beauchamp and Mr. and Mrs. A. G. Mills.

Highest Scoring Dog in Regular Classes: Cali-Col's Monsieur Gendarme. Breeder: G. Fournier. Owner: M. and L. Lunde. Score: 194½.

1979

BOB: Ch. Beau Monde the Iceman. Breeder: R. Beauchamp and P. Craige. Owner: Mrs. C. Porter.

BOS: Ch. Braymar's Pavanne du Chaminade. Breeder: R. and M. Rothman. Owner: N. and D. Morgan.

BW: Knightcap's Brazen Raisin. Breeder: J. Demko and C. Jacobsen. Owner: J. Periotti.

1981 National Specialty Winner, Ch. Rank's Raggedy Andy, bred by Jean Rank and Judy Thayer, owned by Laurie Carlton, Belle Creek Kennels.

Photo by Martin Booth.

1982 BFCA BOB, Ch. Jalwin Just a Jiffy, bred by Ann Hearn, owned by Pauline Schultz.

261

WD: Captiva Ole King Cole. Breeder: Mr. and Mrs. C. W. Cole. Owner: S. Fedder.

Highest Scoring Dog in Regular Classes: Ch. Jindra the Country Fiddler. Breeder-owner: V. Nekic.

1980

BOB: Ch. Crockerly Beau Monde Eclipse. Breeder: R. and J. Blood. Owner: N. Shapland.

BOS: Ch. Lambo of Loch Vale. Breeder: D. Ayres. Owner: J. and D. Ayres.

BW: Keleb Paper Doll. Breeder: K. and L. Bronec. Owner: J. Fausset.

WD: Larkshire the Glow Worm. Breeder: N. and D. Morgan. Owner: J. Wilt and L. Morrow.

Highest Scoring Dog in Regular Classes: Ch. Primo's Prima Tana, C.D.X. Breeder: L. Keator and E. Nief. Owner: F. and J. Cresci.

1981

BOB: Ch. Rank's Raggedy Andy. Breeders: J. Rank and J. Thayer. Owner: N. Makowiec.

BOS: Ch. Crockerly Beau Monde Eclipse. Breeders: R. and J. Blood. Owner: N. Shapland.

BW: Devon How Sweet It Is. Breeder-owner: N. Shapland.

WD: Parfait Coming Home. Breeder: D. Lloyd. Owner: J. Lao.

Highest Scoring Dog in Regular Classes: Ch. Westwynd's Legacy de Lucie, C.D.X. Breeder: M. Westcott. Owner: D. Greening. Score: 197.

1982

BOB: Ch. Jalwin Just a Jiffy. Breeder: A. Hearn. Owners: M. and P. Schultz.

BOS: Ch. Lily Gatlock of Druid. Breeder-owner: B. Keatley and B. Schley.

BW: Craigdale's Ole Rhondi. Breeder: D. Hunter. Owner: L. Morrow and B. Stubbs.

WB: Sarkis T. C's White Magic. Breeder-owners: T. Runyon and M. Sarkissian.

Highest Scoring Dog in Regular Classes: Ch. Sabran Parader. Breeder: Y. Cox. Owner: M. Prestridge.

1983

BOB: Ch. Hillwood Brass Band. Breeder: E. Iverson. Owner: E. MacNeille.

BOS: Ch. Braymar's Pavanne du Chaminade. Breeders: R. and M. Rothman. Owners: N. and D. Morgan.

BIS Ch. Tres Beau Decor, bred by Thomas Keator, owned by Ellen MacNeille. A 1981 National Specialty winner himself and sire of the 1983 BFCA winner.

Ashbey Photography.

1983 BFCA National Specialty winner, Ch. Hillwood Brass Band, son of Tres Beau Decor. Breeder and owner: Ellen MacNeille.

Photo by Klein.

1984 BFCA National Specialty winner, Ch. Camelot's Brassy Nickel, son of Brass Band. Breeder and owner: Pam Goldman.

Ashbey Photography.

263

BW: Devon Puff and Stuff. Breeder-owner: N. Shapland.

WD: Sumarco's Crown of Cromwell. Breeder: S. Miller. Owners: J. Jones, R. Copelin and S. Miller.

Highest Scoring Dog in Regular Classes: Cotton Candy's Bit O'Honey. Breeder: P. Gibson. Owner: R. Roper.

1984

BOB: Ch. Camelot's Brassy Nickel. Breeder-owner: P. Goldman.

BOS: Ch. Paw Mark's Pebbles of Brereton. Breeder-owners: P. Schultz and M. Britton.

BW: Jalwin Just a Dandy. Breeder: A. Hearn. Owners: S. and D. Marrett and A. Hearn.

WB: Tiara's Kandi Girl. Breeder-owner: M. Rubino.

Highest Scoring Dog in Regular Classes: Snow Chien de Neige. Breeder: R. Moffat. Owners: C. and C. Grosbeck.

1985

BOB: Ch. Devon Puff and Stuff. Breeder-owner: N. Shapland.

BOS: Ch. Petit Four Super Trouper. Breeder-owner: J. Hilmer.

BW: Vale Park Perce Neige. Breeder: H. Murphy. Owner: G. Phillips.

WD: Mathers Maximillion. Breeder: S. Miller. Owner: V. Mather.

1986

BOB: Ch. Devon Puff and Stuff. Breeder-owner, N. Shapland.

BOS: Ch. Paw Mark's Talk of the Town. Breeders: P. Schultz and L. Keator. Owner: P. Schultz.

BW: Sumarco Alafee Jazz du Las. Breeders: L. Schuster and C. Jones. Owners: M. and T. Glynn and R. Copelin.

WB: Diamant's Lalique. Breeders: K. Hughes and S. Ezzard. Owner: K. Hughes.

Highest Scoring Dog in Regular Classes: Ch. Cavell Bonaire of Karlane. Breeder: C. Turznik. Owner: K. Schroeder and E. Schroeder.

1987

BOB: Ch. Alpenglow Ashley du Chamour. Breeder: B. Stubbs and L. Day. Owner: J. McClaran.

BOS: Ch. Paw Mark's Lollipop La Bow. Breeder: P, and M. Schultz. Owner: L. and R. Wilson.

BW: Paw Mark's Jet Parade Ex-cel. Breeders: P. Schultz and D. Rentz. Owners: P. Schultz and J. Bryan.

WB: Jalwin Just So. Breeder-owner: A. Hearn.

Highest Scoring Dog in Regular Classes: Somerville's Ruff N'Tuff Stuff. Breeder-owner: J. Somerville.

Ch. Parfait Hellsapoppin of Druid, winner of the 1988 BFCA National Specialty, owned by J. Spilman, B. Keatly, T. Lao and L. Kilduff.

Photo by Missy.

Am., Mex. and Int. Ch. Chaminade Le Blanc Chamour, winner of the 1989 BFCA National Specialty and multiple all-breed Best in Show winner. Owned by Lois Morrow and Carolyn and Richard Vida. Bred by L. Morrow, G. and H. Harrell and B. Stubbs.

Photo by Missy.

265

1988

BOB: Ch. Parfait Hellsapoppin of Druid. Breeder: J. Spilman. Owner: J. Spilman, L. Kilduff, T. Lao and B. Keatley.

BOS: Ch. Westoaks Wizard of Paws. Breeder: S. and J. Witt. Owner: S. and P. Barron.

BW: Gabriel de Lynn. Breeder: W. Phillips. Owner: V. Kandes.

WB: Lady Ashley of Windstar. Breeder: E. Kellerman. Owner: W. and E. Kellerman.

Highest Scoring Dog in Regular Classes: Ch. Beauchien TNT of Dovecoat. Breeder-owner: L. De Gregorio.

1989

BOB: Ch. Chaminade Le Blanc Chamour. Breeders: L. Morrow, B. Stubbs, G. and H. Harrell. Owner: L. Morrow and C. & R. Vida.

BOS: Ch. Chamour Sable du Chaminade. Breeder: L. Morrow, B. Stubbs, G. and N. Harrell, Owner: D. Mason and L. Morrow.

BW: Bunnyrun the High Priestess. Breeders: K. and B. James. Owners: K. and B. James and B. Ribble.

WD: Bichon Haven's Cassanova. Breeders: A. Baldwin and E. Comley. Owner: A. Baldwin.

Highest Scoring Dog in Regular Classes: Sally B's It's About Time. Breeder: S. Alsip. Owner: D. and S. Boyle.

266

18

Bichon Frise
Clubs Across
the United States

THE DEVELOPMENT AND PROGRESS of the Bichon
Frise in the United States has been closely linked to the organization and
activity of the parent club, the Bichon Frise Club of America, Inc., and local
Bichon clubs that were subsequently established in various sections of the
country. The caliber of these organizations and the events they sponsored
decisively affected the conception of the breed as held by the public in general
and the dog fancier in particular.

BICHON FRISE CLUB OF AMERICA

A loosely organized club had been formed in Milwaukee under the
direction of Azalea Gascoigne, but it was the historic meeting in San Diego,
California, with the premier breeders—Gertrude Fournier, Azalea Gascoigne,
Mayree Butler and Goldy Olsen—in attendance that launched the Bichon
Frise Club of America as the official organizational body for the breed, and
the club has functioned solidly in this capacity, without interruption, to this
day.

Mrs. Gascoigne was the first BFCA president and Mrs. Fournier the first registrar, a position she held until 1967, when Mrs. Butler took over those responsibilities. The American Kennel Club had made it clear that one of the major prerequisites for the consideration of breed recognition was the maintaining of complete and accurate Stud Book records, and it is a credit to these women that this work was achieved in such competent fashion. The record-keeping was considerable as indicated by the following statistics.

	Litters	*Individual Dogs*
October 1967	151	414
October 1968	245	646
November 1969	380	985
September 1970	506	1301
November 1971	811	1917

LOCAL CLUBS

The local club structure began with the Bichon Frise Club of San Diego, which was officially organized in June of 1964 with a charter membership of fourteen. Mayree Butler was the first president and Mrs. Fournier was, of course, a charter member. Barbara Stubbs joined in 1967 and Eva and Erwin Schroeder in early 1968. All five are still members of the active Bichon Frise Club of San Diego.

In the latter part of the 1960s, interest in the breed increased, but before the American Kennel Club would even begin to consider recognition for the breed, it was clear that additional local organizations were needed to first indicate a broad geographic interest in the Bichon.

In November 1968 the Mid-Atlantic Bichon Frise Club was formed, with Martin and Roberta Rothman as organizers and Mr. Rothman as the first president. In the interest of centralizing the point of operation, the name was later changed to the Greater New York Bichon Frise Club, a name it retains today. Robert Koeppel and Helen Temmel were early supporters, and Mr. Koeppel continues as president as of this writing.

In July 1969 a meeting was held at the home of Melvin and Marvel Brown in Benton Harbor, Michigan, to bring together Bichon owners of the Midwest. Thirty-five individuals came from the states of Minnesota, Michigan, Wisconsin, Ohio, Indiana, Illinois and Missouri. Mayree Butler and Barbara Stubbs attended as officers of both the national Parent Club and a local club to encourage the group in their goal to share information and constructively further breed interests in this area. The Mid-States Bichon Frise Club was formed, with Marvel Brown as the first president.

As the Bichon population grew in the Midwest, there were soon sufficient numbers of enthusiasts to sustain individual local clubs in concurrence with American Kennel Club policies. Thus, after two and a half years of serving this multistate area, the Mid-State Bichon Frise Club ceased to exist and became separate organizations: the Buckeye Bichon Frise Club (later to become the Western Reserve Bichon Frise Club), serving Ohio with Elizabeth Shehab as organizer and first president; and the Chicagoland Bichon Frise Club, with Virginia Haley as first president. Later the Greater St. Louis Bichon Frise Club was established, with Mrs. Haley at the helm, leaving the Chicagoland group in the capable hands of Dolores and Charles Wolske.

1970 saw the formation of another eastern club, with the advent of the Bichon Frise Club of New England (later the Bichon Frise Club of Southern New England), with Evelyn Farrar as organizer and first president. Doris Hyde was an early supporter, as were Rolande and Donald Lloyd, D.V.M., who maintained the interest and activity in this area through the years.

Two clubs were organized in Virginia during 1971, L'Enfant Bichon Frise Club (later the National Capitol Bichon Frise Club), under the leadership of Stella Raabe, and the Virginia Bichon Frise Club, with Vicki Stowell as organizer and first president.

Two more groups organized in the winter of 1972: the New Jersey Bichon Frise club (Jerome Podell and Mr. and Mrs. Herbert Rothman as founders) and the Bichon Frise Club of Dixie, with Claude and Wynne Hinds and Ann Hearn at the reins.

The mid 1970s saw the advent of the Bichon Frise Club of Dallas (Lee and Sherry Fry, organizers) and the Bichon Frise Club of Northern California, with Norma and Dale Morgan, Leola and Clarke Hoagland and Reneta and Peter Dietz organizing.

The American Kennel Club had a number of requirements to be met before a breed could be considered for recognition. Of utmost importance was maintaining the Stud Book, as mentioned earlier. Also high on the list was the formation of the local Specialty clubs, which would educate and unite Bichon owners in a specific geographical area. The holding of match shows as an ongoing activity was imperative in order to prove the continuity of these groups and to indicate a sustained interest in the breed.

The first recorded Bichon match was held in San Diego in, amazingly enough, July 1961. Even at that early date Gertrude Fournier realized that such match activity would become important. Matches were held in 1962, 1963 and 1964, and from 1965 until 1972 two matches per year were offered in the San Diego area. The Greater New York Club and Mid-States began match-show activity in their local areas immediately after organization. In 1970 these three groups, representing the East Coast, the Midwest and the West Coast, united to host a National Specialty match that was held in Anaheim, California, a significant effort that drew media attention from national dog publications. The other local clubs did their part and held match shows whenever feasible, in addition to participating in the Rare Breed events that had become increasingly popular during this period.

This concerted effort was yet another factor in the rapid acceptance of the Bichon into the Miscellaneous Class, which took place in 1971, and the full breed recognition that followed in April of 1973. Until the advent of the Bichon Frise, no breed had spent so short a period in the Miscellaneous Class.

Without question, it was the intense efforts of the early breeders and national officers and directors, plus the concentrated activities of these first local organizations, that brought the Bichon Frise to the fore. The support and involvement of Richard Beauchamp and his all-breed publication, *Kennel Review,* offered the forum from which serious consideration of the breed evolved. We then had the catalyst that brought it together and made it all work. The Bichon Frise became a recognized breed.

Another standout event in Bichon history was the first Sanction B match held by the Bichon Frise Club of America and hosted by the Bichon Frise Club of San Diego. It was held on April 7, 1973, the first weekend of AKC point competition for the Bichon Frise. The Flamingo Hotel in Las Vegas was the place, Tom Stevenson was the judge and one hundred and eleven Bichons were the participants. An unbelievable array of nationally renowned professional handlers showed the dogs to an audience that included licensed judges and notables of the dog world. It was an extraordinary show—an event still discussed by those lucky enough to have attended. The "Classic Spectacular" became the norm, and through the years Bichon events have earned the reputation of never offering less than the unique and extraordinary in their presentation.

From 1964 through 1969 the Annual National Match was held in San Diego. In 1970 a policy of rotation began, initiated by the parent club; thus from 1970 through 1975 shows were held in Anaheim, New York, Chicago, Las Vegas, Atlanta (GA) and Manassas, Virginia.

Following the required sanctioned events, the American Kennel Club granted a licensed point show to the Bichon Frise Club of America, Inc., in May of 1976, in San Diego. Since that time local clubs have annually hosted the National Specialty week of activities, and 1977 through 1988 have seen these festivities in Silver Springs, Maryland; San Francisco; New York; Troy, Michigan; Boston; Kansas City, Missouri; Seattle; Allentown, Pennsylvania; and Houston. San Diego hosted the fifth and tenth shows in 1980 and 1985 and will host the fifteenth in 1990.

Several of the original local organizations are still hardy and active. A few had periods of inactivity but resurfaced with renewed energy. Totally new clubs have emerged that have proven to be highly successful.

The Bichon Frise Club of Greater Houston was organized in 1985 under the capable direction of Nancy McDonald as president. This is a large group of dedicated and active individuals, who from the beginning have offered activities of consistent quality that have well served Bichon owners in this area.

Dallas Bichon owners joined the Houston group, as their original club had become inactive. However, in time interest in the Bichon grew, and it was obvious that the Dallas–Fort Worth area once again needed a club of its own. Official organization took place in 1987, with Barbara Slattum as president. This group offers the same enthusiasm and quality events as their sister club in Houston.

The Bichon Frise Club of Puget Sound began as the Bichon Frise Club of the Pacific Northwest. It was originally organized by Betty Schuck and

Ginger LeCave in Oregon while serving the entire Northwest area. As time passed, the membership became more concentrated in the Seattle area—hence the name change and the centralizing of activity in accordance with AKC policy. Charles and Sherry Watts and Linda and Berne Thorpe head this group.

Local clubs of record at this time are:

Bichon Frise Club of Dallas
Bichon Frise Club of Greater Houston, Inc.
Bichon Frise Club of Greater Los Angeles
Bichon Frise Club of Northern California, Inc.*
Bichon Frise Club of Northern New Jersey, Inc.
Bichon Frise Club of Puget Sound
Bichon Frise Club of San Diego, Inc.*
Bichon Frise Club of Southern New England, Inc.*
Chicagoland Bichon Frise Club, Inc.*
Greater New York Bichon Frise Club, Inc.
Greater St. Louis Bichon Frise Club, Inc.*
Southeastern Michigan Bichon Frise Club, Inc.

The addresses of local club secretaries and the corresponding secretary of the Bichon Frise Club of America, Inc., are available through the American Kennel Club, 51 Madison Avenue, New York, NY 10010.

*Clubs licensed by the American Kennel Club to hold independent Specialty shows.

Best-selling novelist Barbara Taylor Bradford with her husband, Robert Bradford, a movie and television producer, and their Bichon Frise, Gemmy, age eight years. Gemmy's full name is Ardez Gemeaux de Bradford. *Photo by Cris Alexander.*

19

Celebrities and
Their Bichons

In 1970 ACTRESS BETTY WHITE hosted a weekly television program called *Pet Set*, which was produced by her husband, Allen Ludden. Betty's known love of animals came to the fore, and she obviously enjoyed these half-hour sessions with everything from the mundane to the exotic.

A December show featured dogs all the color of snow, in keeping with the season, plus special guest star actress Eve Arden. Betty had heard of "a new breed," the Bichon Frise, and they were to be highlighted. Thus it was that the author, her son Bruce and seven Bichons from Chaminade made the trip to the Hollywood TV studios.

The television show was Betty White's initial introduction to the Bichon Frise. Her second experience was in Las Vegas in April of 1973, when she attended the Bichon Frise Club of America's first American Kennel Club Sanctioned Match and presented the trophy to the Best of Breed winner, Cali-Col's Scalawag, who of course later became a champion. Her third Bichon encounter brought her to the Johnny Carson Show with Ch. Chaminade Mr. Beau Monde as part of a group of rare or unusual dogs. Years later she acquired her own Bichon Frise, and it was no surprise to learn it was a "rescue" Bichon.

Betty White's long-standing involvement in animal affairs is well known. Medical research, animal protection—all have profited through the years by her efforts. In 1988 she was the recipient of the James Herriot

Candy Spelling (*right*) with her daughter and her Bichon, Shelley.

Television taping of the *Pet Set* program, December 1970. Eve Arden (*left*) and Betty White; asleep in the foreground, Ch. Chaminade Mr. Beau Monde.

Mrs. Sidney (Claire) Pollock with Phillip.

John Forsyth with his wife, Julie, and their Bichon, appropriately named Charlie's Little Angel.

Award, sponsored by the Humane Society of the United States, for promoting and inspiring public concern for animals.

There was always a special feeling for our breed, and somehow the "Golden Girl" and the Bichon Frise seem to be a happy combination.

There are other well-known personalities who have joined the ranks of Bichon owners. Candy Spelling, wife of Aaron Spelling, the highly successful television producer, acquired her Shelley from the Reenroy Bichons of Mayree Butler and has become a true fan of the breed.

Actor John Forsythe and his wife, Julie, named their Bichon Charlie's Little Angel from Mr. Forsythe's TV series, where as Charlie he was heard but never seen. Angel was another Bichon from Reenroy.

Claire Pollock, wife of actor-producer Sidney Pollock, is yet another fan of the Bichon Frise. Phillip, from the Beaujolais Bichons of Marci Harvey, is a relatively new member of the Pollock household.

On the East Coast there can be no bigger devotee of the Bichon Frise than Barbara Taylor Bradford, noted author of the best-selling book *A Woman of Substance.* Born in England, she has lived in the United States for the past twenty-five years. She had previously written nonfiction, but since *A Woman of Substance,* published in eighteen countries, she has devoted herself to fiction.

Ms. Bradford acquired her Bichon, Gemmy, eight years ago from the Ardezz Kennels of Stephanie Ezzard and has been totally enamored of the breed ever since. Two Bichons, Lutzi and Tutzi, appear in her second novel, *Voice of the Heart,* along with a discussion of the origin of the breed, to our knowledge the only time the Bichon has been recognized in fiction. This lovely lady's devotion to Gemmy brought her from London to New York on the Concorde with only purse in hand, to be there for her little friend in a medical emergency—a Bichon owner par excellence.

Suggested Reading
and Viewing

THE FOLLOWING LISTS are a composite of recommen-
dations made by Bichon Frise owners of long standing. Admittedly some of
these books are geared more for the serious breeder and exhibitor, however
many are of a more general nature and would be a fine addition to the library
of any Bichon owner. Some relate specifically to the Bichon Frise. Others
pertain to all breeds but have been found particularly helpful and valuable by
these Bichon owners.

TITLES RELATING TO THE BICHON FRISE

The Bichon Frise Reporter. P.O. Box 6369, Los Osos, CA 93412. An excellent,
bi-monthly breed magazine offering recent winners, records and pertinent articles.

The Bichon Frise Today. Richard G. Beauchamp. Rohman Publications, P.O. Box
48032-K, Los Angeles, CA 90048. A detailed discussion of the Bichon Frise, history,
producers, judging etc. to 1982.

Twenty-Five Years, A Pictorial Review. Published by the Bichon Frise Club of San
Diego, Inc., P.O. Box 97, La Jolla, CA 92038. Pictures and information on nearly 300
of the influential Bichons from the early days to 1985.

Your Bichon Frise. Bichon Frise Club of America, Inc. A comprehensive booklet to
introduce you to the Bichon Frise.

GENERAL KNOWLEDGE AND TRAINING BASICS

Canine Terminology. Harold R. Spira. Howell Book House, New York, N.Y. The definitive book of its kind and the basis for terminology used in Breed Standards as accepted by the American Kennel Club. Superb illustrations.

The Complete Dog Book. Published by the American Kennel Club, New York, N.Y. Gives a brief history, the Breed Standard and pictures of all recognized breeds, health information, nutrition, reproduction and breeding, first aid and training. A "must" for every dog owner, regardless of breed.

Dog Tricks. Carol Benjamin and Capt. Arthur Haggerty. Howell Book House, New York, N.Y. Teaching your dog to do simple and more complicated tricks gives you a way to communicate with him as well as to give him a sense of purpose. Tricks included for children to teach their pets.

Elimination on Command. Dr. M. L. Smith. Smith-Sager Publications, Friday Harbor, WA 98250. Highly recommended by major reviewers. Basic reference for the novice pet owner. Applicable for both the younger and older dog.

How to Housebreak Your Dog in Seven Days. Shirlee Kalstone. Paperback. Bantam Press, New York, N.Y. Recommended by dog trainers.

Mother Knows Best. Carol Benjamin. Howell Book House, New York, N.Y. The responsibility of dog ownership and what every dog's rights should be. Training your dog the natural way as a pup's mother would, to shape your dog into the best possible pet, at home or in public.

The New Dogsteps. Rachel Paige Elliot. Howell Book House, New York, N.Y. Continues as the undeniable classic in the understanding and description of dog gait and movement.

New Knowledge of Dog Behavior. Clarence Pfaffenberger. Howell Book House, New York, N.Y. Learn about the "four critical periods" of puppy development, the ideal time to take puppies from mother and littermates and the best time to develop emotional ties to humans.

Pure Bred Dog/American Kennel Gazette. Monthly magazine published by the American Kennel Club, New York, N.Y. Of general interest to all.

Step by Step About Housebreaking Your Puppies. Jack C. Harris. Paperback. T and H. Publications, Neptune City, N.J. The final recommendation on the subject of housebreaking.

DOG TRAINING FOR PRACTICALITY

Agility Dog Training. Charles L. and Velta R. Kramer. Cascade Press, Manhattan, KS 66502. Training for agility plus the construction and preparation of the obstacles.

Beyond Basic Dog Training. Diane Bauman. Howell Book House, New York, N.Y. The teaching methods presented encourage and cultivate dogs' cognitive abilities. The author believes that dogs learn by trial and error.

278

Training to the Maximum. Max Parris. 7112 Bonny Oaks Drive, Chattanooga, TN 37421. A book in two sections, one a nine-week beginner course and the second a six-months course preparing the dog to qualify for his AKC Companion Dog degree. Several training methods used individually or combined to make your personal dog a better companion.

VIDEOS

Agility Dog Training. Charles L. and Velta L. Kramer. Cascade Press, Manhattan, KS 66502. Video version of book by the same name.

The AKC and the Sport of Dogs. American Kennel Club, New York, N.Y. General information video.

The Bichon Frise: The Breed Standard Series. The American Kennel Club, New York, N.Y. A visual analysis of the new Breed Standard as approved in the fall of 1988. Excellent foundation for anyone wishing to better understand the breed.

Bichon Frise Club of America National Specialties—1987–1988–1989. Sirius Video, 147 North Dubois Road, Ariel, WA 98603. These videos are available as a total package for each Specialty, or the various events may be purchased separately.

Dogsteps—A Study of Canine Structure and Movement. The American Kennel Club, New York, N.Y. The video version of the outstanding work on gait and movement.

Obedience Videos. American Kennel Club, New York, N.Y. "200?" and "Exercise Finished."

Drawing by Rolande Lloyd.